THE MIND OF THE CHURCH
IN THE FORMATION OF SISTERS

THE MIND OF THE CHURCH
IN THE FORMATION
OF SISTERS

SELECTIONS FROM ADDRESSES GIVEN
DURING THE SIX REGIONAL CONFERENCES
AND THE FIRST NATIONAL MEETING OF
THE SISTER FORMATION CONFERENCE,
1954-1955.

EDITOR
SISTER RITAMARY, C.H.M.
MARYCREST COLLEGE
DAVENPORT, IOWA

FORDHAM UNIVERSITY PRESS
NEW YORK • 1956

Nihil Obstat:

JOHN M. A. FEARNS, S.T.D.

Censor Librorum

Imprimatur:

✠ FRANCIS CARDINAL SPELLMAN

Archbishop of New York

JANUARY 20, 1956

LETTER FROM THE CARDINAL PREFECT

March 23, 1955

Sacra Congregazione dei Religiosi
No. 01615/54

Dear Sister Emil,

Through the *Sister-Formation Bulletin,* which has very kindly been sent to us and through reports which have reached us, this Sacred Congregation has learned with great pleasure of the excellent work that is being done by the Sister Formation Conference in the United States, and in particular by the National Committee, of which you are the Chairman.

We are most pleased to hear how much has been and is being undertaken to further the wishes of Our Holy Father in regard to complete preparation—spiritual, intellectual and professional—of Sisters, in order that their own Religious Life and the works in which they engage may be more solid and more fruitful.

It is particularly gratifying to notice the appropriateness of the subjects discussed in the *Bulletin,* and of the Papers read and discussed in the various meetings. Out of such exchanges of ideas and experience will come stimulation to action and a more enlightened approach to the judicious adaptation of Religious Life to modern conditions. It is not necessary, of course, to insist that in regard to this adaptation, the resolutions and decisions of the Conference and of the Congresses have only advisory value. These latter groups assume no legislative or executive power in what concerns such essential elements of the Religious Life as government, formation, discipline and observance, *etc.,* but merely refer their suggestions to the Major Superiors of each Community, to whom alone it belongs to make authoritative decisions.

We realize how much time and effort on the part of yourself and of your co-workers is necessary for the success of a movement as big as this, and we express to you and to all who are collaborating with you, our sincere praise and deep thanks.

Begging God's continued blessing on this all-important work of Sister Formation, and in a special way on the efforts of yourself and your co-workers, I remain

Faithfully yours in Christ,

Valerio Card. Valeri /s/

Prefect

Sister Mary Emil, I.H.M., Ph.D.
Marygrove College
Monroe, Michigan, U.S.A.

FOREWORD
By the Apostolic Delegate

Washington, D. C.
February 15, 1956

The title itself of this volume, "The Mind of the Church in the Formation of Sisters," bears witness of the Sister Formation Conferences and the manner in which the deliberations have been conducted. These are the proceedings of the first series of original conferences on the subject. The Holy Father on September 13, 1951, in a memorable discourse to the many Sisters who had taken part in the First International Congress of Teaching Sisters, pointed out to them the need to follow with careful attention the vicissitudes of the present time, and furthermore the need to know how to adapt themselves to new conditions preserving always those values that do not permit any change. "You," he said to the Sisters, "must serve the cause of Jesus Christ and of His Church as the world of today requires."

The occasion which initiated the organization of these conferences was a panel discussion sponsored by the Teacher-Education Section of the National Catholic Educational Association on the subject of the Holy Father's discourse to the Congress of Teaching Sisters of September 13, 1951.

The title of the papers reported in this volume demonstrates both an enthusiastic determination to carry out in due measure the wishes of the Holy Father and the Sacred Congregation of Religious and likewise the will to be directed into relatively new areas of lengthened and deepened formation programs which would be guided by the wisdom of the centuries embodied in ecclesiastical legislation and in the practice of the orders and congregations of religious men.

Sponsorship of regional conferences by the hierarchy of the United States and their participation in a variety of ways in the programs of the meetings indicate how directly the Most Reverend

Archbishops and Bishops are concerned with the spiritual and professional formation of the religious engaged in school and hospital
work and other activities. In pursuing the high ideals of these conferences it is most fitting that the Sisterhoods should be assisted in
their programs by those whose authority, learning and experience
qualify them to give such help.

Those who have planned these conferences and who have carried them out have been anxious to do their work in accord with
the mind of the Church, preserving statutes, programs and traditions, and yet cautiously pressing on to new horizons in an effort
to extend the kingdom of Christ everywhere. In a sense they have
been like the householder who brings forth from his storehouse
things old and new. The work of the Sister Formation Conferences as it has developed in this country is indeed more than an
educational movement. In the widest and most apostolic sense, it
is an example of the faithful children of the Church working to
enlarge the scope of her influence and helping her to respond to
new needs and new things.

The great needs of the Church in America challenge the dedicated Sisters and Religious to undertake even greater responsibilities for schools and hospitals and social agencies. The zeal of the
Sisters and their initiative have been responsible for the success
of the Sister Formation Conferences, the Sister Formation Bulletin
and this excellent volume of proceedings. The Sisters are agreed
that a basic requisite for answering all of these challenges lies in
sending into the field Sisters whose spiritual and intellectual formation is deep and solid as befits their dedicated and noble service.

May God continue to bless abundantly the fields of religious
work of these generous souls consecrated to our Divine Lord and
to the service of His Church.

⊹ A. G. Cicognani
Archbishop of Laodicea
Apostolic Delegate

CONTENTS

III. ECCLESIASTICAL DIRECTIVES FOR SEMINARIES AND FOR
THE EDUCATION OF RELIGIOUS MEN

IV. SISTER EDUCATION FROM THE VIEWPOINT OF THE SUPER-
INTENDENT OF SCHOOLS

INTRODUCTION

THE SISTER FORMATION CONFERENCES OF THE NATIONAL CATHOLIC EDUCATIONAL ASSOCIATION

Sister Mary Emil, I.H.M., Chairman
Sister Formation Committee,
College and University Department, NCEA

At the NCEA Convention of 1952, in Kansas City, the Teacher Education Section of the College and University Department sponsored a panel discussion under the chairmanship of Sister M. Augustine, O.S.F., of Alverno College on the implications for American Sisters in Pope Pius XII's Discourse to the Congress of Teaching Sisters of September 13, 1951. The statement in the Holy Father's *Counsel to Teaching Sisters* upon which the discussion was largely based was this:

Many of your schools are being described and praised to us as being very good. But not all. It is our fervent wish that all endeavor to become excellent. This presupposes that your teaching Sisters are masters of the subjects they expound. See to it, therefore, that they are well trained and that their education corresponds in quality and academic degrees to that demanded by the State. Be generous in giving them all they need, especially where books are concerned, so that they may continue their studies and thus offer young people a rich and solid harvest of knowledge. This is in keeping with the Catholic idea which gratefully welcomes all that is naturally good, beautiful, and true, because it is an image of the Divine goodness and beauty and truth.

In bringing out the need for Sisters to have a good general education, and an adequate professional education according to the steadily upgraded standards for certification which are being adopted by the states, the panel concluded by pointing out that the major difficulties faced by the sisterhoods in maintaining satisfactory educational programs for their members were three: one of *time* required for the Sisters to complete the degree course, one of *resources* to cover the cost of protracted schooling, and one of generalized *understanding* of the needs and problems in the formation of teaching Sisters. The action recommended with reference to these difficulties was likewise threefold. In order to meet the needs of the schools during the Sisters' training period and in order to make possible the opening of new schools now demanded, there was suggested a generalized policy of supplementing the ranks of religious teachers with a definite ratio of lay teachers, according to need. With regard to the lack of resources, a study was called for to determine to what extent such a lack is impeding the carrying out of the Holy Father's directives. Finally, as a practical answer to the insufficient comprehension of the goals and the present status of Sister education, it was proposed that there be some kind of institutionalized opportunity for an exchange of help and ideas among the motherhouses and colleges engaged in this work.

The lively floor discussion which followed this analysis and these proposals elicited a suggestion from Monsignor John J. Voight, Superintendent of Schools of the Archdiocese of New York, that a survey be made of the current status of teacher education among religious and of the obstacles to the establishment of adequate pre-service programs. Authorization to make this survey was given to a volunteer committee, consisting of **Sister Rose Alice, S.L., Sister Mary Basil, S.S.N.D., Sister Mary Emil, I.H.M., Sister Mary Gerard, O.S.F., and Sister Mary Richardine, B.V.M. Sister Celine, C.R.,** was added to the Survey Committee shortly after its inception. It was understood that the information collected by this committee would be made available to the Mothers General and to the competent ecclesiastical and educational authorities.

The Survey and the Survey Report

On May 29, 1952, the Survey Committee proceeded to address a questionnaire to the 377 general superiors of all teaching communities in the United States. This inquired into the extent of the teacher shortage in schools already accepted by the communities, the number of schools refused for lack of Sisters, the length of the community training program, the intentions of higher superiors with regard to lengthening pre-service training programs, the possession by the community of educational facilities for a four year program of Sister education, and the community policy of lay-teacher ratio. In addition, the free comments of the major superiors were solicited. A second questionnaire, sent out in October, 1952, to twenty-five selected communities, representing 23,000 Sisters, investigated financial matters only, as it was felt that the evidence of financial difficulty yielded by the first questionnaire was too general for maximum usefulness. Points studied here were the percentages of income-producing members in teaching communities, the annual cost of living per capita in parochial houses, salaries in parochial houses, salaries in parochial and diocesan schools, annual cost per capita of maintaining and educating junior professed Sisters in college programs, annual per capita cost of maintaining aged and sick Sisters, and per capita share of community debt.

The information received from these questionnaires, and a compilation of the superiors' general comments were sent in tentative and incomplete form to the delegates to the Notre Dame Religious Congress in August, 1952, and in complete form to the Bishops' Committee on Education in October of the same year.

With regard to the general picture of Sister education delineated by these investigations, it might be said that it was not good. Too many Sisterhoods were sending less than adequately prepared members into their first teaching assignment. Although the delegates assembled in the Teacher-Education Section of the 1951 NCEA convention in Cleveland had decided that a four-year degree program was to be considered "basic" in a Sister's training and that anything short of this was "emergency" level, it was found that only thirteen communities, out of the 255 reporting, had a full Bachelor's degree program in operation. One hundred and eighteen communities had neither educational facilities of their own for the training of their subjects, nor easy access to those of suitable Catholic colleges and universities. Although it is true that the degree programs existed in some of the very largest communities, the figures showed indisputably that there are in almost every religious congregation a very large number of in-service teachers who must strive through a period of from ten to twenty years of summer schools to attain what is now recognized as minimum preparation for their work. It also seems clear that the bulk of American Sisters entering the convent without college training have been educated in this way. That the situation could not be ascribed to a want of vision or of understanding of the need of more adequate training on the part of general superiors appeared clear from the statement of intention made by most of them that they would establish a four-year basic training program as soon as would be feasible, and that they would extend even this preparation if they could.

It was stated repeatedly that the chief obstacle in the way of better Sister training programs was the Sister shortage—a condition which had apparently forced the communities, year after year, to send out Sisters directly from the novitiates without any intermediate period of study. The burden of the Superiors' comments on this point was that the use of lay teachers, in increasing numbers, must be accepted for today's schools, which are over-crowded and understaffed, and in which the task of instruction has of necessity been entrusted to religious whose pre-service formation was notably deficient. The superiors showed awareness that what had been labelled an "emergency" situation was indeed a continuing one, and that plans for the future could not include any expectation of an easing of the pressure of numbers.

Another, and a very great obstacle to adequate Sister education, was the financial condition of the teaching communities. Because Sisters' stipends had failed utterly to keep up with inflation, the communities were struggling to meet greatly increased educational costs on an income greatly reduced in its purchasing power. It was evident that the salaries of the Sisters teaching in the parochial schools were in some cases less than the cost of living for the same Sisters, and were in no case anything like adequate to cover the expense of educating the young Sisters and of maintaining the retired and infirm.

The SEPS Proposal

The Survey Committee, to which Mother Mary Florence, S.L., had been added in September of 1952, felt in the course of the year, as comments came in from all sides on the privately circulated report and its great importance to Catholic education, that the problems raised by this study were too numerous and too weighty to permit of satisfactory handling in the single annual session of the Teacher Education Section of the National Catholic Educational Association. They welcomed the opportunity accorded them by the Superintendents' Department in April of 1953 to hold a joint session by way of a panel discussion of the Survey Report, but they felt that many meetings would be required to make even a beginning on the solutions indicated. They felt further that the Sisters need closed meetings at which the delicate problems involved in the education of Sister students, the conduct and discipline of houses of study, and the details of their administration could be discussed by Sisters only. Although the Survey Report in its final form was prepared as a part of a Master's thesis submitted to Marquette University by Sister Mary Richardine, B.V.M., one of the Committee members, the confidential character of the data had prevented not only the publication of the report but the availability to the public of the detailed analysis of it in the thesis. All of this pointed to a need for some kind of organizational arrangement whereby higher superiors and those engaged in spiritual and intellectual training of Sisters could meet to exchange ideas and to plan programs of mutual assistance.

Because of the phenomenal success of the professional standards movement representative of the public school system, namely the National Commission on Teacher Education and Professional Standards, and the state and local TEPS Commissions, it was decided to refer to the organization proposed, as SEPS—a Sister-Educational and Professional Standards Commission.

This "SEPS" proposal was first made in March of 1953 at the

Midwest Regional Unit Meeting of the College and University
Department, where it was unanimously approved by those present. It was proposed again, this time with a view to action, at the
joint session of the Teacher Education and Superintendents' Department at the 1953 NCEA Convention in Atlantic City. The
following motion was carried unanimously:

> That the present Survey Committee on Teacher Preparation be
> enlarged by the addition of a representative from all interested
> communities, and that it be empowered as an integrating group
> in order to sponsor exploratory regional conferences at interested
> institutions, with a view to the ultimate establishment of Sisters
> Educational and Professional Standards Commissions.

It was further agreed that this proposal was to be presented to
the Executive Committee of the College and University Department, and through it to be referred to the Executive Board of the
National Catholic Educational Association for approval for further action. The SEPS proposal was favorably considered by the
Executive Board of the Association in June, and by the Executive
Committee of the College and University Department in October.
Final action occurred in January, 1954, when the General Executive Board restored initiative on the proposal to the College
and University Department, and the Department communicated
the authorization through its President, Father Cyril F. Meyer,
C.M.

At this time, it was thought well to change the name of the
regional conferences to be held in 1954 and 1955 from SEPS to
Sister Formation. "Sister Formation" indicates the interest of the
Sisterhoods in spiritual as well as intellectual training and includes the integration of both elements in a single program. It
includes in-service as well as pre-service training, and compre-
hends informal formative influences as well as those which are
strictly organized.

Sister Formation Conferences

The first step in arranging for the Sister Formation Conferences
consisted of a general planning meeting held at the Conrad Hil-
ton Hotel in Chicago, on the third day of the NCEA Convention.

Invitations had been sent to each community which had in some way previously indicated an interest in such a meeting, and attendance was limited to mothers general of these communities or their accredited representatives. This group decided to plan conferences within the existing NCEA regions. These conferences were to be two-day meetings, the first day to be an open one and the second day to consist of closed workshop sessions. Since the Survey Committee was to serve as an integrating body during the first year, it was agreed that the regions would consider a suggested program drawn up by the Committee, with the understanding that such programs would be adapted to the special needs of the areas. Provision was likewise made for the establishment in each region of a consultative committee, to consist of a superintendent of schools, a dean of advanced studies, a religious prefect of studies, a religious canonist, two officers of the regional unit of the Department, a Survey Committee member, and a free choice of the region. The final action of this planning group was the selection of six regional chairmen and secretaries who would thereafter be in charge of the conferences in their geographical areas. The first group of regional chairmen were: New England, Sister M. Lucia, O.P.; East, Sister Gertrude, C.R.; Midwest, Sister Mary Hugh, C.S.J.; South, Sister Mary Peter, O.P.; Southwest, Sister Elizabeth Ann, I.H.M., and Northwest, Sister Judith, F.C.S.P.

At the same Convention, the Executive Committee of the Department heard a proposal from the Survey Committee that there be established a separate Sister Formation Section. It was pointed out that such a section, with its own officers, could provide for the national coordination of the work of the regional conferences, and could also provide for a closed Sisters' meeting at the annual Convention. The Committee acted favorably upon this proposal by authorizing a Sister Formation Committee, whose chairman was to be chosen by the President of the Department, Brother Bonaventure Thomas, F.S.C. It was understood that this first authorization was for a maximum of five years, and that the new Committee would be empowered to plan programs for the national conventions. Shortly after the Convention, Brother Thomas appointed Sister Mary Emil, I.H.M., Chairman of the Sister For-

mation Committee. Other members were former members of the
Survey Committee, together with Sister Emmanuel, O.S.F., who
was added at this time. Since then the Committee has been broad-
ened to include Sisters who would represent the total formation
of nursing Sisters and of Sisters in social work. These new members are Mother Anna Dengel, S.C.M.M., superior general and
foundress of the Medical Missionaries, and Sister Frederica Hor-
vath, S.S.S., superior general of the Sisters of Social Service.

First Series of Regional Meetings

In order to plan for the first series of regional Sister Formation
Conferences, Sister Mary Emil, I.H.M., and Sister Ritamary,
C.H.M., editor of the proposed *Sister-Formation Bulletin,* traveled to all the regions in the summer of 1954 to meet with the
Sisters' planning committees and the regional consultative committees on the regional organization of the movement and on the
program for the first year. From these meetings there developed
a unified understanding of the Sister Formation movement, and
a program plan for the first year on the general theme of the
Mind of the Church in the Formation of Sisters. It was thought
that the mind of the Church on this matter could be studied in
two ways—by a careful examination of the pronouncements of
the Holy Fathers and of the Sacred Congregation for Religious
on this very topic, and by an application of the canon law principle of analogy to the ecclesiastical directives for seminaries and
to the actual practice of the Orders of religious men who teach
and who prepare their own teachers. It was decided further that
the Sisters' workshop sessions would be devoted to a discussion of
the principles given on the first day, to an examination of the
training programs of certain Sisterhoods, and to a consideration
of proposed by-laws for the permanent organization of SFC.

The actual Conferences planned in this series of twelve meetings were held in the period from November, 1954 to January,
1955. These meetings were very successful, drawing the participation of 246 religious communities and 170 general or provincial superiors. They were sponsored in every case by the Ordinary
of the place in which they were held. Members of the Hierarchy
who gave addresses and invocations were: Cardinal McIntyre,

Archbishop Connolly, Archbishop Floersh, Archbishop Howard, Archbishop O'Brien, Bishop Dougherty, Bishop Greco, Bishop Helmsing, Bishop Marling, Bishop Sheen, and Bishop Wright. Each of the regional Conferences reported a great and renewed enthusiasm on the part of the Sisterhoods for the earliest possible carrying out of the Holy Father's wishes in the matter of the formation of Sisters. There was keen interest in the organization and program of post novitiate houses of study, or "juniorates." The delegates uniformly expressed satisfaction with the holding of Sister Formation Conferences and their desire for an annual repetition of these meetings. With slight modifications in each region, and on the understanding that these modifications would be incorporated as well as possible into the draft to be submitted at the national convention, the by-laws for the Sister Formation Conferences were approved after discussion item by item.

In order to serve as a publicity organ for the Conferences, and to make possible the exchange of ideas on Sister Formation and the development of a literature on the subject, the publication of the *Sister Formation Bulletin* was initiated in October of 1954, under the editorship of Sister Ritamary, C.H.M., at Marycrest College. Although the *Bulletin* was begun as an organ which would have a very limited circulation among the higher superiors, novice mistresses, and college personnel in charge of the education of Sisters, the demand for it from mission houses, from priests and from others interested in this subject became so great that the publication changed its format from mimeographing to printing after the second issue. At the present writing, which is after the publication of the first five quarterly issues, the subscription list exceeds 2800 and represents every state in the Union and fourteen foreign countries. A most gratifying and encouraging development with regard to the *Bulletin* was the reception, under date of March 23, 1955, of a letter from His Eminence, Valerio Cardinal Valeri, Prefect of the Sacred Congregation for Religious, commending the Sister Formation movement and "the appropriateness of the subjects discussed in the *Bulletin* and of the Papers read and discussed in the various meetings." His Eminence expressed the conviction that "out of such exchanges of ideas and experience, will come stimulation to action and a more enlightened approach to the judicious adaptation of Religious Life to modern conditions."

So that the papers and discussions of the regional Sister Formation Conferences may be preserved and may reach a wider group than the three official delegates permitted to each community from the areas, respectively, of general administration, spiritual formation, and intellectual formation, plans were made from the beginning to issue an annual volume of combined *Proceedings* in which contributions from the various regions would be arranged topically. It is hoped that in this way we may have a permanent collection of materials on this topic. It is hoped too that the diffusion of these volumes may not only provide the stimulation to action and adaptation of which His Eminence, Cardinal Valeri spoke, but may be provocative of more writing in this field. It seems clear that it will require the combined efforts of theologians, philosophers, canonists, psychologists, educators, spiritual directors, and Sisters actually engaged in the work to develop the theory and practice of the effective and integrated total-formation programs which would so greatly benefit the spiritual, intellectual, and apostolic lives of the Sisters.

Second Series of Regional Meetings

It was as a result of such a combined effort on the first year's theme, that the papers and discussions of the first set of regional conferences pointed the way to the theme of the second. One of the topics set for the first series of Sisters' workshop discussions was "Integration: The Relationship of Those Charged with Spiritual Formation and Those Charged with Intellectual Formation." This "Integration" theme proved to be tremendously popular, drawing large numbers of participants, particularly the novice and postulant mistresses. It was found that all the Conference delegates approved of the idea of "integration," but it was found, too, that there was not much content in this notion. Some felt, moreover, that certain remarks in the discussion sections showed that in spite of the nominal approval of "integration" not all the delegated were really convinced that the substance of the unification of spiritual and intellectual elements in the formation of Sisters was truly possible or even desirable. In any event, the poverty of ideas on this point indicated a need for clarifying definitions and objectives and for making some literature along this line. It is hoped that the second volume of *Proceedings,* on the "Integration of Spiritual and Intellectual Elements in the Formation of Sisters," will be a real contribution to the solution of the problem of how to train Sisters for a professed life in which personal spirituality and the work of the apostolate will not seem to be opposed and somewhat irreconcilable aims. It is also hoped that it will provide a framework within which the Conferences can go on, in another year, to discuss problems of curriculum in the pre-service education of Sisters.

Sister Formation Session, NCEA Convention, 1955

The Sister Formation Committee, whose members have been assembling once or twice a year to plan their activities, met jointly with the regional chairmen of the Conferences for a three-day session in Monroe, Michigan, in February of 1955. The agenda covered among the other items described at length in the rest of this chapter, the planning of the first meeting to be held under the auspices of the Sister Formation Committee at an NCEA Convention. It had been understood that these meetings were to be closed, for Sisters only, and were to be devoted to such educational problems as could and should be discussed from the standpoint of a religious community. It was decided to devote the first such session to community problems involved in the graduate education of Sisters, this being a topic which had not been covered in any of the regional conferences. It was thought that the chief community problems here involved the selection of suitable Sisters for graduate study, the arrangements made for these Sisters during the actual period of their studies, and the optimum utilization of these members after their return to their communities.

The Sister Formation session of Easter week, 1955, which was a first gathering of major superiors, college personnel, and spiritual formation personnel ever to be held as a closed meeting in an NCEA Convention, drew an overflow crowd of more than 350 Sisters. Papers on the topics planned in Monroe were read by the Rev. Edwin A. Quain, S.J., Academic Vice-President of Fordham

University, and Sister Emmanuel, O.S.F., Dean of the College of St. Teresa and Vice-Chairman of the Sister Formation Committee. The chairman took this occasion to make a progress report on SFC to date, and to read to the delegates assembled the commendatory letter of His Eminence, Cardinal Valeri. The remainder of the business meeting was devoted to a discussion of the by-laws or "Regulations" which will form a pattern for the conduct of the Regional Conferences. These were adopted in the form proposed, with two minor amendments, which are indicated in the NCEA Bulletin of 1955. They were likewise approved, in the form of Regulations, by the Executive Committee of the College and University Department.

Other Sister Formation Activities

The Directory of Catholic Women's Colleges Having Facilities for the Education of Sisters. This brochure, which has now come out in two editions, is the work of Sister Mary Gerard, O.S.F., of Alverno College, and is one of the most significant accomplishments to date of the Sister Formation movement. It is an effort to meet the needs of 118 small communities having no educational facilities of their own and no ready access to Catholic colleges or institutions, by listing the Catholic women's colleges which are able to take in Sisters of other communities, preferably at reduced rates. The compilation and checking of the many tables which go to make up the two directories was a monumental task, but the labor of Sister Mary Gerard and of Sister Mary Basil, S.S.N.D., who arranged the graduate section of the second edition, as well as the generosity of the donors who made the publications possible, would seem to have been amply rewarded by the great interest manifested in this project and the wide distribution of the *Directories* as well as by the growing awareness of the colleges and motherhouses having facilities of their own, of the importance of sharing these resources with the communities which do not. Eighty-six women's colleges list themselves as willing to take in Sisters at greatly reduced rates; twenty-one graduate schools offer very substantial reductions to Sisters; and thirty all-expense scholarships are offered by the women's colleges.

The Vocation Survey

This project grew out of the preparation for a discussion in the Northwest Conference of 1954 on the subject of the relation of Sister-Formation standards to recruitment to the Sisterhoods. The research, planned and directed by Sister Judith, F.C.S.P., involved the administration to 14,000 students in high schools, colleges, and schools of nursing, of a questionnaire to test attitudes of students toward the Sisters. Publication of the results and interpretations of this study will soon take place, and the report is expected to furnish valuable empirical evidence of the importance of improved Sister formation as a part of the answer to the vocation problem.

Juniorate Study

This project was suggested at the Midwest Conference of 1955, and was carried out by Mother Mary Florence, S.L. It involved a careful investigation, by questionnaire, of current practices in post-novitiate houses of study, or "juniorates." It is felt that this piece of research will have great value, not only in the hitherto unavailable data which it collects, but in the suggestions it offers to the very large number of communities which are just now planning or instituting such programs. This survey was published in the December, 1955, issue of the *Bulletin*.

In-service Study and In-service Formation Committees

The early work of the Survey Committee and the Sister Formation Conferences was concerned rather exclusively with the pre-service training of Sisters. This was not because of any want of appreciation of the needs of in-service teachers, nurses, and social workers, who have cheerfully borne the heat and burden of doing their work and acquiring their professional preparation under the most difficult circumstances. It was due rather to simple physical limitations of time and resources. Just as SFC is concerned with all the Communities—not with a view to imposing or urging any uniform pattern or answer upon them, but in order to help and stimulate each one to make progress from the point at which it finds itself at the present time, to the next stage which

seems desirable to it in the improvement of the formation program—so SFC is interested in all the Sisters—those in service as
well as those whose active apostolate is still in the training stage.
In an effort to do something for the Sisters in service, however,
it is felt that the individual needs and differences are so great,
that little can be urged by way of action to help the teachers and
nurses in this group, until we have more exact information on
what they themselves, in great numbers, feel they need by way
of time, materials, courses, helps, and guidance of all kinds. To
that end, "In-service" committees are being erected in all the
regions. The work and study of these groups will be coordinated
by Sister Elizabeth Ann, I.H.M., of Immaculate Heart College,
Los Angeles. It is likewise planned at this point that the 1956
national NCEA Convention session under the auspices of the
Sister Formation Committee will be devoted to this topic.

Cooperation with NCTEPS and local TEPS Commissions

SFC, from its beginning, has had the most cordial possible relations with NCTEPS. The personal idealism of Dr. Stinnett and
his associates, and their accomplishments by way of raising standards for their profession generally, have afforded useful and inspiring patterns to what is in a rough way a parallel movement
in the NCEA. NCTEPS has been most interested and helpful.
Delegates from SFC were invited to both the Albany and DeKalb
Conferences, and the Chairman of the Sister Formation Committee was the guest of the Commission at its own meeting in August, 1954. The commission has been very generous in making
its materials and services available to the Sisters. SFC members
have been invited to take leadership roles and to present papers
at TEPS Conferences.

Curriculum Study

Perhaps the most ambitious single project of SFC to date is the
large scale study which has been begun of best practices and felt
needs in the Sister training institutions of this country and of
Europe. This research is being done by three full-time persons:
Sister Emmanuel, O.S.F., dean of the College of St. Teresa, on
leave of absence, and Sisters Mary Emil, I.H.M. and Xaveria

I.H.M., on leave from Marygrove College. Sister Emmanuel is at present studying Sister formation in Europe. Sister Mary Emil and Sister Xaveria are studying the curricula used in the education of Sister-students in colleges and motherhouses in this country, and are visiting a large number of these institutions for this purpose.

These data are being gathered to serve as background material for the construction of an ideal curriculum in Sister education by a group of sixteen Sister educators in a workshop to be conducted for three months in the summer of 1956.

This curriculum will be a joint effort by outstanding Sisters from all academic fields. The objectives and patterns suggested by this group, it is hoped, will form the subject matter for discussions in a third set of regional conferences in 1956-57. This entire project is being financed by a grant from the Fund for the Advancement of Education.

Acknowledgments

Because of the very large number of priests, Sisters, and lay persons whose help has in some way or another provided the critical impetus or assistance without which SFC could not have continued on a national scale or in individual regions, it is almost impossible to make a listing of the most important ones. In a hundred ways advice or assistance has been "most important" at certain times, and it is impossible for many reasons to give recognition to all these friends. Nevertheless, at the risk of notable omissions, the Sister Formation Committee would wish to express its gratitude to the members of its national consultative committee, His Excellency, Most Rev. Bryan J. McEntegart, Rt. Rev. Msgr. Henry C. Bezou, Rt. Rev. Msgr. Frederick G. Hochwalt, Rt. Rev. Msgr. John J. Voight, Very Rev. Paul C. Reinert, S.J., Rev. Allan P. Farrell, S.J., Rev. Cyril F. Meyer, C.M., Rev. John F. Murphy, and Brother W. Thomas, F.S.C., who have given generously of their time to attend meetings and to offer advice by mail. Without the vision and courage of the Executive Committee of the College and University Department and its two Presidents, Father Cyril Meyer, C.M., and Brother Bonaventure Thomas, F.S.C., who saw the implications of SFC for Catholic education, the present formal structure of the movement could not exist. Important leadership, encouragement, and financial assistance have been given at crucial times by His Eminence, Francis Cardinal Spellman. The chairmen of the Teacher-Education Section under whom SFC began—Rt. Rev. Msgr. Felix N. Pitt, Sister M. Josetta, R.S.M., and Sister Mary Gerard, O.S.F. gave indispensable support and cooperation. Special help and support have been given at various times throughout our work by Rt. Rev. Msgr. Joseph A. Gorham, Rt. Rev. Msgr. Francis X. Fitzgibbon, Rev. Robert J. Henle, S.J., Brother Gregory, F.S.C., Rev. Edward A. Kammer, C.M., Rev. Edwin A. Quain, S.J., Rev. Edward B. Rooney, S.J., Very Rev. William E. McManus, Dr. Alvin C. Eurich, Mr. T. H. Keating, Dr. Bernard J. Kohlbrenner, Dr. T. M. Stinnett, and Dr. John O. Riedl.

In every region, members of local consultative committees and speakers for the regional conferences have traveled long distances and given important and substantial assistance. The members of the Hierarchy and the priests and religious who have written articles for the *Bulletin* have shown similar generosity. The mothers general and provincial of the country have gone to great pains to answer questionnaires, to cooperate with all SFC projects, to write many personal letters of advice and encouragement, and to participate in the regional conferences. In every case the spirit of apostolic solidarity manifested by the Sisterhoods has been heartwarming. Special gratitude should be extended to the major superiors of the members of the Sister Formation Committee and the regional chairmen for the splendid cooperation which they have given, and in particular to Mother Mary Magdalen, C.H.M., Mother Mary Alcuin, O.S.F., and Mother Anna Marie, I.H.M., for the contribution of community time which they have permitted their Sisters to make to the national cause of improved Sister formation.

The great success achieved in a short time has thus been due to the generous help of many friends. In another way, it has been due to the prayers of the Sisters in every part of the country, the white-veiled ones, perhaps, in particular, and of the little children whose petitions were enlisted. In still another sense, however, it must be said that although the accomplishment may have been noteworthy organizationally, the real work has hardly been begun. It will be on its way when we have adequate professional pre-service training for all Sister teachers, nurses, and social workers, when the juniorate movement has developed to a point at which we can say that it represents the spiritual flowering of the novitiate training and parallels spiritually the intellectual enrichment of the pre-service college program, when we have made an honest and completely realistic appraisal of the difficulties experienced by the Sister in service to continue or complete her professional training, to continue to nourish her spiritual life with solid dogmatic and ascetical truths, to keep up with current events and thought, and to acquire and maintain a modicum of general culture. At that point we may begin to think of what an influence 154,000 Sisters could be in the spiritual, intellectual, and apostolic life of the Church and of our nation.

-❖-I-❖-

INVOCATIONS AND WELCOME
ADDRESSES

INVOCATION

His Eminence, J. Francis Cardinal McIntyre
Los Angeles, California

We have come together to discuss problems of your profession
and your life—I might say your life of profession, because as educators yours is a great mission. Your primary consecration in life,
of course, is a spiritual one—your own salvation and the salvation
of others. This is a dual purpose. Today you have come together
to discuss these primary interests in your life so that the whole
"curriculum" of your life, the efforts of your life, will be accomplished.

Our Lord said to His Apostles, "Go forth and teach all nations." [1] You share in that apostolate, in that commission to teach
all nations of all colors, of all kinds. And that is your consecration, to teach—no matter in what—whether you are engaged in
pedagogy as such or in other fields; whether you are commissioned
to teach in a school, or in a hospital, or among the poor. You
are always teaching, teaching everybody all things that God has
given us. We first teach the things of God, then the things of life,
the things of nature, learning in general. Each has a commission
to teach, and we know full well that if we use the qualities of
mind and body that God has given us, if we give them diligently

1

to our vocation we may be sure that God will be with us and will
crown our work with success. We may not be a success in the
eyes of the world, but only in His eyes, because it so often happens that a teacher working in her classroom may be unknown to
all, but she is known in the mind of God.

I am very happy to come today. I am happy that you have assembled to discuss these problems, to discuss them intelligently,
prayerfully. We are gathered together, if necessary, to change our
point of view, to make better these elements in our lives.

As we study the ideals of pedagogy, let us always remember
that ideals are strange things that are never attained, because
once they are reached they cease to be ideals. Even in viewing
our spiritual ideals we are always reaching out for a higher standard of relationship between ourselves and Almighty God.

The ideals of method and pedagogy as prescribed by some of
our secular educators do not have the objective that you have in
your spiritual life. They are human objectives, sometimes ques-
tionable objectives; but we must look at them with good judgment. Good judgment and common sense are your gift from God.
We are devoted to God's work; therefore, we may be sure that
our deliberations will be blessed. May God bless you in your discussions.

FOOTNOTES

1. Matthew 28:19.

INVOCATION

The Most Reverend Joseph P. Dougherty, D.D.
Bishop of Yakima
Yakima, Washington

Since it may be said that fundamentally the purpose of the Conference for which we are assembled today is to study the means
by which women in holy religion may participate more fully in
the general priesthood of Christ, we should join them in stirring

up the grace which was given all of us by the imposition of hands in the Sacrament of Confirmation—the enduring sacrament through which we share in a higher degree than at baptism in the general priesthood of Christ, and which makes us official witnesses to the truth of the Christian faith. Our Sisters are par excellence witnesses to Christ by reason of their identification with the priestly and teaching office of their bishops; and it is most important, therefore, that taking full advantage of the grace of their Confirmation, they should be formed spiritually and intellectually for their vocation of giving witness to Christ in the classroom, in the hospital, and in areas of social action. As St. Thomas Aquinas says (Summa Theol. III, Q lxiii, a. 5):

> "Christ's faithful have a share in His priesthood, in the sense that as Christ has the full power of a spiritual priesthood, so the faithful are likened to Him by sharing a certain spiritual power with regard to the sacraments and to things pertaining to divine worship."

And he continues, saying that Confirmation advances the Christian to the status of an adult with the right and duty of actively sharing as co-workers with Christ in His priestly function. If this is true of the average lay person who is confirmed, how much more intimate must be the sharing in the priesthood on the part of the religious Sister by reason of the dedication of herself to God through her vows and her more immediate identification with the pastoral office of the bishop of the diocese in which she resides.

ADDRESS OF WELCOME

The Most Reverend Charles H. Helmsing, S.T.D.
Auxiliary Bishop of St. Louis
St. Louis, Missouri

The official welcome is coming from our beloved friend, Father Reinert, but I believe it my duty to congratulate you in the name of the Archbishop, and to voice the hope that the work of this Sister Formation Conference will be fruitful. Because of His Excellency's vast experience in diocesan administration, he realizes how important the spiritual formation of our Sisters is; but at the same time he never forgets their intellectual formation. Almost any problem touching our religious can be traced to the lack of solid spiritual and intellectual formation. Shortly after His Excellency's arrival in the archdiocese, he sent me to teach some Sisters the truths of the catechism because of his conviction that they showed a lack of appreciation of the dogmas of the Faith. It is the mind of the Holy See to train Sisters in theology. Thank God this desire is being heeded. The Sisters must have a solid grounding in the Faith, but they must also be formed intellectually if their work be such that we may never blush when comparisons are made.

However, you would not be at this meeting, nor would you have spent your money, nor given up your very busy occupations, did you not appreciate that this spiritual and intellectual Sister Formation is vitally necessary. Much of our unity of purpose and the fruitfulness of much of the Church's work of education and charity depends upon the content and purpose of this gathering.

It is a joy for me to represent the Chief Shepherd of the archdiocese in welcoming your conference to St. Louis.

INVOCATION

The Most Reverend Fulton J. Sheen, D.D.
Auxiliary Bishop of New York
New York, New York

What is the difference between France and the United States in their political, economic, and national life? You are the difference, Sisters. Think of the great wisdom of the early bishops of the United States, who insisted on religious schools. And now the influence of America is much wider than our state; it is extending even to the missions where 50,000 elementary schools have been established by us. We know well that the future of Africa and Asia and all other mission lands depends on the educators and the education of youth. Maybe in the eyes of God—in fact, I am sure of it—you are doing more for the Christ-life in the United States than we priests.

Oh, yes! We have more power. But remember that power operates in two ways. (Permit me to seem learned here.) There are two ways in which power operates: *ex opere operato,* by the very fact that something is done; for example, you turn on the faucet, and water comes out; and *ex opere operantis,* which depends upon the worker; for example, playing tennis in the novitiate, painting, and the like. When we operate as priests, we operate *ex opere operato* in administering the Sacraments. The power does not come from us. Even if we were unworthy, we could not interfere with the grace of God. Sunlight that comes through a dirty window is not polluted because the window is dirty, and neither is the grace of God restrained because it comes through us. The merit is not our own either. It is only because we are acting as instruments of Christ.

But with you it is different. You operate *ex opere operantis.* All your effectiveness depends on the way you are prepared. It depends upon your preparation and your lives. Your whole efficacy is due to your formation. Hence the importance of a gathering of this kind.

I once asked Cardinal Mercier to give me some good advice for being a teacher, and he said, "Tear up your notes at the end of every year," because you are always tempted to go back to the yellow pages.

Another suggestion: Create an environment for each subject. Just as in order to breathe you have to depend on something that is extra-corporal, the air; your stomach depends on food outside; your eyes need light—so in order to breathe in any subject you have to have a tremendous intellectual environment. Surround yourselves with many books on the subject you teach. Never limit yourself to one textbook. A textbook is the deathknell of knowledge. I once saw a reference in a textbook to St. Thomas Aquinas; it had been quoted from another textbook, and that from another, and that from a fourth, and the original book had misquoted St. Thomas! Read everything you can on the subject so that the student is getting something that is not in the book. After all, he can read the book more quickly than you can give it to him. He can read it in six hours; he can read it ten times in sixty hours.

Again, be conscious of the fact that we need not only intellectual virtues. Man also has a practical intellect, that of choosing and willing. We very much stress intellectual convictions and intellectual requirements; let us not forget that we are sent not to the bright students alone, but for character formation in Christ, and not everyone has brains. Where would we get delivery and grocery boys? Suppose they had a high I.Q.: What would we be doing? It is foolish to ask that everyone before us have brains. Brains are a gift of God. I know of three boys thrown out of religious schools—one boy kept dirty books in his desk; another boy drew during geography class; the third boy was a fighter. Those boys were Stalin, Hitler, and Mussolini. After all, what is redemption but the renovation of a *felix culpa?* Remember that all people have tremendous energy, enough to be very good or bad. All your convents are filled with potential devils. All the criminals in the penitentiaries are potential saints. The Little Flower said she would have been the worst woman in the world if she had not followed grace. All of our power is born by taking the tangled threads and weaving out of them the tapestry of holiness.

Be not conformed with the world. We must have and we must obey all the legal requirements of education. But remember that all standardizations refer to quantity and not to quality. A yardstick can be used to measure mud, and a yardstick can be used to measure gold. There is too often a tendency to confuse quantity with quality. So we tend to add extra courses. All our courses should be united and built up, as St. Thomas says, like a pyramid.

Finally, your influence as a teacher comes from your spirit. In other words, it is something that goes out of each and every person as it is in them. And what is to go out of you? The spirit of Christ to all the young. You are Sisters, and what does this mean? When the Blessed Mother pushed through the crowd to see a Son who was preaching by day and praying by night, and the crowds told Him His mother was there, Christ said, "Who are my mother and my brethren? . . . Behold my mother and my brethren. For whoever does the will of God, he is my brother and sister and mother." [1] What makes you Sisters? The foundation of the word "Father" for a priest and "Sister" for you is to do His Will. Increasing detachment is necessary. We made our triple vows—your flesh, things, and the pride of your own mind. So we begin to change; we can get along without things, and this is our vow of poverty; without the things of the flesh, and this is chastity; without our own will, and this is obedience. But not without the Divine Will; this purifies our will so that it is completely and totally dedicated to Our Lord. If there is anything we have to bear in mind it is this: We have to resist the temptation of believing that we have to make compromises with the youth of the world in order to win them. Let me tell you that anyone who thinks that way does not know the world. Why has Communism swept the world? Because all of these philosophies offered an absolute to the young. They knew, better than we are conscious of, that the youth of the world is sick and tired of a milk and water liberalism. Youth wanted to surrender itself, to believe that there is something so evil that one should fight against it; something so good that they could give up anything in order to get it. The fault is ours, the fault of leadership that has not seen this in youth. There are thousands of letters that come to me every year from the young— "What can I do?" In general, the youth of the country wants it, and the youth of the world wants it, and it is happening that the spirit of sacrifice which the youth wants is not being taught them as it should be taught. The result is that the Communists have taken up the cross; they have not Our Lord, but they have the cross, and that is what they are preaching. The western world has Our Lord, but without His cross.

Teacher formation is fire, and fire involves light and heat. This light is truth and the heat is love. Communists have the heat but not the light. Christ was the fire, and He meant that we be a flame. From this conference may there come a great burning zeal to communicate this light, that people may feel that we love the truth. Be in love with God, and you are formed as you should be.

FOOTNOTES

1. Mark 3:35.

ADDRESS OF WELCOME

The Very Reverend Paul C. Reinert, S.J.
President, Saint Louis University
St. Louis, Missouri

All of us, I am sure, are grateful for the cordial greetings and welcome from His Excellency, Bishop Helmsing, delivered to us in the name of Archbishop Ritter and the Archdiocese of St. Louis. It is my privilege and joy to reiterate His Excellency's warm welcome and to say specifically that Saint Louis University, though happy to have you here on any occasion and for any reason, is particularly gratified at your presence here today because of the high purpose for which you have come.

Why are we so happy? Because we are convinced that this Sister Formation movement will prove to be one of the greatest single contributors to the genuine progress and the prestige of Catholic education in recent decades. The program of training for the Sisters which will grow out of these conferences will provide what I consider the two basic essentials for such progress and prestige. As the Chairman of the National Committee, Sister Mary Emil, I.H.M., has emphasized so often, this movement is directed first and foremost to the spiritual formation of our Sisters, to a combination of instruction in theology and to the constant inspiration to the practice of virtue in accordance with the spirit of a given community. As its most important objective, therefore, this movement wishes to assist each community in imparting to its young Sisters basic theological knowledge, a genuine ardor for perfection, and an opportunity to apply in the period of training what they have been instructed and exhorted to do.

Then, as its second great objective, the Sister Formation movement wishes to enlarge the opportunity for Sisters to acquire the intellectual virtues, particularly through the pursuit of a well-planned course of collegiate study. From this course of studies, it is hoped, will result the formation of a religious woman who can think for herself, who is eager to continue her education independently through reading and study, and who has a love and an appreciation of the things of the mind.

It is my conviction that the Catholic teacher cannot actively and effectively achieve the objectives of our schools unless she possesses both these essentials: the spiritual understanding and appreciation, founded in her own deep religious life, of what Catholic educational ideals are and how they differ from and go far beyond purely secular objectives, and at the same time the professional attitude which every true teacher must have and without which her spiritual ideals will remain ineffective. What is true in the life of a medical doctor, a scientist, a scholar, is equally true in the life of a teacher: a professional attitude is essential. What are the characteristics of this professional attitude? First, a teaching Sister must have academic competence; she must know well what she is teaching; she must know her own powers and limitations within that field of knowledge; secondly, she must have a sense of responsibility. Realizing that truth and knowledge are sacred things, she must teach as well as possible in order to be faithful to her profession. Never must she tolerate low or mediocre attitudes or standards of achievement for this would be contrary to her professional integrity. Thirdly, a professional attitude includes a restless dissatisfaction with present performance. Hence, she must be interested in research and experimentation, always desirous of doing a better job than is being done at the moment.

Sisters teaching in our Catholic schools who have received a training of this kind will be Catholic education's most precious jewel and possession. They will give the bishops of this country who ultimately are responsible for Catholic education an assurance that this delegated duty is being performed well. They will inspire and lead and win the respect of the lay teachers who necessarily will become an integral part of our teaching from kindergarten to graduate school. They will provide Catholic parents with the assurance that their children could never secure an equal education outside the walls of a Catholic institution because added to the spiritual influence on their children, so desperately needed today, the professional competence of the Sisters will surpass those in non-Catholic, public, or private schools. Thus these parents will be convinced that it is worth the ever-growing cost and sacrifice which they will be called upon to face in order to bring our Catholic educational system to new heights of excellence. Finally, Sisters trained according to the ideals of the Sister Formation movement will provide our Catholic colleges and universities with the kind of student who can be developed into the dynamic leadership in science, education, industry, and government which the Church and the United States need so desperately.

These are the reasons why your coming here is most welcome and most auspicious. May your deliberations be blessed with wisdom and courage.

NOVA ET VETERA: NEW GOALS IN THE EDUCATION OF OUR TEACHING SISTERS

The Reverend Edwin A. Quain, S.J.
Vice President, Fordham University
New York, New York

It is a source of great personal pleasure to me to have the opportunity to extend a most cordial welcome to Fordham to this group who perhaps bear upon your shoulders the greatest responsibility and certainly the heaviest burden, that is being carried by anyone in the field of Catholic education in the United States today. There are just short of four million students in the Catholic schools of the United States. They are being taught by 123,015 teachers. Out of that total of 123,015, 89,391 are Sisters. In this eastern area designated by the Catholic Directory as the Middle Atlantic States, comprising New York, New Jersey, and Pennsylvania, there are 1,206,882 students. There are 33,932 teachers. Out of this total of nearly 34,000, 24,597 are Sisters. Since nearly 3,000,000 of our total school population are in elementary schools throughout the United States and almost a million in this Middle Atlantic area, it is clear that more than 75 percent of the students in Catholic schools in the United States this year sit in classrooms facing a nun in her religious habit. It is an eloquent testimony to your undoubted faith in God and your dedication to your apostolate that the Catholic Church in the United States has been able all through our life time to act as if the supply of teaching Sisters was permanently inexhaustible. I would not pretend to spell out for you what this has meant in the way of burdens financially, the effect it has had on the religious life of your communities, and the feeling that it must give you that there are always more problems than there are solutions.

Your presence here today at Fordham is a further testimony to the vigor and vision with which you address yourselves to your present problems—the spiritual, cultural, and professional training of the Sisters who are engaged in teaching. The motives that have caused the organization of various educational conferences and associations are as varied as is the human capacity for enhancing one's self-importance, but I am sure that there is no educational conference that has so clamored for existence as the group that brings you together today, the Sister Formation conference of the National Catholic Educational Association. Too often in the past we have, as I have said, assumed that there was a limitless supply of Sisters to go into the classroom. We have also assumed, unfortunately, that their training, spiritual, cultural, and professional, would somehow or other get done in spite of the annually increasing burdens that have continually been put upon your communities. No one needs to be told of the self-sacrifice, devotion, religious spirit, abnegation, and at times real hardships that have been endured by you and the Sisters of your communities in making our contribution to Catholic education. I need not remind you that the movements for an eight hour day, a minimum wage, and adequate leisure time have not, as far as one can notice, trickled down into the convents attached to our Catholic schools. In view of all this, I must confess that I marvel at the fact that you have come together today, not to look back on the past and to concentrate on what you have done, but to see how you can do more and better what you have been doing, and what you will inevitably be called upon to do to a greater extent in the next generation.

The magnitude of your task, I am sure, would frighten you if you had not the great advantage of looking back upon the dynamism of your own origins. Each of you from your knowledge of the history and spirit of the founders of your communities can look back and recognize the clear understanding they had of the needs of the times in which you were founded. You can there also recognize the heroically courageous steps that were taken to meet the needs of those times with new institutions and new ways of doing things in the face of great physical, financial, and ideological obstacles. Every founder of a religious community was a man or woman with a vision and a mission. They were precursors. They would be the first to admit that they did not complete the work they set out to do. In the light of that vision and mission, it is your task to conform the founders' ideals and spirit to the needs of today. Needless to say, this does not mean abandoning their ideals. It means, rather, completing and rounding out that spirit and those ideals and aiming at the perfection of your founder's vision by a more perfect realization of the ideal that they sketched for you. *Filii sanctorum sumus*—we are the sons and daughters of the saints and the grace and courage and initiative that is inherent in the spirit that each of you cherishes will not be lacking to you in our times, to face with equal vigor and courage the problems that the world of today brings to us.

When we survey the opportunity that is yours in the picture of Catholic education in the United States today, I do not think you could exaggerate your appreciation of the possibilities for good that lie within your communities. We who are in the college and university section of Catholic education are all aware that for all of our lifetime the heart and soul of Catholic education has lain in the elementary schools, largely in the hands of the Sisters. The growth, however, and the development of Catholic education will not be a true improvement unless there is a parallel growth and expansion of the teaching communities and of the training that they are capable of giving to their Sisters. No one, I am sure, would be tempted to delude himself in the belief that merely putting a woman in a religious habit, in the front of a classroom, automatically makes her a competent professional teacher. Parallel to your own deepening realization of the close connection between your personal sanctification as part of your vocation there must necessarily be an understanding of the fact that the means by which we have chosen to bring souls to God must be used by us with the greatest possible professional competence.

In the words of Our Holy Father, Pope Pius XII, spoken last fall:

> "The first consequence for you of the deepening of your Christian life will naturally be a more elevated notion of your educational mission and a greater professional consciousness. We mean a more ardent will to achieve the greatest possible competency in your own field or in anything pertaining to either theory or practice." [1]

Last January in his address to the Fifth Inter-American Congress on Catholic Education at Havana, Our Holy Father said:

> "Good teachers, then, should have perfect human formation, intellectual and moral. For the teaching office is a lofty position which calls for educational discernment and for goodness of heart, for a capacity of intuition and delicacy of spirit, for adaptability and adjustment, as well as human depth, capable of bearing all for love of neighbor. Good teachers need a professional competency which should be at least above average, and better yet, outstanding on all levels of instruction and in each of the specialized fields, if it is not to be unworthy of a mission which serves not merely the people and the State, but also God, the Church, and souls." [2]

The need for a thorough professional training is not merely the obligation of the Sister who runs the kindergarten but it extends all through to the senior year of college. Largely unrealized as yet, as you well know, are the plentiful talents among the members of your community who could take their place at the highest levels of scholarship in their fields of intellectual interests. For the past fourteen years I personally have had some opportunity to recognize the sacrifices made by many communities in this area for the graduate training of members of their community. I have also come to a keen realization that among the most competent and hardest working graduate students that I have ever had, have been the Sisters whose work I have had the privilege of directing.

We at Fordham hope that we will be able to make a contribution to Catholic education by doing everything we can to help in producing outstanding experts and leaders in all areas of education among the Sisters who can come to us for training. Many of you, I am sure, are aware of the very practical assistance and I might say stimulation that has been given us at Fordham in helping the teaching Sisters of this archdiocese to enhance the cultural and professional training of teaching Sisters. For this we are indebted to the vision and generosity of our Cardinal Archbishop and his diocesan consultors.

I have often been struck at national educational meetings by the impression made by the large number of Sisters who are to be seen everywhere in the crowds at those meetings. I have often also thought that it must bring home to those outside the Church the tremendous contribution that the Sisters are making to American education. In some such organizations it is inspiring to see that Sisters now sit upon the executive committees and the highest commissions in regional educational associations, but in proportion to the number of Sisters engaged in teaching, those who can by training take a commanding position are unfortunately all too few.

If by this time I have not dwelt too long on the problems that face you, and perhaps brought you to a state of discouragement of ever being able to measure up to your responsibilities, I should like most earnestly to stress one more point—to stress the obligation of the religious superior to appreciate the individual Sister, whom you put into the classroom, *as a person.* The obligation lies upon you to come to know each of the members of your community whom God has given you for your work for souls, to realize her fullest capacities, to make the maximum use of her time and the talents that God has given to her. Obviously not every nun who steps into a classroom can have an educational training through the Ph.D. However, the training of any single Sister must be planned intelligently with a view to the most pressing need, with cognizance taken of her intellectual capacity, her health, and of the other obligations that she may have to carry while pursuing her training in higher education.

God in His wondrous Providence has blessed us in the United States with more than 154,000 Sisters; 90,000 of them are now engaged in teaching. Perhaps another 10,000 are in the period of their spiritual and educational formation. Is it possible that this very large number for whose training you are responsible has, of its own weight, forced many of you to consider your available candidates merely as a group, the individual Sister undistinguishable amidst the crowd? Is it possible that the noble ideal of the selfless anonymity of the humble religious has prevented you from undertaking what your position in Catholic education in the United States today demands: the searching evaluation of the talents that have been given you for intellectual eminence for those most blessed by Almighty God? Have the long years essential to adequate cultural and intellectual training been sometimes looked upon as an escape from, and neglect of, the work of the community? I am afraid that the wearying labor of intellectual preparation has sometimes been considered as a part-time job that must be done in addition to a full-time task in the classroom or in the community. I can assure you from my own personal experience and from that of my students, that there is no more taxing or salutary work of abnegation than the labor and self-discipline that is required for truly outstanding work in intellectual things. The position that you actually hold in the educational structure of the United States today demands that there be outstanding experts among the Sisters in the field of elementary, secondary, as well as in college and university education. The time is, I believe, upon us when the communities of Sisters must face the task that the religious Orders and communities of men have so bravely undertaken of the adequate intellectual and cultural training of their members.

The representatives of religious Orders of men will, I am certain, assure you today that their efforts at developing by careful individual selection among their members, educational and scholarly leaders, have never been incompatible with the true spirit

of the religious life. I know that in our case we Jesuits have seen
this task as an expression of true and enlightened zeal for the
greater Glory of God. God will not be outdone in generosity,
nor has His Hand been shortened in these our times. If you approach this problem on the home front, with the courage and determination you have given to your labors as missionaries in foreign fields, the Hand of Almighty God will not be lacking to your
need.

In conclusion I should like to quote His Holiness, Pope Pius
XI, in an address to the superiors of priests, both secular and religious:

> "Wise encouragement and help should be given to those mem-
> bers of the clergy, who, by taste and special gifts, feel a call to
> devote themselves to study and research, in this or that branch
> of science, in this or that art; they do not thereby deny their
> clerical profession; for all this, undertaken within just limits and
> under the guidance of the Church, redounds to the good estate
> of the Church and to the glory of her divine Head, Jesus Christ.
> And among the rest of the clergy, none should remain content
> with a standard of learning and culture which sufficed, perhaps,
> in other times; they must try to attain—or, rather, they must
> actually attain—a higher standard of general education and of
> learning. It must be broader and more complete; and it must
> correspond to the generally higher level and wider scope of mod-
> ern education as compared with the past." [3]

In the words of Our Lord and St. Matthew: "And so every
scribe instructed in the kingdom of heaven is like to a man that
is a householder, who bringeth forth out of his treasure new
things and old." [4]

Nova et Vetera—the dynamic and apostolic spirit of your founders joined to the intellectual resources of our times—to the upbuilding of the body of Christ which is His Church.

FOOTNOTES

1. "Aims of an Italian Teachers' Union," *The Pope Speaks,* I (First Quarter, 1954),
   13, *AAS,* 46 (1954).
2. "The Secret of Good Schools," *The Pope Speaks,* I (First Quarter, 1954), 20,
   AAS, 46 (1954).
3. "On the Catholic Priesthood," (N.C.W.C. translation), pp. 40-41, *AAS,* 28 (1936).
4. Matt. 13:52.

·II·

APPLICATIONS
TO THE AMERICAN SCENE
OF RECENT PRONOUNCEMENTS
OF THE HOLY FATHER
AND THE SACRED CONGREGATION
OF RELIGIOUS

**SOME RECENT PAPAL PRONOUNCEMENTS
ON THE TRAINING OF TEACHING SISTERS** [1]

The Most Reverend Joseph M. Marling, C.PP.S., S.T.L.
Auxiliary Bishop of Kansas City
Kansas City, Missouri

Those responsible for the program of these Sister Formation conferences deserve commendation for their wisdom in suggesting a paper dealing with the recent papal pronouncements on the preparation of Sisters for their role as teachers. It is not alone that we acknowledge the Holy Father to be Vicar of Christ, assisted in his teaching office by the Holy Spirit. The earthly wisdom of our recent Pontiffs is known to all. Especially is this true of our present Holy Father, whose ability to analyze the gravest problems and propose vital remedies of a practical character has amazed the world. Faced, then, with a situation that is critical in connection with our parochial school system—the prime source of the fine spirit of our Catholic people—we turn to the papal

17

statements on Sister-training, with the assurance that they will provide principles of guidance for every discussion pertinent to this complex and thorny problem.

Twenty-five years ago in his masterly encyclical on the *Christian Education of Youth,* Pope Pius XI laid down the fundamental principle: "Perfect schools are the result not so much of good methods as of good teachers; teachers who are thoroughly prepared and well grounded in the matters they have to teach; who possess the intellectual and moral qualifications required by their important office." Our present Holy Father, in a radio-message to the Fifth Inter-American Congress on Catholic Education at Havana, on January 12, 1954, repeated these words of his illustrious predecessor and continued: "Good teachers, then, should have perfect human formation, intellectual and moral. For the teaching office is a lofty position which calls for intellectual discernment and for goodness of heart, for a capacity for intuition and delicacy of spirit, for adaptability and adjustment, as well as human depth, capable of bearing all for love of neighbor. Good teachers need a professional competency, at a minimum above average and better still, outstanding on all levels of instruction and in each of the specialized fields, if it is not to be unworthy of a mission which serves not merely the people and the state, but also God, the Church, and souls."

These words should be pondered in the current rush to build parochial schools. Brick, mortar, and tiled walls do not make a school; nor does the finest philosophy of education. "Perfect schools," says the Holy Father, "are the result of good teachers; teachers who are thoroughly prepared and well grounded in the matter they have to teach." Better that a school remain on an architect's board or in a pastor's fancy, than that it be staffed by poor teachers, ill-prepared teachers, or teachers quite unfamiliar with the tasks assigned them. This is emphatically implied by both Pope Pius XI and Pope Pius XII.

On September 15, 1951, our present Pontiff addressed the First International Congress of Teaching Sisters in Rome. The following year he repeated certain words of that message, and expatiated upon them, in speaking to the superiors general of religious communities of women from all over the world. The result is two statements, so expressive that they should adorn the mast of the entire Sister Formation movement.

"Many of your schools are praised," said our Holy Father to the teaching Sisters, "and described to us as very good—but not all. It is our fervent wish that all strive to become excellent. This presupposes that your teaching Sisters are masters of the subjects they expound. See to it, therefore, that they are well trained, and that their education corresponds in quality and academic degrees to that demanded by the State. Be generous in giving them all they need, especially where books are concerned, so that they may continue their studies and thus offer young people a rich and solid harvest of knowledge. This is in keeping with the Catholic idea which gratefully welcomes all that is naturally good, beautiful, and true, because it is an image of the Divine goodness, beauty, and truth. Most parents entrust their daughters to you because their consciences bid them do so. But this does not mean that the children should suffer by receiving in your schools an education of inferior value. On the contrary, you must do all that you can to assure parents that their children are getting the best education from the very elementary classes on. And then, do not forget that knowledge and good teaching win the respect and consideration of the pupil for the teaching Sister. Thus she can exercise greater influence on their character and spiritual life."

In the fall of 1952 His Holiness spoke in similar vein to the superiors general. *"The formation of your Sisters for the task incumbent upon them:* Here let there be no parsimony; take a broad and generous view. Be it question of education, pedagogy, the care of the sick, artistic or other activities—the Sister should entertain the conviction: 'My superior is making possible for me a formation that will put me on equal footing with my colleagues in the world.' Make it possible for them, and give them the means to keep their professional knowledge and training up to date. On this point we have also elaborated during the past year. We repeat it in order to underscore the importance of this requirement for the interior peace and for the work of your Sisters."

Though hours could be spent in profitable study of these two statements, we must confine ourselves to a simple listing of the salient points. In the first place, the Holy Father emphasizes that the Church never places a premium upon merely average results, nor advocates inferior goals in the natural realm just because her true mission lies in the supernatural sphere. What is naturally good, beautiful, and true, as His Holiness indicates, must be honored as an image of the Godhead. Those who defend mediocrity in the natural order, even in the name of supernatural striving or supernatural achievements, neither speak nor act the mind of the Church.

The Sovereign Pontiff urges that our Sisters enter the classroom with an education that meets the most rigorous requirements of the State. Here is an accurate measuring rod. In recent years our states have raised their standards so notably that soon certification, even in the case of elementary teachers, will be only for those with four college years of preparation. This is the minimum objective, therefore, toward which the Holy Father would have us bend every effort in the interests of our teaching Sisters.

Secondly, His Holiness distinguishes between knowledge and good teaching, pleading that both prevail in our schools. There is question, then, of general and professional training for our Sisters. The modern bias toward methods that detracts from content in teaching, we need not endorse. Nor are we obliged to place identical stress on the pedagogical disciplines in the case of primary grade and high school teachers. But the presence of both liberal and technical training for our Sisters is plainly part of the papal command.

In the third place, the Holy Father notes that a Sister's development is not complete with the termination of pre-service training. She must keep pace with the progress in her chosen field; the newest discoveries must not be strangers to her. Over and beyond this is the growth which experience, study, and reflection produce. To this process of maturity the Pontiff urges superiors to contribute by providing tools, removing obstacles, and creating an atmosphere which fosters intellectual and spiritual advancement. The completed structure envisioned by the Holy Father is striking. From it one may judge the type of foundation that he prescribes.

Finally, His Holiness computes the practical advantage flowing from Sisters in our classrooms who are adequately prepared for their tasks. The children will be trained to be perfect Christians. In an address to the Union of Italian Teachers on September 4, 1949, Pope Pius XII had said: "By a perfect Christian we mean the Christian of today, child of his own era, knowing and cultivating all the advances made by science and technical skill—a citizen and not something apart from the life led in his own country." Moreover, the pupils will have greater confidence in their instructors and thus surrender more readily to their influence. We may ask if this does not imply that young girls will be more attracted to the religious state if the Sisters who teach them manifest that poise which only skill in any undertaking begets.

The Holy Father also observes that parents make sacrifices to send their children to our schools, and that this grants a title in justice to an education for their offspring, in no way inferior to that of the public schools. Lastly, there is thought of the Sister herself. Peace of mind and deep satisfaction with religious life are the natural results of efforts in the classroom that are crowned with success by reason of ability and suitable training. Then is the work truly an apostolate and not merely drudgery. Health, longer years of activity, and a vocation made secure are other blessings that His Holiness must have in mind when he mentions the interior peace that flows from proper formation.

It is important to add that the Holy Father would have all Sisters trained in fullest conformity with the spirit of their institutes. On many occasions he has praised the Founders of the various communities, and described their mode of life as a precious inheritance, under no circumstances to be dissipated or set aside. The Church is enriched and her children blest by the many types of spirituality which the diverse congregations evince. It has been said that the most successful innovator is he who worships most fervently at the shrine of tradition. This is surely true of our Holy Father. Nothing essential to the spirit of a religious institute would he have sacrificed. Yet he pleads that those accidentals be swept away which represent only attachment to the past, and stand squarely in the path of progress.

Nor may we imagine that His Holiness would have intellectual formation interfere with spiritual advancement. Any effort of a religious that is devoid of spiritual motivation is an anomaly. It is thus that Pope Pius XII, in dealing with the High Mission of the Teaching Brother, wrote on March 31, 1954: "We desire that they perform their task not only with the greatest alertness, diligence and devotion but, above all, animated by that supernatural spirit by which human efforts flourish and bring forth salutary fruits. . . . What is most important is this—that they draw supernatural strength from their religious life which they ought to live most intensively, by which they can form to Christian virtue the students committed to their care." It would be easy to show in everything the Holy Father has said or written that intellectual and spiritual development go hand in hand, stimulating, sustaining, and enriching each other toward the realization of what St. Paul has called "perfect manhood . . . the mature measure of the fullness of Christ."

To turn to the Sacred Congregation for Religious is to hear echo of the Holy Father's words. Naturally there is more attention to specific details. First, there is the Decree of November, 1929, with norms for the teaching of religious in the novitiate, and the training after noviceship for those who will instruct youth in religion. Clearly advocated for religious teachers are pedagogical and professional competency, a sound Catholic philosophy of education and life, and the ability to formulate and appreciate a curriculum that is adequate from the standpoint of doctrinal Catholicism.

At the Congress for Superiors General of Religious Congregations of Women, held at Rome in 1952, one of the basic topics was the formation of Sisters. The unofficial summation of the Congress, which the Superiors received, calls for higher institutes of learning similar to those which have always existed for men. Theology, philosophy, canon and civil law, pedagogy, and psychology are subjects to be taught to those who direct consecrated souls. There is to be a course in Orientation, given in the individual Institute or in a house where several communities can come together, that will make the religious familiar with the current needs and trends in her field of activity. Reviews are to be available which treat in a general and specific manner of things which the Sister should know for her work. Finally, pertinent documents of the Holy See are to be placed in the hands of the Sisters for careful study and assimilation.

It would be interesting to trace the latest developments in connection with the Institute recently established in Rome for Sisters from the various congregations throughout the world. Difficulties have naturally attended its birth but there is promise of excellent results. It does manifest in a striking manner the concern of the Holy See for the intellectual and spiritual life of the Sisters. One other unrelated procedure of the Sacred Congregation for Religious deserves mention. Into Constitutions for religious women, now reaching Rome for approval or revision, there is injected a norm prescribing training for the junior professed in houses where it is possible for them to work for a diploma honored by the State.

It is profitable to ask to what extent our teaching Sisters attain the ideal expressed by our Holy Father. If comparison is to be made with the past the answer will be very optimistic. Not too remote are the days when the standards were low, preparation meager, and technical methods unknown. It is easy to remember when our university campuses swarmed in the summertime with aged Sisters forced to acquire disciplines which had been denied them in their younger years. Rather than dim the record of our parochial school system, these facts increase its lustre, just as they accentuate the heroism of the religious women who bore their burdens with such fortitude. But it was with joy that a new era was heralded with its promise of high achievement after a protracted struggle with pioneer conditions.

It would be idle to dilate here upon the factors which have produced the new crisis with our overcrowded classrooms, overworked Sisters, far too few teachers, and periods and methods of teacher preparation that may deserve censure. These difficulties have brought us together. They are familiar to us, as they are to the Holy Father. One may say that His Holiness has had them in mind in offering counsel concerning Sister formation. The steps you have taken are surely in harmony with his wishes—the formation of the Section on Teacher Education within the framework of the NCEA, with its fine papers, discussions, and surveys; the establishment of the Sister Formation Conference with its modest but excellent bulletin and the various regional meetings. What further practical measures are indicated in line with the papal advice?

First, it would seem that there is need for a gigantic effort to make the Church in this country conscious of the seriousness of the problem. Bishops, priests, educators, Sisters, and lay people must be made to think deeply about it. It is a crisis all must face, not only the Sisters. We boast, for example, of the eagerness of our lay people to provide a Catholic education for their children. They make certain sacrifices to bring this about. But the vast majority of them have no true picture of the financial obligations involved. They know the cost of current construction and maintenance and that Sisters subsist on a pittance. But not even an idle thought is given to the cost of motherhouses, the training of teachers, the care of incapacitated Sisters. If these things were before them they would appreciate the burdens which they must actually assume if their children are to enjoy a parochial school training.

The need which escapes our lay people most successfully is, of course, vocations. Here there is call for ceaseless instruction. In its broadest aspect the problem is one of making our homes and our lives more truly Catholic. In a worldly atmosphere vocations wither and die. The drawing of candidates to religious life is thus a daily task, one associated with our every action. Still, there is much to be done by way of education and inspiration, and here the primary role is that of the priest. If I were speaking to priests alone, I should develop at this point my conviction that it is this phase of the pastoral office that priests most often neglect.

The great shortage of Sisters in comparison with our school needs and ambitions is common knowledge. The temptation is therefore at hand to rush Sisters into classrooms before they are properly trained. Bishops, pastors, school superintendents, and Mother Superiors acknowledge that proper preparation is essential, but often an emergency is proclaimed and theory surrenders to practice. Two suggestions are made at every parley—a more equal distribution of Sisters, and the employment of qualified lay teachers. Actually these schemes go hand in hand, for lay teachers are more available in certain areas. The distribution of Sisters is not, therefore, a purely geographical proposition, but one that depends upon the supply of capable substitutes from the ranks of the laity.

These are topics which cannot adequately be handled here. Two observations, however, are in order and both follow the Holy Father's advice. Nothing can be done in these matters unless there is a united approach to the problem. There must be agreement between bishops themselves, and between pastors and religious superiors, or there will be merely discussion without action. In the second place, the employment of lay teachers would seem to lie at the very heart of the great movement, designated Catholic Action by recent Pontiffs, and urged by them as the finest program for our times. In a message to the Lenten preachers of Rome, our Holy Father has spoken of lay people as "capable of multiplying the strength and capacity of the clergy." Is this not an excellent description of the lay teacher in our schools? Therefore, is not the presence of these teachers regarded by our Holy Father as one answer to our most pressing need?

We have said that the Pontiff's request that the standards of the State be met in the preparation of Sisters for the classroom is equivalently a plea for four years of college study. The recent survey conducted by the Section on Teacher Education of NCEA shows graphically how distant is this ideal at the moment. We may leave to the experts the content of such a degree program, realizing that they will be guided by familiarity with educational needs and a sound Catholic outlook. But let us urge that the pre-service degree be sought.

Is it not possible to work out a time limit within which communities will guarantee it to their Sisters? Prudence demands that the limit vary according to existing conditions and difficulties. The stringent and uncompromising introduction of a degree program that would lead to the immediate closing of established schools would show zeal not tempered with wisdom. On the other hand, if we continue building new schools and expanding existing installations without any consistent and serious thought to Sister-training, we are courting disaster.

In conclusion, let me express my high regard for these Sister Formation conferences and their obvious achievements. I am sure that they bring great joy to our Holy Father, who has advocated so frequently that the various religious institutes gather to analyze their mutual problems. Were he present this morning he would probably repeat to you the beautiful words which he spoke to the Union of Italian Teachers on September 4, 1949: "Have courage and confidence. No matter how great the undertaking and how arduous the goal, the Christian educator is to leave nothing undone to attain it. You have sufficient human means, but above all you are rich in supernatural assistance through the grace which you and your pupils can abundantly obtain from the flood tides of the sacraments and prayer."

FOOTNOTES

1. Reprinted by permission from *American Ecclesiastical Review*, CXXXII (March, 1955), 145-53.

THE TEACHING SISTER IN THE CONTEMPORARY WORLD

The Most Reverend Thomas A. Connolly, D.D.
Archbishop of Seattle
Seattle, Washington

Confusion concerning the basic questions of human living is universal in our secular colleges and universities. The intellectual life of the country is feeding on the slow poison of agnosticism and skepticism and atheism in religion, of materialism in philosophy and laxity in moral values. Among too many people, the very existence of God is questioned when it is not openly denied. The Name of God may not be so much as mentioned in the classroom; but the enemies of God, under the guise of academic freedom, are free to carry on their nefarious campaign against Him and His interests. Knowledge of a Personal God and Divine Providence are considered as fables by modern irreligious philosophers and professors. The spiritual nature and immortality of man's soul are subject to ridicule if they are discussed at all. Such an attitude and atmosphere have not only been the fundamental cause of advancing immorality but they have been responsible for the shift in the basis of morality itself.

The modern secularist teaches that morality is a convention. To him, standards of morality are as public tastes. What the people do as a class is moral. The judgment of mankind, not the Law of God, is the last appeal. Things are right or wrong just as we wish to see them.

This tragic condition of our public and national life has had particularly harmful effects on the home and the family. There are a number of the classroom problems that affect and afflict the teaching Sister today to the general disregard for the moral law and the lack of any idea of a personal, individual responsibility to God. In many instances, the school instead of being an extension of the home has become its substitute—a role that it was never intended to play.

It serves our purpose merely to present for your consideration the fact that in many instances the home and family life have long since departed from the Christian ideal. We have witnessed the process of its decay over the past thirty years, from the Flaming Youth period of the twenties, through the depression thirties when the welfare State sapped it of much of its pride and self-respect, on into the war-torn forties when we saw our younger children appear at school with the keys to their respective homes dangling from chains about their necks, when we witnessed them changing five and ten dollar bills for a twenty-five or fifty cent luncheon in our school cafeterias, when we came across them running loose in the streets at all hours, completely free from parental guidance and supervision. Father was in the Armed Services or working one shift in a defense plant while Mother worked another. Today we are reaping the harvest of these baneful influences that have contributed to the general lowering of moral standards and the teaching Sister in her classroom bears the brunt of the burden.

The recognition of this sad state of affairs by God-fearing Catholic parents is one of the elements that has contributed in no small measure to the greatly increased enrollment of children in our schools; it is responsible for the present change of attitude of many Catholic parents toward the question of religious education in that they no longer consider it a duty but rather that they insist upon their rights to have their children enrolled in a Catholic school or college; so much so that their capacity for sacrifice seems to be almost inexhaustible where the spiritual and moral training and education of their children are concerned.

Our entire system of Catholic education has made tremendous strides in recent years. A little more than a generation ago we had 1,800,000 pupils enrolled in our Catholic elementary schools whereas today we have over three and a half million; there were about 130,000 students in our high schools and today we have about 600,000; in Catholic colleges and universities we had some 38,000 where today there is an enrollment of some 275,000. This, of course, is a manifestation of the tremendous stride that Catholic education has made in recent years. But what of the future?

Ten years from now if we are to continue to educate only half of our Catholic children, percentage-wise we shall have just as many children in our schools as we have today. However, this will mean that we shall have to recruit and train and prepare for the classroom over 60,000 additional teachers and to finance and build and equip 43,000 additional classrooms. This is not an emergency; it is only the beginning of a normal trend. The Catholic school construction program of the past decade has been astounding in its magnitude, but its future course is terrifying in its aspect to all who have the responsibility of supplying adequate facilities and properly trained personnel. The latter necessity in itself constitutes a problem of almost insurmountable proportions.

Even though a greatly stepped-up vocation program in church and school has been successful in enlisting the services of a large number of candidates for our teaching communities, in justice to both pupil and teacher, some well defined system or method of "Sister Formation" must be devised and utilized; if not, the ideals and the scope of Catholic education as outlined by the Sovereign Pontiffs of the past thirty years will fail of proper realization. The present picture of Catholic education in the United States is patent proof that our communities are making greater strides and more serious efforts to realize the educational ideals of the

Church. But such attempts, laudable though they are, fall far short of providing a proper solution to the problem in question.

An increasing number of our young teaching Sisters are almost at the breaking point. They are assigned to overcrowded classrooms of half-disciplined children whom they are expected to supervise and educate; during their spare moments, they must correct papers, keep records, make out report cards, list contributions to the ever growing number of school collections, and engage in a number of extra-curricular activities. A Sister's holidays are spent by attending workshops and teachers' meetings and what has come to be called Saturday school, to secure an extra credit or two toward the acquisition of her state teaching credentials. Not infrequently, she is called upon to teach catechism in her own or a neighboring parish. During her summer vacation, when she has a right to expect some rest and relaxation, her time is spent in teaching in a religious vacation school, in following the exercises of her annual retreat, and in attending summer school at an institution of higher learning, probably located in some abominably hot, humid section of the country. It is too much to expect from any human being. It is not a pretty picture, but it does present us with a solid argument for the complete re-orientation of our position with regard to the problem of proper teacher training and "Sister Formation."

When I was invited to participate in this conference, I examined a number of the volumes of the convention proceedings for the purpose of securing some information regarding the "movement," if such it may be called. I was surprised to note that although references were made from time to time over the years regarding the necessity of an adequate teacher training program in our novitiates and colleges, no definite or concerted action was ever taken. It was less than a year ago that a serious effort was made to promote some interest in the problem and to provide a workable solution to it. Whatever group was responsible for the establishment of the Sister Formation Conferences will earn the undying gratitude of every teaching community in the nation. It constitutes one of the most important developments in the field of Catholic Action. It should have been initiated ten or twelve years ago for it comes up for consideration now at a time

when the demand for teachers was never greater and the enrollment and prospective enrollment of children in our schools was
never higher.

The purpose of the Conference, of course, is to improve not
only the preparation, the intellectual and spiritual formation of
our teaching Sisters, but also their continuing training and formation while they are actively engaged in teaching.

You are all familiar with the injunction issued by our Holy
Father to the International Congress of Superiors General in
1952 and repeated last Fall. The institution of the Sister Formation Conference is entirely in harmony with that mandate.

This movement may be classified in some quarters as a luxury
item which we can ill afford at the moment in view of our pressing educational needs, but it is precisely because of that need that
our thinking along these lines must undergo a change. We must
recognize the situation for what it is and realize that the future
welfare of our Catholic educational system in the United States
may be jeopardized unless proper and prompt steps are taken to
translate this plan into action. Although we of the Pacific Slope
have witnessed an unprecedented growth in population in the
past decade, second to none in the country, I would willingly post-
pone or delay our school construction program for several years so
that our young novices might have the opportunity of securing
adequate spiritual and intellectual training for the important educational tasks that lie ahead of them. Whatever hardships will
be wrought from the adoption of this program will be, indeed,
acute but only temporarily. In view of the tremendous prospects
in the entire field of Catholic education, no time is to be lost.
Those in charge of the preparation and training of teaching Sisters should make immediate plans and devise at once a suitable
program to meet the pressing needs of the present and the future.

The entire operation will require the united, whole-hearted
cooperation of bishops and pastors as well as definite financial assistance in the form of an ample increase in salary over what is
now paid to the teaching Sister. It will necessitate the establishment of juniorates in the vicinity of our Catholic institutions of
higher learning or the institution of "extension courses" in novitiates that are located at some distance from our Catholic edu-

cational centers. These are only a few of the important details that must be worked out if the Conference is to meet with the success that it merits.

The enthusiasm manifested here today gives rise to the ardent hope that what is said at this conference will not end up between the covers of an educational manual to be decently interred on some dusty bookshelf. May I add that the spiritual encouragement of constant prayer for the happy achievement of your goal will, I am sure, be readily forthcoming from all who stand to benefit from the establishment of this program.

APPLICATION TO THE AMERICAN SCENE OF THE PRONOUNCEMENTS OF THE HOLY FATHER

The Most Reverend Charles P. Greco, D.D.
Bishop of Alexandria
Alexandria, Louisiana

The Sisters teaching in our Catholic schools have been, under God, one of the main factors of the magnificent progress of the Catholic Church in America since the turn of the century.

* * *

The Sister-teacher has spiraled in importance with the phenomenal growth of the Catholic school system and with the realization of the indispensable need of Christian education, both on the part of our own Catholic people and of so many non-Catholics who are becoming aware of the baneful effects upon modern society of an education without God.

* * *

The demand, past and present, for the Sister-teacher has increased far beyond the supply, precisely because of the phenomenal growth of the Catholic schools and because this growth promises to become more gigantic in the years immediately ahead. Add to this situation the fact that vocations to the Sisterhood have not kept pace with the school expansion program and you will find the reason why 205 religious communities refused 4,227 requests for Sisters to open new schools during a recent period of five years.

Fortunately a large number of pastors have lined up with the latest trend, and in fact with what is the only answer to an otherwise insoluble problem—the hiring of lay teachers to supplement the dearth of Sisters. This acute shortage of Sisters will be allayed when every elementary Catholic school, especially in the more substantial parishes, will hire at least 25 percent lay teachers.

It is very encouraging to note that within the first two years that this solution was proposed the over-all picture for the whole country showed that elementary Catholic schools had 7.6 percent lay teachers; high schools had 15 percent lay teachers; colleges had 46 percent lay teachers.

These percentages have now increased very substantially. Some dioceses have as much as 30 and 40 percent lay teachers in their parochial schools.

While the Sister-teacher, the mainstay or backbone of our Catholic school system, is under unprecedented demand, she is also under ever increasing fire, both by friend and foe.

The foe wants her liquidated from the classroom—in fact from the educational system of the land. This foe abhors our Catholic schools. But we do not fear him. Our country being what it is, we shall always have our Catholic schools. The friend is he who is ever pressing for higher standards on our schools. This friend is the pupil, his parents, the State, the Church itself.

Because of the great demand Sisters have been sent into the classroom without the proper preparation. This danger still exists. No one is fooled, however. The Sister not thoroughly prepared cannot do justice to her calling and to her grave responsibility in the classroom. In fact, she is a liability to herself, to the pupil, the school, her community, to the Church.

*   *   *

The Church has spoken clearly and forcefully on the importance of thorough preparation on the part of our Sister-teacher, through the voice of the Popes. To quote Pius XII:

"Sisters who are teachers and educators must be so ready and so up to the level of their office; they must be so well versed in all with which young people are in constant contact, in all which influences them, that their pupils will not hesitate to say: 'We can approach Sister with our problems and difficulties; she understands and helps us.' " [1]

And Pius XI says:

"Perfect schools are the result not so much of good methods as of good teachers, teachers who are thoroughly prepared and well grounded in the matter they have to teach; who possess the intellectual and moral qualifications required by their important office." [2]

* * *

It is proposed for your consideration and adoption, therefore, that no young Sister be sent into the classroom, before she has received the Baccalaureate degree. This may cause a hardship to the schools for a few years after the adoption of this rule, but once this period is over, the school program can be resumed in its normal course, with the difference, however, that the Sister-teacher then entering the classroom will be "thoroughly prepared."

This will ensure less defections from the religious life, because our Sisters will then be relieved of strain and worry, and from the double pressure arising from inadequate preparation, of teaching and studying at the same time.

Moreover, a satisfied customer is the best advertiser. A happy contented Sister, radiating joy, cheerfulness, and sunshine around her, is the best "sales lady" of the religious life.

One of the heavy obstacles to this program is, of course, the finances. Keeping the young Sister from two to four years at college will entail considerable expense which religious communities are unable to absorb. It will therefore be necessary to work out some satisfactory and feasible plan between the superiors, pastors, and Catholic women's colleges.

FOOTNOTES

1. "Counsel to Teaching Sisters," September 15, 1951, (N.C.W.C. translation), p. 7.
2. "Christian Education of Youth," (America Press edition), p. 30.

THE APPLICATION TO THE AMERICAN SCENE OF PRONOUNCEMENTS OF THE HOLY FATHER AND THE SACRED CONGREGATION OF RELIGIOUS ON THE EDUCATION OF SISTERS

The Most Reverend Edward D. Howard, D.D.
Archbishop of Portland
Portland, Oregon

Few things can be so difficult as the position of the Holy See when it addresses itself to the entire world. No two countries are alike, nor are any two dioceses. While there is a certain similarity in the rules and constitutions of all religious communities of women, there is an unquestioned difference in their traditions, their customs, and their approach to problems. Even when rules and constitutions are identical, as in two houses in different countries, national and racial tradition exert their influence. So we often find a greater resemblance between two houses of different communities in one country than between two houses of the same community in different parts of the world.

When the Holy Father speaks to religious, each community must promptly and immediately adapt its ways to his directives. Yet, often if not always, the adaptation will vary with the countries where the community is working. So it is the duty of the hierarchy of each country to point out to religious how the Holy Father's words may find application on the local scene. The Holy Father implied as much when he told the superiors of communities of men that, "Priests, whether religious or secular, ought so to exercise their office as to be auxiliaries of the bishop." "For," he said, "the exemption of religious in no wise conflicts with the principles of the divinely given constitution of the Church, nor is it at variance with the law whereby the priest must obey the bishop." [1]

The principle which the Holy Father stated regarding communities of men applies as well to institutes of women. Obviously it is not the bishop's place to institute changes in the rules or customs of exempt religious. That is the duty of the higher superiors and their councils, subject, of course, to the approval of the Holy See. The Holy Father makes this clear in his address to the International Convention of Teaching Sisters: "It is possible," he says, "that some details of the school schedules, certain regulations—simple application of the Rule, certain customs which were, perhaps, in harmony with past conditions but which today merely hinder educational work, must be adapted to new circumstances. Let superiors and the general Chapters proceed in this matter conscientiously; with foresight, prudence, and courage, and, where the case demands, let them not fail to submit the proposed changes to the competent ecclesiastical authorities." [2] It is the bishop's function, then, to point out to the various Sisterhoods where the particular rules or customs impede or retard the work which the good of souls demands. It is the duty of the higher superiors to weigh well the words of the successors of the Apostles, who, to quote Saint Paul, "Watch to render an account of your souls." [3]

Before descending to particulars, it might be well to determine the underlying motive—the unifying principle of all the Holy Father's words to religious. I believe this principle is identical with what we may call the theme of his pontificate. Pius XII is concerned to bring religion to men—not merely to the devout who now discharge their duties, but to all classes of society, including those who, up to now, have been impervious to the Church's influence. It is not the devout who suffer the most if religious communities fail to meet the needs of modern times. It is the less devout, the careless, the fallen-away, the irreligious, who will never be brought to accept Christ's sovereignty, unless a certain necessary adaptation is made. Everyone of you has noticed the fearful dichotomy between religion and life that characterizes our modern days. Those who retain a perfunctory respect for religion have no concept of the role God intends it to play in human life. To them, it is something apart—a garment to be taken on and off at will. So the newsstand displays Bishop Sheen's books in one rack and some lewd publication in another. The theater which features a nativity tableau at Christmas will make an appeal to all that is worst in man on New Year's Eve. It is the God-assigned function of religious to permeate the world with the leaven of Christ's Gospel. They shall fail wretchedly if they attribute to worn-out observances a sacredness which the founders themselves did not mean them to possess. As Monsignor Larraona points out in his evaluation of the First National Congress of Religious in the United States, "All Founders accomplished what they did . . . because this was an obligation imposed on them by the grace of God and the realization of their vocation. To do today as they would do in our place, what they would do if they were living in our times—in this way we shall continue their work." [4]

In applying the words of the Holy See to the American scene, I do not think we shall be guilty of pride if we say that here there has been a definite trend to make religious life meet the needs of the modern apostolate. We have not done all we could, certainly, nor is it zeal alone that makes us a rather adaptable people. There is something about American life that favors change—even glorifies it. As Catholics, we have had to protest the inordinate worship of change that sometimes makes it an end in itself. American willingness to revise, revamp, and renew is good in itself, as long as revision, revamping, and renewal have sound reasoning behind them.

To change—for the mere purpose of changing—is dangerous and unreasonable. We must be quick to change where change is necessary or advisable. We must be adamant and unyielding where it is not.

One of the things that concerns us most is the operation of our schools. Catholic schools are means whereby we bring men to heaven. They are instruments whereby we save our own souls. If your vocation in life is Christian education, you cannot perform this work negligently. To be remiss is to run the risk of losing your soul.

The Holy Father has never questioned the motives of religious engaged in education. He takes it for granted you work for the glory of God and the good of souls. Yet he is concerned that some may yield to the false principle that providing instruction in religion excuses one from meeting the standards of education outside the Church. "Many of your schools," he told the International Convention of Teaching Sisters, "are being described and praised to us as very good, but not all. It is our fervent wish that all endeavor to become excellent. This presupposes that your teaching Sisters are masters of the subjects they expound. See to it, therefore, that they are well trained and that their education corresponds in quality and academic degrees to that demanded by the State." [5]

We in America are accustomed to hear comparisons between Catholic and public education, which reflect rather favorably on the former. It is safe to say that most Catholic schools do a reasonably good job; yet there is danger of taking the praise that accrues to the system as a whole and applying it to every school, every teacher, and ever classroom. Let us be realistic. Our schools, regardless of how they compare to others, stand in need of improvement. Unless we work constantly to better them, we shall find them growing worse. In every diocesan school system there are weak spots. Religious vows, religious habit, religious motivation are not enough to improve education. Human nature is such that we must have standards, goals, and measures of achievements. It is the clear wish of the Holy Father that the standards of the state in teacher training be regarded by us as minimum. The children of this world must not be wiser in their generation than the children of light. [6]

Those teachers who are outstanding in the public schools are not content with obtaining their credentials. They are ever on the alert to know more about the psychology of children. They read avidly about modern experiments in education. That which is good, they seek to retain and apply in the classroom. That which is mere novelty, they quickly learn to discard.

Is it too much to ask that all religious engaged in teaching, both men and women, become students of education? Can we be fair to our children if we are not? The fact that public education is not religious does not make it evil. Much of it is naturally good. We shall grow stale and stagnant if we do not watch developments in education. With the ballast of Catholic teaching to steady us, we shall find in public education many things to use in the Kingdom of God. Would the Holy Father ask us to acquire an education corresponding in "quality and academic degrees to that demanded by the state," [7] if these did not possess, in his mind, a real value?

I think we express the mind of the Holy Father when we say that rules and customs must never keep the priest, the Brother, or the Sister, from giving to students everything a modern teacher is expected to give. One of the tenets of modern education is that child-training is not the work of the teacher alone. We in Catholic education have always held this theory, yet our practice is not invariably consonant with our beliefs. Too often the labor of the day, the early hour of rising, the multiplicity of spiritual exercises, have caused us to dispense ourselves from meeting with parents. To say we are available for consultation in our classroom is not to be realistic. Many a modern parent works longer hours than we. If we are to know our children, we must know their parents—or at least try to know them. When parents, after a day that is long and hard, are willing to come to the parish hall to discuss their children's education, it is our duty to be there to meet them, to greet them, to mingle with them, to hear them out, to question them, to offer counsels that may help them in their God-assigned task of rearing "the perfect man in Christ Jesus." [8]

As part of his plan for bringing religion to all men, the Holy Father is insistent that we try to understand modern youth. Apparently not all of us succeed in doing so, for in his address to the International Congress of Teaching Sisters, the Pope remarks: "To try to reform young people and convince them by making them submit, to persuade them by force, would be useless and not always right. You will induce them very much better to give you their confidence if you, on your side, strive to understand them and to make them understand themselves. . . ."

"Understanding young people," he continues, "certainly does not mean approving and admitting everything they maintain in their ideas. . . . It consists fundamentally in finding out what is solid in them and accepting this trustfully and without remorse or anger; in discovering the origin of their deviations and errors which are often nothing but the unhappy attempt to solve real and difficult problems; and, finally, in following closely the vicissitudes and conditions of the present time." [9]

Most religious do try to understand youth. But for some it is not easy. There is such a difference between the docile child of the intermediate grades and the self-assertive individual of the upper grades and high school. We shall have to bear in mind the Holy Father's words. You will not persuade youth by forcing it. You will not convince it by repressing it.

When the modern young man and woman bitterly criticize the way that we, their elders, have handled many situations, we shall have to admit that in some cases they are right. We have not given them the happiest kind of background—what with one general depression and two hellish wars. Sometimes we complain of modern youth's lack of reverence. The Holy Father has a comment on that: "But young people of today are not solely to blame for their present attitude," he says. "In childhood, they have lived through horrible things and they have seen many ideals formerly held in high esteem break down miserably before their eyes. In this way they have become distrustful and aloof." [10]

You who have taught youth, and adolescent youth especially, have some awareness of its problems. One of the greatest of these is purity. While a classroom teacher would err in trying to usurp the place of the parent or confessor, she should still know how to answer certain questions. The morality of dating, of going steady, of courtship should be known to her. Her approach to problems of purity must be sound, realistic, and practical. If she feels inadequate to discuss these things, her superior should provide for her instruction by persons with a background of theology and proven ability in guidance.

A second problem of youth is the acceptance of Church teaching. In childhood they believed without question what was told them. In earlier and later adolescence, their tendency to think for themselves sometimes conflicts with their duty to accept on faith. Here the teacher must be sympathetic. She must not be shocked when a boy blurts out in class, "How do we know Christ worked all these miracles?" or, "What proof can you give me that the Pope is infallible?" Questions do not imply that faith is wavering; they may only indicate that faith is seeking a reasonable basis. So again, the teacher must be properly instructed. Her training in religion must be geared to her needs as she faces a room full of modern youth.

A third problem of youth is vocation. Too often this word has but one meaning for priests and religious—persuading youth to enter the convent or clerical life. You know, of course, that vocation in its broader sense means the choice of a way of life. We speak of marriage, religious life, and single life in the world, as different types of vocations. Is it asking too much that religious teachers be well informed about all three? It is not enough to tell a girl, "Since you are not willing to be a Sister, I suppose your vocation is to get married." Youth must be taught the beauty, the magnificence of Christian marriage. They should be brought to see it as Christ sees it—a means whereby one soul leads other souls to God. They should be taught the dignity and splendor of parenthood; the sacredness of sex-life, lived in the way God wills. They should receive sound counsels on matters of family financing. They should be warned of the problems involved in making two lives one. In their religion classes they should learn, not how to battle with straw men, but how to teach their own flesh and blood. If one sharp criticism may be made of our religion courses, it is this—we do not equip future parents to teach religion in their homes. The young graduate of the Catholic college will find himself quite helpless if he tries to train his baby by telling him five ways to prove the existence of God.

I mention these problems of youth by way of implementing the words of the Holy Father. If youth are "to approach Sister with . . . problems and . . . difficulties," [11] it is important for Sister to know in advance what those difficulties are.

While speaking of youth and vocations, we should make some reference to the Holy Father's words on the spiritual training of young religious. To his mind, one reason for the shortage of vocations is that modern youth "deems it too hard to give up free choice and the power over one's own will, as the vow of obedience by its very nature requires." [12]

The Pope would have us react to this situation, not by growing arbitrary, but by forming a proper concept of obedience and seeking to transmit it to those who contemplate religious life. Obedience is not simple subjection, but a "free immolation of freedom." [13] We obey, not through force, but because for Christ's love, we made a choice to obey. "No one is bound by office," the Holy Father says, "to undertake the evangelical counsel of perfect obedience, which has its root in the surrender of power over one's will. One may, if he wishes, adapt his way of life to this new rule. . . . Let no one unwillingly be impelled to a vow of this sort. But, if he wishes it, let no one discourage or detain him." [14]

Problems of obedience, and of other counsels as well, will be solved rather readily if the superior is both fair and motherly. In his address to the International Congress of Religious in Rome, the Holy Father brings out the difficulty a superior faces in trying to balance severity and goodness. "All the more reason," he says, "for you to cultivate motherly sentiments. You are right in saying that the vows have exacted from your Sisters, as from yourselves, a great sacrifice. They have renounced their family, the happiness of marriage, and the intimacy of the hearth. This is a sacrifice of high price, of decisive importance for the apostolate of the Church, but a sacrifice all the same. The noblest and the most refined of your Sisters feel this detachment in the most lively fashion. . . . But the Order ought to replace the family as much as it can; and you, superiors general, are called in the first place to breathe into the common life of Sisters the warmth of family affection." [15]

The fact that a superior should be motherly does not mean she should coddle her subjects. Sometimes a young religious, feeling keenly the sacrifices she is asked to make, tends to minimize in her thinking the sacrifices and the trials of those who are called to marriage and family life. A favorite text of the novice mistress might well be the words of the first Holy Father, "Resist ye, strong in faith, knowing that the same affliction befalls your brethren who are in the world." [16]

As the Holy Father's health declines, and we realize he cannot remain with us much longer, we are grateful to God for this movement he has inaugurated—to adapt religious life to the needs of our times. We see here no trend to change religious life, but only to renew its spirit. This means we must recall our first objectives: Christian perfection and the good of human souls.

FOOTNOTES

1. Allocution to the General Convention of all Religious Orders, Congregations, Societies and Secular Institutes, Rome, December 8, 1950.
2. Address to the International Convention of Teaching Sisters, Rome, September 13, 1951, (N.C.W.C. translation), pp. 6-7.
3. Heb. 13:17.
4. Evaluation of The First National Congress of Religious in The United States. IV, 183-184.
5. Address to the International Convention of Teaching Sisters, Rome, September 13, 1951.
6. Luke 16:8.
7. See note 5.
8. Col. 1:28.
9. Address to The International Convention of Teaching Sisters, Rome, September 13, 1951, pp. 4-5.
10. *Ibid.,* p. 4.
11. *Ibid.,* p. 7.
12. Allocution to the General Convention of all Religious Orders, Congregations, Societies and Secular Institutes, Rome, December 8, 1950.
13. *Ibid.*
14. *Ibid.*
15. Address to the Higher Superiors of Orders and Religious Institutes of Women, at the International Congress in Rome, September 15, 1952.
16. I Peter 5:9.

RECENT PAPAL PRONOUNCEMENTS AND THEIR APPLICATION TO THE AMERICAN SCENE

The Right Reverend Monsignor Philip E. Donahue
Vicar for Religious Archdiocese
of Philadelphia, Pennsylvania

The importance of the religious life in the Church has always been stressed but never more so than by Our Beloved Holy Father, Pius XII. Since the very beginning of his pontificate he has been giving frequent expression to his appreciation of the religious life and its value to souls by urging the members of the various orders and institutes to make full use of the means provided them for their personal sanctification and to intensify their zeal for souls in their direction of their particular apostolate.

His pronouncements include:

1) The Letter on the House of Theological Studies for Sisters in Rome.

2) Letters on the Congress of Religious in Rome, 1951.

3) The "Sponsa Christi," 1951.

4) Address to The First International Congress of Teaching Sisters, September 15, 1951.

5) Letters to Mothers Superior on the Formation of Religious Women, 1951.

6) Letters on the Congress of Religious of the United States, Notre Dame, August, 1952.

For this paper I have drawn mostly on the address to The First International Congress of Teaching Sisters.

The two great points stressed by the Holy Father in his pronouncements are renewal and adaptation: a renewal of the primitive spirit of each religious institute, and its adaptation to the needs of today.

The Holy See has insisted that the spirit of the institute, its proper end and scope, be carefully safeguarded and preserved. The renovation must be internal and spiritual. Meeting that need, however, may demand and justify readjustment in the accidental structure of the internal life of the institute as well. Certain things do not admit of change because they belong to the substantial element of the religious institute: such things as the juridical personality, the essence of the vows, the special scope and characteristic of the institute, and the common laws of religious life as found in the Code of Canon Law.

But in regard to the methods and techniques used in the field of the apostolate, great adaptation is possible and desirable. The importance of the religious teacher to the apostolic work of the Church was expressed by the Holy Father at the beginning of his address to Teaching Sisters, September 15, 1951.

The record of the teaching Sisters in this country has been one of constant adaptation to the needs of time and place while always preserving the spirit of the various founders and foundresses. It seems possible that the Holy Father might have had in view the Sisters of the United States as a model for the Sisters throughout the world. Most of the Orders originally came to this country from Europe. The pioneers met the challenge of an apostolate often among people of the frontier by combining a real religious life and fervent community spirit with an extraordinary adaptability to the temperament and needs of the people. That God blessed their lives and their work is evidenced in the active Catholic faith we find in America now. It would be impossible for us to estimate how much of our Catholic heritage is due to the work of the Sisters in the classrooms of our parish schools, high schools, private schools, and colleges.

The first practical directive that the Holy Father gives to teaching Sisters is on the question of understanding the modern girl. He answers immediately the objection made by secularists that being a religious is a handicap to a teacher. The fact is that the religious teacher is in a better position to understand modern youth than are most other teachers. Your habit, the vow of chastity, your rules and constitutions render you all the more fit and capable where the instruction and education of today's young people are concerned.

Parents who have the primary right in the education of their children are of this opinion, as is shown by the fact that so many, often those who care little or nothing for religion, choose to send their children to the Sisters' schools. The demand is so great that even with increased numbers of vocations we never have enough Sisters for all the needs. We can expand our school facilities only by sharing the nuns more widely through the employment of more lay teachers.

A real part of your apostolate is fostering vocations. It is not necessary to water down the high ideals of the religious life in order to attract girls to the convent. With all its weaknesses American youth is generous and will respond to a noble challenge, whatever the cost to self might be, if properly presented.

Understanding young people does not mean approving everything and admitting all that they maintain in their ideas, their tastes, their whims, and their false enthusiasms. It rather consists fundamentally in finding out what is solid in them and accepting this trustfully; in discovering the origin of their deviations and errors which are often nothing but their own unhappy attempt to solve real and difficult problems; and finally, in following closely the conditions of the present time.

Chastity and virginity, which imply the inner renunciation of all sensual affection, do not estrange souls from this world. They rather awaken and develop the energies needed for wider and higher offices beyond the limits of individual families. The Holy Father points to the fact that there are many teaching and nursing Sisters today who are nearer to life than the average person in the world.

Your constitutions, too, followed in letter and spirit, bring to the Sister all she needs and must do in our time to be a good teacher and educator. It is possible that some details of the school schedules, some simple applications of the rule, certain customs which were perhaps in harmony with past conditions but which today merely hinder educational work, must be adapted to new circumstances. Superiors and the General Chapters are to proceed with this matter conscientiously, with foresight, prudence, and courage; and where the case demands, they are not to fail to submit the proposed changes to the competent ecclesiastical authorities.

You wish to serve the cause of Jesus Christ and of His Church in the way that meets the needs of today. Therefore, it would not be reasonable to persist in customs and forms that hinder this service.

The Holy Father expresses his fervent wish that all Sisters' schools become excellent and tells the Sisters that this presupposes that your teaching Sisters are masters of the subjects they expound, that they be well trained, and that their education corresponds in quality and academic degrees to that demanded by the State. He asks superiors to be generous in giving the Sisters all that they need, especially where books are concerned, so that they may continue their studies and thus offer young people a rich and solid harvest of knowledge. You must do all you can to assure parents that their children are getting the best education right from the elementary classes. Knowledge and good teaching win the respect and consideration of the pupils for the teaching

Sister, and she can thus exercise a greater influence on their character and spiritual life.

You are reminded that you are always to keep in view the object of the school and of education, which is the formation of the perfect Christian. For the Sisters here it is to apply this principle to the American conditions, to exercise such spiritual and moral influence and so to train the children in your schools that when they are left to themselves they will remain firm in their faith as Catholics and put this faith into daily practice. Your entire school and educational system would be useless were this object not the central point of your labor. God has called you to the vocation of educating boys and girls and making them perfect Christians. In this He demands your complete dedication.

Never was there such a time as the present when a girl had to be won, according to her convictions and will, for Christ's cause and a virtuous life, remaining faithful to both despite all temptations and obstacles. Our Holy Father warns you never to allow material advantages, personal authority, wealth, political power, or similar advantages to induce you to renounce your educational ideals and betray your vocation.

The Holy Father appeals for harmony and generous accord among the different religious congregations. Mutual knowledge and encouragement can only be to your mutual advantage.

Your mission is not an easy one. In influencing the inner formation of your pupils your vocation is your powerful ally. Living faith, union with God, the love of Christ with which every Sister has had the chance to fill herself in the spirit of her Congregation from the first day of the novitiate; the vow, not only of chastity, but especially that of obedience; a common task under one guidance in the same direction—all these things act strongly on young minds, always supposing that you live up to your vocation.

Be true to your vocation, therefore, Our Holy Father tells you, and your own sanctification will be assured and the success of your teaching apostolate guaranteed.

◆III◆

ECCLESIASTICAL DIRECTIVES FOR SEMINARIES AND FOR THE EDUCATION OF RELIGIOUS MEN

RELIGIOUS CLERICAL FORMATION AND SISTER FORMATION

The Reverend Joseph F. Gallen, S.J.
College of the Sacred Heart
Woodstock, Maryland

We can aptly begin our meeting by borrowing a thought of Pius XII. There is no doubt that progress has been made in the education and formation of Sisters. Our spirit, therefore, should not be one of discovery and reform but of greater progress. We are to direct our thoughts and efforts, not to the merely necessary or barely sufficient, but to the perfect.[1] The state of perfection implies not only personal perfection but also perfection in God's work.

The topic assigned to me may be entitled, "Religious Clerical Formation and Sister Formation." The comparison is not new. Father Larraona, the Secretary of the Sacred Congregation of Religious, stated in 1951 that the teaching apostolate of Sisters had a distinctive similarity to the priestly ministry.[2] There is nothing in the *Code of Canon Law* on the studies or professional formation of members of lay institutes, Brothers, nuns and Sisters. The same silence is verified with regard to non-clerical studies in cler-

47

ical institutes. The aim of this talk is to give the pertinent legislation and especially the mind and spirit of the Church on undergraduate clerical studies of religious men. This is to serve as a basis of conjecture to the mind of the Church on the education and formation in lay institutes and as a partial foundation for your practical discussions on this same point. My instructions were to emphasize the reasons for the legislation on clerical studies. Since these reasons are not found in the *Code of Canon Law* but in documents of the Holy See issued before and after the Code, this talk will necessarily be, in great part, a documentation.

Duration of Undergraduate Clerical Studies

Presupposing the completion of high school, canon law commands two years of the humanities (first and second year of college), at least two years of philosophy, and at least four years of theology for religious destined for the priesthood.[3] Exactly the same norm is true of diocesan clerical studies.[4]

There is also an added period of clerical formation immediately after the completion of the seminary course. This period is only of counsel, not of strict obligation, but it is a counsel strongly urged by Pius XII and the Sacred Congregation of Religious for both diocesan and religious priests. The words of Pius XII to the bishops of the world on this point are: "We urge you, Venerable Brethren, as far as circumstances may permit, not to rush inexperienced priests into the life of full activity."[5] On the time of this added formation, he states: "Accordingly, We heartily approve the plan of assigning for several years the newly ordained priests, wherever possible, to special houses."[6] "Several years" demand a minimum of two years. The Sacred Congregation of Religious had already urged the same practice for religious priests.[7]

The undergraduate preparation for the priesthood is thus at least eight years of obligatory study and training after high school and two years of counselled limited activity and further formation after the completion of the seminary course.

The reason for the obligatory duration was expressed in the same words by Leo XIII and the Sacred Congregation of Seminaries and Universities: "The preparation for the priestly duties must be long and arduous, since no one becomes familiar with things of such great moment easily or rapidly."⁸ The same Congregation also phrased this purpose as follows: "The work of the formation of a worthy ecclesiastic is arduous and prolonged, but the fruits that are gained are no less useful to the Church and no less consoling to the heart of a bishop."⁹

The reasons given by Pius XII and the Sacred Congregations of Religious and of Seminaries and Universities for the highly recommended added period of formation are: the dangers that exist at the beginning of the priestly life; the insufficiency of seminary training for the increasing needs of the people; the necessity of training in doctrine, technique, and in new forms of the apostolate; the need of competent and experienced individual guidance in the ministry and also in the spiritual lives of young priests; and the need of learning the necessities, dangers, and difficulties of our times.[10]

The subjects I would suggest for your thought and discussion under this heading are the following: Is it not in accord with the mind of the Church that the young Sister should finish her undergraduate schooling and training before beginning to teach? Is not teaching also a great work and one that demands a proportionately long and arduous preparation? Is the ill-prepared and unformed teacher in accord with the norm of excellence of Catholic education stated by Pius XI in his *Encyclical on Christian Education?* Are religious superioresses guilty of the imprudence that Pius XI censured in religious superiors who wish to abbreviate clerical studies that they may apply their subjects more quickly to the sacred ministry? He declared that the defect of such a rapid and inverted preparation can scarcely ever be remedied in later life and that the utility is later proved illusory by the diminished aptitude of the subject for the sacred ministry.[11]

I almost sense the familiar rebuttal that springs to the lips of many: "But we need the Sisters." "What of the thousands of children who must be given a Catholic education?" Let the Holy See answer. In an Instruction of April 26, 1920, to the Ordinaries of Italy, the Sacred Congregation of Seminaries and Universities repeated a recommendation of the Sacred Consistorial Congregation that newly ordained priests be assigned as prefects in minor seminaries. One reason for the recommendation was that it would give the young priests one or two years of added study, formation, and initiation in the sacred ministry. The Sacred Congregation proposed to itself and answered the one difficulty that existed against the recommendation, that is, the immediate need of priests in the active ministry. The Congregation maintained that this difficulty was outweighed by the good of giving later a perfectly and solidly formed priest, that the profit of the added formation of one or two years was immensely greater than the good of supplying the immediate necessity, and also that the delay in supplying the immediate needs would be only for one or two years. The system would be in full operation at the end of this time, and the same number of priests would then be assigned yearly to the life of full activity.[12] We can add that it appears to be idle to oppose the necessity of teachers against the longer preparation of Sisters. The Catholic population in the United States is not decreasing; the demand for teachers will not decrease in the future. If the longer preparation cannot be given now, when will it be possible to give this preparation?

We may add here some pertinent and important details of clerical studies. Canon law forbids religious superiors to assign any duties to the students of philosophy or theology that would be an obstacle or impediment in any way to either their study or classes.[13] Canonical authors are quick to explain that the usual violation of this law is the appointment of such students as teachers or prefects in the schools of the institute.[14] Furthermore, the Code explicitly grants superiors the faculty of dispensing students from some community exercises, including choir, if this is judged necessary for their advance in study.[15] The length of the scholastic year in clerical studies is nine months, which gives a summer vacation of three months.[16] In a letter of July 16, 1912, to the Ordinaries of Italy, the Sacred Consistorial Congregation decreed that there should be four hours of class daily in seminaries. Four and a half hours daily were permitted only if there was a full holiday each week. These hours were to be broken, not all consecutive. The Sacred Congregation opposed a greater number of hours as impossible and gave as the reasons: the religious exercises obligatory in seminaries and the interruption of labor and rest necessary to avoid harm to the physical health of the students.[17] Care of the health of the students is to be exercised in all seminaries, and it is at least not unusual for one of the officials to have the special duty of prefect of health.[18]

Is the life of the young and sometimes even of the older Sister in dark and even frightening contrast to this sensible legislation, regulation and reasoning of the Holy See? She is confronted daily with the exhausting task of six or seven hours of teaching young children, of extra-curricular activities, preparation for classes, several hours of religious exercises, domestic duties in the convent, and sometimes of added parochial duties. She may have to attend classes for her own education on some afternoons and on Saturdays. Her Christmas vacation is frequently taken up in great part by a second retreat, and her Easter vacation is sometimes devoted to the annual retreat. In the summer she is faced by summer school for her own education, her annual retreat, and sometimes by catechetical schools. In such a regime we can seriously doubt that she is capable of being soundly educated by the extra classes during the year and the summer school. We can affirm with certainty that sufficient care is not being taken of her physical and mental health and that she is not being given the maternal government demanded by Pius XII.[19] With equal certainty we can hold that her spiritual life is endangered. She is faced by an impossible life. Something has to break, and experience proves, at least usually, that the first thing to weaken in such circumstances is the spiritual life.

Purpose of Undergraduate Clerical Studies

The essential purpose of undergraduate clerical studies is to educate and train a competent and worthy priest for the sacred ministry. This purpose was expressed by Urban VIII, in 1624, "that they may later be useful workmen for the Church" [20]; by Benedict XIII, in 1725, "that they may be worthy, skilled, useful workmen" [21]; by Pius X, in 1910, "the formation of a priest worthy of the name." [22]

In 1940 the Sacred Congregation for the Oriental Church made a comparison with regard to this purpose, which we can summarize as follows: If lawyers, civil officials, doctors must study for years and obtain a prescribed degree, if even those engaged in the manual arts must serve a long apprenticeship, certainly the ministers of Christ need a much longer and much more careful formation both because of the sublime dignity of their office and the most important duty of directing souls.[23]

Is not the office of the Catholic teacher also sublime, also most important? That office is to form the mind, the heart, the soul to this life and especially to eternal life. Is the Sister being given a formation that is commensurate with her purpose and that can stand unashamed before the preparation required for a lawyer, a doctor, before that demanded and enjoyed by her secular colleagues in the teaching profession? We religious live in the day of a great movement in the Church, the renovation and adaptation of the religious life, initiated and fostered constantly and intensely by Pius XII. Does not this movement demand that we no longer look to secular agencies and persons for leadership, that the principle of our life, our work, our advance, our progress be within, not without?

If we go into this purpose in greater detail, we realize that clerical formation is a training in knowledge and in sanctity. Knowledge is of less importance but it is of great importance. The purpose of the formation in knowledge is not to produce merely a skilled spiritual mechanic, a man unlettered outside the sacristy and sanctuary. It is the intention of the Church, emphasized by Leo XIII,[24] that the priest be a man of culture, of wide and varied learning. Pius XII stated: "Seminarians are to be formed in piety and virtue and are also to acquire a literary and scientific learning that will later enable them to exercise an efficacious and fruitful ministry among all classes of citizens. A priest must be thoroughly familiar with sacred doctrine but he also cannot be ignorant of the knowledge possessed generally by cultured men of his own nation." [25]

To teach is to transmit culture. This is especially necessary in our country and age when, to paraphrase Pius XII, so many men work at machines and a much greater number think and live as machines.[26] Every Catholic teacher should be distinguished by a strong family resemblance to her mother, the Catholic Church, the mother of culture and the devoted parent of the liberal arts.

Is the extension, the summer school, the discontinuous type of education of Sisters apt to produce a person of information and methods rather than one of culture? Is the attainment of culture generally possible except in a continuous, prolonged, properly directed and properly regulated course of studies?

Seminary training is a preparation in knowledge but, in the language of Pius XI, it is infinitely more a preparation in sanctity.[27] Canon law sufficiently emphasizes this purpose and demands that common life be observed perfectly in religious houses of study, and this under the most severe penalty of privation of the ordination of the students, that only edifying religious be assigned to such houses, that the superior exert constant and careful vigilance to secure the most perfect observance of the religious exercises, that the students be committed to the care of a spiritual director of outstanding prudence, charity, spirituality, and religious observance, and that the professors are not only to be competent but also of conspicuous prudence and spirituality.[28] The law on diocesan seminaries is perfectly parallel.[29] The preeminence of this purpose does not escape canonical authors, who follow Clement VIII in classifying the period of clerical studies of religious as another noviceship.[30] However, it is especially in the constant directives of the Roman Pontiffs that the preparation in sanctity receives its adequate expression. Leo XIII and Benedict XV aptly summarized the purpose of diocesan seminary training not as mere observance of regulations, not as a mere morally upright life, but as the formation in the students of the living image of Jesus Christ.[31] In the thought of St. Pius X, the purpose of the seminary is to form the student in priestly sanctity, and the distinction between the priest and the merely upright man should be as great as that between heaven and earth.[32] This purpose must be intensified for clerical religious, since Pius XII has clearly removed any possible doubt from the proposition that it is the obligation of the religious, not of the cleric, to strive for complete evangelical perfection.[33]

Thus the training in priestly sanctity, in the religious sanctity of the religious priest, demands this long noviceship of at least eight years. Pius XII stated to a gathering of members of the Society of Jesus: "As a long space of time is required to establish the sturdy oak, so prolonged patience is always necessary for the formation of the man of God. Therefore, the generous daring of young men that impels them immaturely into action must be curbed. Too hasty activity destroys rather than builds up and is harmful both to the subject and to the apostolic works themselves." [34]

In law the Sister is no less the woman of God. She shares equally with religious men the obligation and the glory of striving for complete evangelical perfection. Is she not being rushed immaturely into action? Is it conducive to her purpose of personal sanctification to hurry a young Sister into the life of full activity after only a year and a half or two years and a half of postulancy and noviceship? You must be aware that at times even postulants and second-year novices are assigned to this life of full activity. In the case of the novices, this practice, as customarily carried out in fact, is clearly contrary to an important instruction of the Sacred Congregation of Religious.[35] Are these facts in accord with the principle of Pius XII quoted above? In his *Encyclical on Sacred Virginity,* the same Pontiff demands the long segregation of the seminary and scholasticate for diocesan and religious priests and then asks the question: "What gardener in planting trees exposes his choice but weak cuttings to violent storms that he may test the strength that they do not yet possess? The students of the sacred seminary and the scholastics are certainly to be considered like young and weak trees that must first be planted in places of shelter and prepared gradually for resistance and conflict." [36] Should not our age of the equality of woman have proved to us that she is the equal of men also in weakness? that she, too, needs a long segregation in the shelter of eternal things before she is strong enough to live eternal things even satisfactorily in the attractions and allurements of the things of time?

One House of Studies in Every Clerical Institute

The law of the Code is that every clerical religious institute is obliged to have at least one house of studies for philosophy and theology.[37] It is even somewhat probable that each province should have such a house.[38] The same law is true of every diocese for the diocesan clergy.[39] The reason for this norm is that the

Popes have identified the necessity of a seminary in every diocese with the necessity of seminary training itself.[40] We may add that a seminary in every diocese and a house of clerical studies in every religious institute are, generally speaking, more conducive at least to spiritual formation and evidently permit greater control, direction, and supervision. This canonical norm prompts the following subject for your thought: Should not every congregation of Sisters have its own juniorate where, immediately after the noviceship, the young professed complete their undergraduate intellectual formation and continue their spiritual formation? An observation must be added here. In commanding a seminary in each diocese and a house of studies in every clerical religious institute, the Church manifests that she has no excessive fear of educational inbreeding. This difficulty will be overcome by having the juniorate teachers make their graduate studies outside their own institute.

Exception to the Preceding Norm

According to canon law, if a religious institute or province cannot have a suitable house of studies for philosophy or theology or it is difficult to send the students to their own house of studies, they are to be sent to the house of studies of another province of the same institute, or of another religious institute, or to a diocesan seminary, or to a Catholic university.[41] In the same circumstances, a diocese is to send its seminarians to the seminary of one or several ecclesiastical provinces (regional).[42] These canons suggest the following thoughts for your consideration: the sending of the junior professed to the juniorate of another province, or to the classes of the juniorate of another institute, or to the classes of a Catholic college or university, or to those of a diocesan college for Sisters, or finally to a central house of studies for all the provinces of the same congregation.

One very important caution may and should be added here. A seminary is not a day school. By a seminary or clerical house of studies, the Church means a house where the students reside day and night. Otherwise, their principal purpose, the continued spiritual formation of the students, would have to be classed as a practical impossibility. If we apply this concept to congregations

of Sisters, the following conclusion seems to be evident: If congregations send their junior professed to classes outside their own
institute, these young professed should reside in the one house
of their own institute, under the direction of a mistress of juniors,
whose office is to be analogous to that of the spiritual director in
diocesan seminaries and clerical houses of study. If this is not
done, the principal purpose of a juniorate, the continued spiritual
formation of the young professed, will also be a practical impossibility. A well known authority on the law of religious, the Dominican canonist Pruemmer, has a pertinent thought on this matter: "Experience proves sufficiently and superabundantly that
clerical studies suffer when the students are scattered in small
houses that serve only secondarily for studies; therefore, they are
to be assembled in larger formal houses whose principal purpose
is the promotion of studies." [43] We can well add that their spiritual formation suffers even greater damage.

Separate Education for Junior Professed

It is the repeated and insistent teaching of the Roman Pontiffs
and the Roman Congregations, also in our day, that there is no
such thing as a mixed seminary, that is, an educational establishment for both seminarians and secular students. The words of
Pius XI on this point are: ". . . sacred seminaries are to be used
only for the purpose for which they were instituted, the proper
formation of sacred ministers. Therefore, not only must there be
no place in them for boys or young men who manifest no inclina-
tion for the priesthood, since such association does great harm to
clerics, but the religious exercise, the plan of studies, the method
of government must all tend to prepare the mind of the student
in the proper manner for the performance of his divine office.
This must be the sacred law of all seminaries and it admits of
no exception." [44] There are eminent canonists who maintain that
the seminary is not to be classed as mixed if seculars are confined
to attendance at the classes.[45] However, the Sacred Congregation
for the Oriental Church declared in 1940: "The doctrinal, moral,
and ascetical formation of the students is to be imparted in seminaries, that is, in colleges or houses devoted exclusively to the
preparation of students for the priesthood and properly estab-

lished and directed to this purpose." [46] Therefore, the doctrinal formation also is to be exclusively for seminarians. This principle was affirmed more clearly for Italy by the Sacred Consistorial Congregation in 1912 and the Sacred Congregation of Seminaries and Universities in 1920: "Care is to be taken also that the classes be reserved to seminarians or aspirants for the priesthood, since the seminary classes, also of minor seminaries, should have the distinctive spirit and orientation demanded for aspirants to the priesthood." [47] The latter Congregation also gave the essential reason for the principle, which we can summarize as follows: As the formation of a Catholic must animate every Catholic teacher and be the soul of every Catholic classroom, so the formation of the priest must animate every seminary professor and be the soul of every seminary classroom; education is formation, not the mere imparting of knowledge, and every class must be a training in both knowledge and virtue.[48] This doctrine of the Sacred Congregation is certainly not new; it is the basic concept of Catholic education. The reasons for the separation given by Popes and the Sacred Congregations are also: Clerical education is something entirely different from that of the laity, and the association of the two is a cause of loss of vocations, fatal to clerical formation, and the cause of great harm to clerical students. The distinction and separation of ecclesiastical and lay education are to be carefully pondered in the following emphatic words of Leo XIII: "For this reason the education, studies, and manner of life, in brief all that appertains to priestly discipline, have always been considered by the Church as something complete in themselves, not only distinct but also separate from the ordinary norms of lay life. This distinction and separation must remain unchanged also in our times, and any tendency to unite or confuse ecclesiastical education and life with lay education and life must be judged as reprobated not only by the tradition of the Christian centuries but by the apostolic teaching itself and the dispositions of Jesus Christ." [49]

Thus the subject for your consideration here is: Should not the classroom for the young Sister also have a distinctively religious spirit and orientation? Should not the religious formation of the Sister animate all her teachers and be the soul of every class she attends? Is the classroom of secular girls the suitable place for the education of the young Sister just out of the noviceship?

Financial Support of Juniorates

In his Apostolic Exhortation on Priestly Sanctity, Pius XII stated: "What is more, Venerable Brethren, We heartily commend the plans that you will discuss to insure that priests be provided not only with means to meet their daily needs but also with assurances of assistance for the future—as we are happy to see done in civil society—particularly for cases in which they may fall ill, be afflicted with chronic ill health, or be weakened by old age. Thus you will relieve them of all anxiety for the future." [50] If we apply again the principle of comparison, the salary of Sisters should be sufficient to provide for their daily necessities, at least all ordinary medical care and old age. It should also provide at least in good part for their formation. It is inherent and essential in every centralized religious institute that there should be an annual tax on every house for the general and provincial expenses, and a very great part of such expenses is the education and support of subjects in the states of formation. This tax is a necessary item of the budget of every convent, and the income of any convent of a school or institution that does not belong to the institute is to be derived at least principally from the salaries of its Sisters.

Education and Formation of Subjects As Part of the Internal Government of the Institute

The canons on clerical houses of study apply to all clerical religious institutes, even if diocesan. These canons nowhere prescribe any intervention of the local Ordinary, but, on the contrary, they place houses of study under the authority of the superiors and the general chapter of the particular institute.[51] The reason is evident. The education and formation of subjects in any religious institute, pontifical or diocesan, clerical or lay, is a matter that by its very nature clearly appertains to internal government, that is, to the authority of the superiors of the institute. The admitted concept of internal government in canon law is that it includes not only the general relation of subjects to superiors but also the admission of subjects into the congregation and to the professions, their education and formation, appointment to various offices and employments, and transfer from house to house.[52] External authority and other persons outside the institute may and have helped, but the right, the obligation, and the responsibility for the education of subjects fall on the superiors of the congregation. I believe it is necessary to emphasize this point. In this matter higher religious superioresses are too prone to wait for those outside the institute to take the initiative, whereas they themselves have the responsibility for action.

As a brief conclusion, we may appropriate a thought of Pius XI: "There is perhaps nothing that the Church has promoted through the course of the centuries more actively, maternally, and carefully than the suitable training of her priests." [53] In our own country, where Catholic education is so important a part of the Church and of Catholic life and where Sisters are so essential a part of that Catholic education, there is perhaps nothing that we should promote more actively, generously, and progressively than the proper education and formation of the Sisters.

FOOTNOTES

1. Address to the General Congress on the States of Perfection, Dec. 8, 1950, *AAS*, 42 (1951), 34.
2. Opening Address, First International Convention of Teaching Sisters, September, 1951, p. 14.
3. Can. 589, Sec. 1.
4. Can. 1364-1365.
5. *Menti Nostrae*, Sept. 23, 1950, *AAS*, 42 (1950), 692.
6. *Ibid.*
7. Instruction of the S.C. of Relig., Dec. 1, 1931, *AAS*, XXIV (1932), 77-78, *Canon Law Digest*, I, 478.
8. Leo XIII, Encyclical Epistle, *Etsi Nos*, to the Bishops of Italy, Feb. 15, 1882, *Enchiridion Clericorum*, n. 434; S.C. of Sem. and Univ., Letter, *Vixdum haec Sacra Congregatio*, to the Bishops of Germany, Oct. 9, 1921, *Ench. Cler.*, n. 1123.
9. S.C. of Sem. and Univ., Instruction to the Ordinaries of Italy, Apr. 26, 1920, *Il Monitore Ecclesiastico*, 33 (1921), 146.
10. Pius XII, Motu Proprio on the Pontifical Institute of St. Eugene, April 2, 1949, *AAS*, 41 (1949), 165-166, Bouscaren, III, 61-63; Instr. of the S.C. of Relig., Dec. 1, 1931, *AAS*, 24 (1932), 77, Bouscaren, I, 478; S.C. of Sem. and Univ., Instr. to the Ordinaries of Italy, Apr. 26, 1920, *Il Monit. Eccles.*, 33 (1921), 149-150; cf. S. Consist. Congr., Circular Letter to the Ordinaries of Italy, July 16, 1912, *Ench. Cler.*, n. 867.
11. Apostolic Letter, *Unigenitus Dei Filius*, to the Supreme Superiors of Orders of Regulars and other Societies of Religious Men, Mar. 19, 1924, *AAS*, 16 (1924), 143.

12. S.C. of Sem. and Univ., Instr. to the Ordinaries of Italy, Apr. 26, 1920, *Il Monit. Eccles.,* 33 (1921), 149-150; S. Consist. Congr., Circular Letter to the Ordinaries of Italy, July 16, 1912, *Ench. Cler.,* n. 867.

13. Can. 589, Sec. 2.

14. Abbo-Hannan, *The Sacred Canons,* I, 607; Beste, *Introductio in Codicem,* 401; Coronata, *Institutiones Iuris Canonici,* I, 764; Creusen, *Religious Men and Women in the Code,* n. 262; Vermeersch-Creusen, *Epitome Iuris Canonici,* I, n. 743.

15. Can. 589, Sec. 2.

16. Cf. S.C. of Relig., Declaration, Sept. 7, 1909, ad III, *Enchiridion de Statibus Perfectionis,* 275-276; Declaration, May 31, 1910, *Ench. de Stat. Perf.,* 282-283.

17. S. Consist. Congr., Circ. Letter to the Ordinaries of Italy, July 16, 1912, *Ench. Cler.,* n. 870.

18. Cf. Micheletti, *Constitutiones Seminariorum Clericalium,* 37-38; 54-55; 86-88; 118-119.

19. Address to the Congress of Mothers General, Sept. 15, 1952, *AAS,* 44 (1952), 825-826.

20. Apostolic Letter, *Universalis Ecclesiae,* Nov. 23, 1624, *Ench. Cler.,* n. 129.

21. Apostolic Constitution, *Creditae Nobis,* May 9, 1725, *Ench. Cler.,* n. 199.

22. Motu proprio, *Sacrorum Antistitum,* Sept. 1, 1910, *Ench. de Stat. Perf.,* 293.

23. Decree on the Proper Formation of the Oriental Clergy, Jan. 27, 1940, *AAS,* 32 (1940), 153.

24. Letter, *Plane quidem intelligis,* to the Cardinal Vicar of Rome, May 20, 1885, *Ench. Cler.,* nn. 461-462; Letter, *Obsequii pietatisque,* Apr. 21, 1901, to the Superiors and Students of the Sacred Seminaries of Milan, *Ench. Cler.,* n. 613.

25. Letter to the Cardinals, Archbishops and Bishops of Spain, June 29, 1941, *AAS,* 34 (1942), 226.

26. Allocution to Teachers of the Order of Discalced Carmelites, Sept. 23, 1951, *AAS,* 43 (1951), 736.

27. Address to the Students of the Pontifical French Seminary of Rome, Nov. 9, 1936, *Ench. Cler.,* n. 1510.

28. Can. 587, Secs. 1-2; 588; 1360, Sec. 1; 1366, Sec. 1.

29. Can. 1360, Sec. 1; 1366, Sec. 1; 1367; 1369, Sec. 1.

30. Clement VIII, Constitution, *Cum ad regularem,* Mar. 19, 1603, *Ench. de Stat. Perf.,* 104; Chelodi, *De Personis,* n. 275; Schaefer, *De Religiosis,* n. 1023; Wernz-Vidal, *Ius Canonicum,* III, n. 332.

31. Leo XIII, Encyclical Epistle, *Quod multum,* to the Bishops of Hungary, Aug. 22, 1886, *Ench. Cler.,* n. 473; Encyclical Epistle, *Fin dal principio,* to the Bishops of Italy, Dec. 8, 1902, *Ench. Cler.,* n. 703; Benedict XV, Encyclical Letter, *Ad beatissimi,* Nov. 1, 1914, *Ench. Cler.,* n. 919.

32. Exhortation to the Catholic Clergy, *Haerent animo,* Aug. 4, 1908, *Ench. Cler.,* n. 824.

33. Address to the General Congress on the States of Perfection, Dec. 8, 1950, *AAS,* 43 (1951), 29.

34. Allocution to the XXIX General Congregation of the Society of Jesus, Sept. 17, 1946, *AAS,* 38 (1946), 383.

35. Instr. on the Second Year of Noviceship, Nov. 3, 1921, *AAS,* 13 (1921), 539-540.

36. Encyclical on Sacred Virginity, March 25, 1954, *AAS,* 46 (1954), 185.

37. Can. 587, Sec. 1.

38. Can. 587, Sec. 3.

39. Can. 1354, Sec. 1.

40. Cf. *Ench. Cler.,* nn. 217, 383, 543, 1086.

41. Can. 587, Sec. 3.

42. Can. 1354, Sec. 3.

43. *Manuale Iuris Canonici*, Q. 220, 2.
44. Apostolic Letter, *Officiorum omnium*, on Seminaries and Clerical Studies, Aug. 1, 1922, *AAS*, 14 (1922), 451-452.
45. Cappello, *Summa Iuris Canonici*, II, p. 432; Coronata, *Institutiones Iuris Canonici*, II, 290; Vermeersch-Creusen, *Epitome Iuris Canonici*, II, n. 702.
46. Decree on the Proper Formation of the Oriental Clergy, Jan. 27, 1940, *AAS*, 32 (1940), 154.
47. S. Consist. Congr., Circular Letter to the Ordinaries of Italy, July 16, 1912, *Ench. Cler.*, n. 868; S.C. of Sem. and Univ., Instr. to the Ordinaries of Italy, Apr. 26, 1920, *Il Monit. Eccles.*, 33 (1921), 169-170.
48. *Ibid.*, 170-171.
49. Encyclical Epistle, *Fin dal Principio*, to the Bishops of Italy, Dec. 8, 1902, *Ench. Cler.*, n. 693.
50. Apostolic Exhortation, *Menti Nostrae*, Sept. 23, 1950, *AAS*, 42 (1950), 698.
51. Can. 587, Sec. 1.
52. Cf. Beste, p. 420.
53. Encyclical on the Catholic Priesthood, Dec. 20, 1935, *AAS*, 28 (1936), 37.

ECCLESIASTICAL DIRECTIVES FOR SEMINARIES AND FOR THE EDUCATION OF RELIGIOUS MEN

The Reverend John F. Zimmerman, C.M., J.C.D.
Kenrick Seminary, St. Louis, Missouri

My assigned topic, "The Ecclesiastical Directives for Seminaries and for the Education of Religious Men," must at first sight seem completely foreign to the subject matter of this Institute. To indicate the reason for its inclusion in the program, it was further suggested that my topic be confined to two points—the first, a brief explanation of the principle of analogy of law; and the second, a summary of Church law and practice in regard to the education of religious men, indicating the reasons for such regulations, in such wise that a basis may be laid, in later sessions, to determine which of these reasons apply to the education of Sisters. This we have attempted to do.

The Principle of the Analogy of Law

Notwithstanding the good will and diligence of the legislator, there remain deficiencies—*lacunae*—in his legislation. Since laws necessarily provide for the general situation, they fail at times to provide for particular cases, inevitable in the social and juridical interrelations of those for whom the law was made.[1] It is to meet the exigencies of these cases, that the Code of Canon Law, in Canon 20, supplies four objective sources to remedy the absence of norms, not only in general, but also in particular law. This canon gives us the authoritative way, the legal method of supplying law. Canon 20 reads as follows:

> "If there is no explicit provision concerning some matter, either in general or in particular law, a norm of action must be taken, unless there is question of applying a penalty, from laws given in similar cases, from the general principles of law applied with equity proper to Canon Law, from the style and practice of the Roman Curia, and from the common and constant teaching of approved authors." [2]

The case involved in this canon is one in which there is no law at all, either explicitly or implicitly expressed, and yet, one in which a norm of action must be found. In such a situation the legislator indicates that we must have recourse exclusively to the sources which he enumerates. These supplementary sources are the following:

1) *Laws given in similar cases.* Analogy between laws as a supplementary source of law has always been recognized in every judicial system. The axioms expressing this principle are found in the Glossa to the Old Canon Law (*Corpus Iuris Canonici*): "Where the same reason for the law exists, there the same disposition of law should prevail"; and "Of like things (in like cases), the judgment is to be the same." Obviously, then, we are justified in making use of this analogy of law in the matter under consideration in this Institute, for other than the canons pertaining to the training of novices in religious institutes of women, there is found no legislation on this matter in Part Two, "Concerning Religious" of the Second Book of the Code of Canon Law.

2) *The general principles of law.* The general principles of law, that is, of canon law and of natural law, are to be applied in accordance with the equity proper to canon law "with justice tempered with mercy."

3) *The style and practice of the Roman Curia.* By this is under-

stood the customary procedure employed by the various dicaster-
ies of the Roman Curia for expediting matters presented for their
consideration.

4) *The common and constant teaching of canonists.* To be a
common opinion the matter must be treated *"ex professo"* by at
least six authors of repute. If such a common opinion has been
persevering, it is constant and therefore meets the requirements
of this canon as a supplementary source of law.

Canon 490, which states that the provisions of the law in which
religious are named in the masculine gender apply equally to
women religious, unless the contrary is obvious from the context
or from the nature of the matter involved, also justifies our use
of analogy of law in the matter of Sister Formation. The norm
of this Canon is strictly applicable to all the legislation in the
second part of the second book of the Code, but it may also be
applied, if the context justified it, in reference to legislation in
other parts of the Code, as well as in post-Code documents of any
sort.[3]

The Canon Law in Regard to the Education of Religious Men

Title XII of the second part of the second book of the Code of
Canon Law treats of studies in clerical religious institutes. This
title in five canons, Canon 587 to Canon 591, very briefly treats
of the formation of clerical religious and members of clerical institutes of the common life. To this may be added the canons on
the curriculum in diocesan seminaries, as given in Title XXI,
"On Seminaries" of the fourth part of the third book of the
Code,[4] and various encyclicals of recent popes, such as the *"Menti
Nostrae"* of Pope Pius XII.

The opening canon, Canon 587, of Title XII on studies in
clerical religious institutes, requires that every clerical institute
shall have houses of studies, approved by the general chapter or
by the superiors, to which shall be assigned only religious conspicuous for the observance of religious discipline. The studies
referred to by this canon are those constituting the curriculum
of the philosophical and theological courses. The common life
must be observed in this house of studies, and if it is not, those
who study there cannot be promoted to Orders. The basic reason

for this legislation seems to be that the young religious be strengthened in their observance of the obligations of the religious life, by the example of the older religious who are their instructors and be shielded from those customs and abuses which might be a source of scandal to them.

This interpretation is strengthened by the third and fourth paragraphs of this canon, which allow young religious to be sent elsewhere for studies, to other houses of studies or to Catholic universities, but which require that these religious must live in houses of their institute, or of some other institute or seminary, but never in private houses. (Canon 587, #3 & 4).

During the whole course of studies, the students of religious institutes must be entrusted to the special care of a spiritual prefect or master who must train them in the ways of religious life by suitable direction, instruction and exhortation. (Canon 588). This prefect or master shall be endowed with the qualities of the Master of Novices, at least in the degree in which they are required of his associate. This prescription very fittingly can be applied, by analogy of law, to houses of studies, or juniorates, which several of our American communities of religious women have established. Certainly under the direction of such a competent mistress, the young religious more adequately and more fittingly will be formed to the spirit of their community, and will acquire a deeper and more lasting appreciation for the fundamentals of the religious life.

Canon 589 deals with the curriculum and the duration of studies, stating that, after a thorough instruction in the preparatory branches of study, the humanities, the young religious shall devote themselves to philosophical studies for at least two years, and to theological studies for at least four years, in accordance with the instructions of the Apostolic See. Upon cross-reference to Canon 1,365 on the curriculum of Major Seminaries, we find that the theological course must include, besides the study of dogmatic and moral theology, the study of Sacred Scripture, Church history, canon law, liturgy, sacred eloquence, Gregorian chant, pastoral theology, catechetics and the administration of the Sacraments.

Certainly this curriculum of clerical religious houses of studies does not pertain to houses of studies of religious women, but when we reflect that these courses are specified not only to prepare the religious clerics for Holy Orders, but also to deepen their own spiritual life, might there not be some application of these to the formation of religious women? Specifically, besides the courses in theology, which many communities have already introduced, perhaps a summary general introduction to the Sacred Scriptures, both the Old and New Testaments, as specified for the clerical religious students in the philosophical course, by the Instruction of the Biblical Commission of May 13, 1950, (A.A.S., Vol. 42, p. 495), could be adapted for juniorates of religious women. Many communities have also introduced a course on the tract "On Religious" in the second part of the second book of the Code of Canon Law.

The second paragraph of Canon 589 further orders that no offices or duties shall be imposed on the professors or students which might take them away from their work of teaching or studying or interfere in any way with their classes. Offices forbidden to students include those of teaching or of acting as prefects of discipline in schools. Moreover, the superior general, and in particular cases, other superiors also, may exempt them from some exercises of the community, including even the recitation of office in choir, whenever this seems necessary for the efficient pursuit of study.

This prescription prohibiting incompatible offices very fittingly can be applied to institutes of religious women. Worthy of note, also, I think, is the exemption from some community exercises, including the recitation of office in choir, which can be granted to students "whenever this seems necessary for the efficient pursuit of study."

Title XII concludes with two canons requiring an annual examination on the sacred sciences for five years following ordination, and in every formal house a monthly conference in which a moral and a liturgical case is solved. While these canons would have no immediate application to the training of religious women, perhaps again, the basic reason for these canons, the continued pursuit of the sacred sciences, may form the basis for practical application to the continuing formation of religious women while they are actively engaged in teaching and in the other works of their apostolate.

One final directive can be drawn fittingly from the exhortation of our present Holy Father, Pope Pius XII, *"Menti Nostrae"* of September 23, 1950. From the section dealing with the formation of seminarians, religious and diocesan, I would like to quote these words of our Holy Father, words which are equally applicable to religious women, during their period of formation:

> "Let directors have no fear in keeping them in contact with the events of the day which apart from furnishing them with the necessary material for forming and expressing a good judgment, can form material for discussions to help them and to accustom them to form judgments and reach balanced conclusions." [5]

The same exhortation *"Menti Nostrae"* should be a source of encouragement to you in your work of advancing the spiritual and intellectual formation of young religious women by the study of the sacred sciences. For our Holy Father goes on to say:

> "The masters of the spiritual life state that the study of the sacred sciences, provided they be imparted in the right way and according to correct systems, is a most efficacious help in preserving and nourishing the spirit of faith, checking the passions, and maintaining the soul united to God." [6]

FOOTNOTES

1. Abbo-Hannan, *The Sacred Canons* (St. Louis: Herder, 1952), I, 41.
2. Cicognani, *Canon Law*, 2nd rev. ed., 1934, p. 621.
3. Abbo-Hannan, *op. cit.*, I, 494.
4. Canons 1364 and 1365 of the Code of Canon Law.
5. *Menti Nostrae*, Sept. 23, 1950 (N.C.W.C. translation), pp. 31 ff., *AAS*, 42 (1950).
6. *Ibid.*

ECCLESIASTICAL DIRECTIVES FOR SEMINARIES AND FOR THE EDUCATION OF RELIGIOUS MEN

The Very Reverend Monsignor Warren L. Boudreaux, J.C.D.
Pastor, St. Peter's Church
New Iberia, Louisiana

We have come from far to debate a question. To determine, first of all, whether we have the vision to debate it, and then, whether we have the courage to follow that vision.

Men have long debated the proposition, and condemned it, whether there was or should be a double standard of morality—one for women and one for men. We have come to debate whether there shall be a double standard of training—one for religious men and one for religious women.

All laws and directives of the Church proposed for the training of seminarians and clerical religious are destined to achieve two things: One of them is holiness. The other is learning.

Whenever these two qualities were most present in the clergy, the Church prospered most. I do not pretend to defend this thesis here. I will only ask the doubting to search their history book and to find that it is true.

That is why the laws of the Church have required of seminarians that:

   a) they acquire a secular knowledge according to the needs of the time;
   b) they have at least two years of philosophy;
   c) they have at least four years of theology, both dogmatic and moral;
   d) they be well trained in the study of Sacred Scripture, Church history, canon law, liturgy, sacred eloquence and chant, and pastoral theology.

And all this time there is a program of spiritual formation.

And yet, with all this, there is a growing feeling that this is not nearly enough, and the Church, if not by legislation, at least by supplication, is asking for more and more training. And why?

Because the Church is no longer accepted in general as the

teacher and the Mother of men. Whether deserved or not, those fields which were especially hers are now challenged in the eyes of public opinion, and she is deserted on many sides.

The field of guidance and counseling is being assumed by the psychiatrist and the psychoanalyst; the field of charity by the Red Cross, the Community Chest, the Public Welfare; the right of the Church to teach is being questioned on all sides, so much so that it is the sorrow and the anguish of today's priests that they feel that the real world exists and that it is taking shape without them, and that they are strangers to it. They are aware that there is the danger, individual and social, that the world is becoming a swarm of slaves, even satiated ones, over whose lives and minds a minority of omnipotent technicians may soon have complete dominion.

In trying to correct the situation in France, where it was said an abyss separated priest and people, Cardinal Suhard wrote in *Priests Among Men:*

> "If the priest wants to be not only a learned man or a scholar, but the *doctor* (teacher) of the city, as his priesthood makes it a duty for him to be, he must acquire a culture which will enable him to see the world, men and things from God's point of view, that is to say, to save them and consecrate them in their entirety. It can be seen how, without paradox, the priest's interior life, as also his learning, is literally a public function and a social ministry." [1]

There are many such quotations, from which I shall select just one more: Pius XII said in the encyclical *On The Sacred Priesthood:*

> "The dignity of the office he holds and the maintenance of a becoming respect and esteem . . . demand more than purely ecclesiastical learning. The priest must be graced by no less knowledge and culture than is usual among well-bred and well-educated people of his day. That is to say, he must be healthily modern . . ." [2]

And so it is, you take a boy in his teens, or even younger, and you train him for years and years, with a general secular education that surpasses that of the average secular college, plus his specialty in the religious sciences, and all the years of formation taught him by his spiritual directors and imbibed through his own studies and you send him out a man—twenty-four years old, and even then you suspect he is not sufficiently prepared.

And what of a Sister? After two years of training in many instances she goes to a classroom with a high school education and a child's knowledge of catechism, to face the same problems as a priest.

Does a Sister receive infused knowledge from God? I have in general never noticed it. Is it less important that she be that much the lesser trained than a man? Nobody will concede it. Can a greater mistake be made in the confessional than in a classroom? I doubt it. Is a Sister that much different that we may expect her to carry so heavy a burden, without training equal or nearly equal to that of a man in her same position?

In the adapted words of Shylock in *The Merchant of Venice:*

"Hath not a Sister eyes? Hath not a Sister hands, organs, dimensions, senses, affections, passions; fed with the same food, hurt with the same weapons, subject to the same diseases, healed by the same means, warmed and cooled by the same summer and winter as a priest is? If you prick her, does she not bleed? If you tickle her, does she not laugh? If you poison her, does she not die?" [3]

Why are there so many Sisters whose lives are frustrated? Because besides carrying burdens they are not prepared to carry, their spiritual formation has been warped, through the reading and studying of pious drivel, or the instructions of well-meaning but poorly informed mistresses of novices, who did the best they could, but had not themselves had the advantages of proper training and theological education for so vital a function.

So that in many, many instances, a Sister is professed for ten or fifteen years before, through crowded summer courses and continual assault upon her nervous system and emotional life, she has anything like the training she should have had before she first left the motherhouse.

Mostly because of the frequent pleas of bishops and pastors for more Sisters in the schools, hospitals, and so on, there will be no solution to this problem, unless we will all have the courage to face the problem with honesty and courage. I am not here to propose a solution to this problem but since I have gone this far, and the die is cast, I may as well say what will have to be done:

1. We will have to realize that mother superiors are going to have to start saying "No" for a while to requests for more Sisters and more schools.

2. The period of training will have to be lengthened.

3. Mistresses of novices will have to be specially trained by intense courses in philosophy and theology, including ascetical theology from sound authors—not that of the rare mystic who would be the last person in the world to impose such principles on others.

4. Financial assistance will have to be given, either through increased salaries or diocesan collections or other means devised for many communities to give the Sisters, who serve the Church so well, at least a fair chance to be what we expect them to be.

And, therefore, I pray that "your charity may the more and more abound in knowledge and in all understanding." [4]

FOOTNOTES

1. In Emmanuel Cardinal Suhard, *Priests Among Men (Integrity* reprint), p. 79.
2. *Menti Nostrae,* Sept. 23, 1950 (N.C.W.C. translation), p. 40, *AAS* 42 (1950).
3. cf. *Merchant of Venice* III, 1.
4. Phil. 1:9.

ECCLESIASTICAL DIRECTIVES FOR THE EDUCATION OF SEMINARIANS AND OF MEN IN RELIGIOUS COMMUNITIES

The Reverend Thomas Brockhaus, O.S.B.
Mount Angel Abbey
St. Benedict, Oregon

It might reasonably be asked why the First Northwest Regional Meeting of the *Sister* Formation Conference should schedule a talk on "Ecclesiastical Directives for the Education of *Seminarians* and of *Men* in Religious Communities." Surely, if the Church's

Code of Canon Law * had included a section on the educational formation of *Sisters,* such a topic as "Directives for the Education of Seminarians" would lose much of its interest for the purposes of this day's gathering.

But it is precisely because the *Code of Canon Law* includes no special provision with respect to professional formation for teaching Sisters, that we shall examine the Code's prescriptions regarding religious clerics and seminarians, to discover principles and practical norms for our guidance in developing a program for the education of Sisters. This procedure has its sanction in the *Code of Canon Law* itself, which provides for just such supplementary norms in Canon 20. "If there is no express prescription of law, either general or particular, regarding some certain matter, the norm is to be taken, except in applying penalties, from laws enacted for similar cases, from the general principles of law tempered with canonical equity, from the style and practice of the Roman curia, and from the common and traditional opinion of teachers." [1]

The reason why we are compelled to start from Canon 20 and not from Canon 490, which states, "Whatever is prescribed for religious imposes the same obligation on women as on men, even though express mention is made only of men, unless the context or the nature of the matter plainly indicates the contrary," [2] is that in the present instance it is the "nature of the matter" which "plainly indicates the contrary." For the canons on the formation of men religious, like those for seminarians, have as their object preparation for holy orders and the clerical state.

Since Sisters do not aspire to the clerical state, the canons on the education of men in religious communities are not binding upon nuns according to the rule of Canon 490. But since, as we shall see, the ecclesiastical directives for the education of the clergy have in great part to do with their preparation for teaching, the supplementary norm of Canon 20 borrows these directives and offers them for our guidance in formulating a program for the formation of Sisters.

For convenience we shall group the directives selected from canon law under six headings: the House of Studies; the Seminary; the Administrative, Teaching and Counseling Staff; the Curriculum; Saint Thomas; and Catechetical Training and Pedagogy.

The House of Studies

Canon 587 prescribes in S 1: "Every clerical religious institute should have its houses of studies, approved by the general chapter or by superiors," [3] and adds, from Canon 554, S 3: "in which only such religious should be stationed as are exemplary in their zeal for observing the rule." [4]

"S 2. In the house of studies the perfect common life must be maintained; otherwise the students may not be promoted to orders." [5]

"S 3. If the institute or province is unable to maintain properly staffed and equipped houses of studies, or if, in the judgment of superiors, it is difficult to send their subjects to them, they should send their students to a properly conducted house of studies of some other province or institute, or to classes in the diocesan seminary, or to a Catholic university." [6]

"S 4. Religious who are sent away from their own monastery to make their studies are not allowed to live in private homes, but must take up their abode either in some other house of their institute, or if that cannot be done, in the house of some other male institute, or in a seminary or in some other pious house in charge of men in sacred orders, which has been approved by ecclesiastical authority."

The "common life" referred to in S 2 above is described by Father Adam C. Ellis, S.J., (in *Canon Law: A Text and Commentary* by Bouscaren and Ellis) in two senses: the wider sense, which means dwelling together under a common roof, sharing a common table and lodging with fellow members of a society subject to a designated superior and bound by a definite rule; [7] and the stricter sense defined in Canon 594, which describes the proper manner of practicing religious poverty, legislating for food, clothing, furniture, and the handling of money.[8] All of these elements are required in the house of studies.

The following Canon, 588, adds in S 3: "Superiors should see to it that the regulations prescribed for all religious in Canon 595 be observed most perfectly in the house of studies." [9]

Canon 595 reads: "S 1. Superiors should take care that all religious:

"1. make a retreat each year;

"2. unless lawfully impeded, daily assist at Mass, make their meditation, and carefully perform the other pious exercises prescribed by the rules and constitutions;

"3. go to confession at least once a week.

"S 2. Superiors should promote frequent and even daily reception of Holy Communion among their subjects, and every properly disposed religious must be allowed freely to approach the Most Holy Eucharist frequently, and even daily.

"S 3. If, however, a religious has, since his last sacramental confession, given grave scandal to the community or committed a serious and external fault, the superior may forbid him to receive Holy Communion until he shall have gone to confession again."

We further read in Canon 589, S 2: "During the time of their studies, the teachers and students are not to be assigned duties which will call them away from their classwork or interfere with the school in any way. The superior general, and in particular cases other superiors as well, may use their discretion in exempting them from certain community exercises, especially from the night offices in choir, whenever this seems necessary for the success of their studies." [10]

We must not omit here a provincial statute binding upon all religious in the Northwest. Decree 174 of the Fourth Provincial Council of Portland in Oregon states: "We strictly forbid religious of either sex, including those who are exempt, to attend any non-Catholic school without written permission of the local ordinary, which will be but rarely granted and is a matter of conscience for superiors."

The Seminary

Just as religious institutes must have their houses of studies, so must dioceses have their seminaries. Canon 1354 prescribes:

"S 1. Every diocese should have in a suitable place chosen by the bishop a seminary or college, where, according to the resources and extent of the diocese, a certain number of young men are trained for the clerical state.

"S 2. In the larger dioceses there should be two seminaries: a minor one where boys make their preparatory studies, and a major one for the students of philosophy and theology.

"S 3. If it is impossible to establish a diocesan seminary, or to obtain adequate training, especially in philosophy and theology, in the one which is established, the bishop should send his students to the seminary of some other diocese, unless an interdiocesan or regional seminary has been established by papal authority." [11]

The Administrative, Teaching and Counseling Staff

Canon 1358 prescribes: "There should be in every seminary a rector for discipline, teachers for instruction, a procurator, distinct from the rector, for financial administration, at least two ordinary confessors, and a spiritual director." [12]

Canon 1360, S 1, requires that the priests to be chosen for the offices of rector, spiritual director, confessors, and teachers in the seminary be not only learned but outstanding for their virtue and prudence, so that they may be a help to the students both by word and example.[13]

Canon 1366, S 1, adds that, other things being equal, the professorial chairs in philosophy, theology, and canon law be assigned by preference to those who have been awarded the doctorate by some university or faculty recognized by the Holy See; or in the case of religious, to those who have a corresponding testimonial from their major superiors.[14]

In an apostolic letter addressed to the superiors general of religious orders and societies of men on March 19, 1924, Pope Pius XI said: "We recommend particularly to you to see to it that well-qualified professors be chosen to teach the higher subjects among you; men who by the ordered purpose of their lives will stand out as examples, and who are thoroughly learned in the subjects which they are required to teach. Hence, every professor or lecturer should have completed with honor the course in philosophy, theology, and the allied branches, and should have sufficient skill and talent for teaching. Be mindful, too, of that provision of the Code: 'There should be separate and distinct professors at least for Sacred Scripture, dogma, moral, and Church history' [15] (Canon 1366, S 3)." [16]

The Curriculum

Students preparing for holy orders pass through a curriculum arranged to provide thorough training in orderly thinking, a solid and well-rounded knowledge of revealed religion, and the professional polish and specific skills useful for the sacred ministry. To attain these ends is the purpose of the laws enacted for houses of studies and for seminaries.

Canon 589 states in S 1: "Religious who have completed their preparatory studies shall apply themselves diligently to the study of philosophy for at least two years and of sacred theology for at least four years according to the instructions of the Holy See. They shall follow the teaching of St. Thomas as prescribed by Canon 1366, S 2." [17]

Canon 1366, S 2, reads: "Professors must follow faithfully and uncompromisingly the method, teaching, and principles of the Angelic Doctor in their lectures on rational philosophy and theology and in their instructions of the students in these subjects." [18]

Canon 1365, S 1, prescribes: "Seminarians shall devote at least two whole years to the study of rational philosophy and related subjects.

"S 2. The theology course shall extend over at least four whole years, and in addition to dogmatic and moral theology it shall include especially Sacred Scripture, Church history, canon law, liturgy, sacred eloquence, and chant.

"S 3. Lectures must also be given in pastoral theology, with practical exercises especially in the method of teaching catechism to children and to others, of hearing confessions, visiting the sick, and assisting the dying." [19]

Saint Thomas

Pope Pius XII summarized the reasons for following the principles and method of St. Thomas in a speech on June 24, 1939, to the clerical students in Rome, when he said: ". . . the wisdom of Aquinas throws a vivid light upon the truths of natural phi-

losophy and wonderfully binds them together in a firm and co-
herent unity; it is excellently adapted to explain and defend the
dogmas of the faith; finally, it is sufficiently effective to check and
to conquer the principal errors which are rampant in every
age. . . ."

On August 12, 1950, in his encyclical *Humani Generis,* the
Holy Father explained at greater length: ". . . as we well know
from the experience of centuries, the method of Aquinas is sin-
gularly preeminent both for teaching students and for bringing
truth to light; his doctrine is in harmony with divine revelation,
and is most effective both for safeguarding the foundation of the
faith, and for reaping, safely and usefully, the fruits of sound
progress." [20]

The Church would have us build our intellectual structure
solidly, from the ground up. Modern scientific investigation with
its objective observation of facts and gathering of data, supple-
ments and completes the groundwork laid by St. Thomas. We
must always refer to him for the "why" even though scholars of
a later age supply us with the "what" and the "how" of new
facets of reality.

Catechetical Training and Pedagogy

Thus far we have concerned ourselves with selected areas of the
Church's legislation, requiring first of all that institutions of
higher learning be established and maintained for seminarians
and religious clerics. We have glimpsed briefly at the recollected,
scholarly, and definitely religious atmosphere of these institutions
—staffed by a personnel marked out for holiness and prudence as
well as learning and the ability to communicate knowledge to
students: actions speak louder than words. We have surveyed the
curriculum for at least two years of philosophy and four of theology—at least six years in all—and have taken special pains to discover the reasons for the Church's insistence on following the
principles and methods of St. Thomas Aquinas.

Now, to complete the picture, the remainder of our discussion
of the Church's directives will be devoted to its detailed practical
instructions on the actual teaching of catechetics and pedagogy.
Selection of these particular topics is necessarily arbitrary—since

there are similarly detailed instructions on the teaching of Sacred Scripture, religion, Latin, sacred chant, canon law, and Catholic Action, English translations of which are readily available in Bouscaren's *Canon Law Digest* [21] but the directives on the teaching of catechetics and pedagogy provide typical examples. They point up the Church's desire to keep abreast of new developments in practical teaching techniques, which nevertheless are not permitted to encroach upon the traditional staple courses in its educational program.

A letter of the Sacred Congregation of Studies addressed on September 8, 1926, to the most reverend ordinaries reads in part as follows:

"The *Code of Canon Law*, in Canon 1365, S 3, provides that in the course of theology which must be maintained for at least four years 'there shall also be lectures in pastoral theology, with practical exercises particularly in the manner of teaching catechism to children and others.' . . .

"Since the teaching of most profound matters especially to the uneducated and ignorant in language suited to their understanding is a most difficult as well as a most necessary task, a long and diligent preparation for so great a work is to be made. This must be done in seminaries; *for it is for this that they are established.* But in order to undertake the task of teaching the people rightly and with success, it is not sufficient to have a doctrinal training merely, which consists in the knowledge of the truths to be taught, and which is acquired by the study of theology, especially of dogma, but a certain pedagogical training also is required, as regards the manner in which those truths are to be taught; and this is imparted both by suitable instruction and by practical exercises.

"The words of Pope Pius X in his memorable encyclical *Acerbo Nimis* of April 15, 1905, are here in point: 'It is far easier to find an orator who will speak copiously and beautifully than a catechist whose teaching is in every respect what it should be. Therefore, whatever be the facility in thought and expression with which a person is naturally endowed, let him remember this: he will never treat of Christian doctrine to children or to the people with profit to their souls unless he prepares and makes himself ready by much reflection . . . the more untutored one's hearers

are, the more care and diligence he must use to adapt those sublime truths, in themselves so remote from the common grasp, to
the dull minds of the uneducated, to whom they are as necessary
as they are to the wise for the attainment of eternal beatitude.'...

"Let the professor of pastoral theology give frequent instructions on the manner of teaching Christian doctrine; and let the
clerics themselves have practical exercises in preparation for this
great work, either in the seminary or in churches, as prudence
may suggest." [22]

In another letter to the most reverend local ordinaries three
years later, on August 28, 1929, the same Sacred Congregation of
Studies reaffirmed the need for a special course in catechetics and
asked the ordinaries to inform the Congregation of what actual
steps had been taken in the seminaries to comply with the directives.[23]

Finally, on December 21, 1944, the Sacred Congregation of
Seminaries and Universities issued further instruction to the most
reverend ordinaries, saying in part:

"The training of seminarians in pedagogy, didactics, and catechetics has always been the object of many cares and grave solici-
tude on the part of this Sacred Congregation.

"It is clear from the pages of the Gospel, from the letters of the
Apostles and from the whole history of the Church, that the priest
of Christ is not only a minister of worship and an official of the
liturgy, but also an educator, an instructor, charged with the
training of minds and consciences. In fact, in the commission of
Christ to the Apostles, the *magisterium* or teaching office precedes
the Sacramental and liturgical ministry: *Going, therefore, teach
ye all nations, baptizing them in the name of the Father, and of
the Son, and of the Holy Ghost* (Matt. 28, 19).

"In obedience to this divine command the Apostles actually
placed the *magisterium* before all other activities; so that St. Paul
could say: *Christ sent me not to baptize, but to preach the Gospel* (I Cor., 1, 17).

"The reason for this precedence of the teaching office is evident: a soul cannot be endowed with grace until it has been enlightened with truth.

"It follows that, for priests, *pedagogy*, dealing with education
in general, *didactics*, which is concerned in general with teaching

and method, and *catechetics,* that is, didactics applied to the teaching of religion, are of primary importance.

"It might be objected that the basic laws of education are easily learned by experience, and that in the field of pedagogy good natural dispositions joined to the Christian virtues and aided by grace have always borne abundant fruits. But it is also true that art perfects nature, and religious education may truly be called the *art of arts.*

"The importance of this preparation has greatly increased in recent times.

"It is clear, therefore, that today more urgently than in the past, there is need of giving to candidates for the priesthood proper training also in the matter of pedagogy and didactics.

"Hence the following provisions are made:

"I. *The Course in Philosophy*

"A theoretical-practical course in pedagogy and didactics shall be established (two years, one hour a week); this may be entrusted to the professor of philosophy, inasmuch as these subjects are closely connected with psychology and ethics. . . .

"Thus future priests will at least not be inferior to the teachers in elementary schools, who in their normal training have had courses in pedagogy and the history of education, and they will also be better able to make their way in the various departments of the sacred ministry, especially in the teaching of religion.

"It will be very useful to have the seminarians explain in the form of lectures—to high-school students, educated persons, and members of study clubs—some of the theses which are studied in the course of philosophy and which confute the errors of the present day (for example, the theses on the spirituality and immortality of the soul, the freedom of the will, the end of man, the moral law and its sanctions, and so on). Likewise the seminarians should be made to discuss among themselves under the direction of the professor the best methods of presenting and effectively proving these truths, so that they will become accustomed to put their theoretical course into practice.

"II. *The Course in Theology*

"A practical course in catechetics is to be established, with special reference to the teaching of religion in schools. It is less a question of establishing such a course, since it is already included in pastoral theology, than of increasing its effectiveness and making it more specific. Accordingly, two of the four hours assigned to pastoral theology shall be given to catechetics.

"The students of theology shall develop in writing and orally the theological subjects which have a connection with catechetics, not only in the form of homilies and explanations of the Gospel, but also by way of lectures to students of various schools, under the direction of the professor; and they shall discuss the best method of giving such lectures.

"Moreover, practical exercises in catechetical teaching are to be introduced where they are not already in use (cf. Canon 1365, S 3), not only in a parish but also in a public or private school or in the seminary itself. . . .

"Let the candidates for the priesthood be persuaded that the teaching of religion is not only the teaching of the most noble of the sciences but is also the bestowal of the *word of life,* which the Lord will bring to fruition in the hearts of the listeners. It is therefore not merely a task of teaching, for which scientific preparation would be sufficient, but it is above all an apostolate in which the grace of God and the cooperation of good example on the part of the teacher are indispensable." [24]

Some of those present who have majored in education need not take alarm at the scant eight semester hours prescribed to cover their field. Actually, our American seminaries have in great part allowed more time for their education courses.

FOOTNOTES

* References to the actual text of the Canon Law will be made to the page on which the canon concerned is found in: *Codex Iuris Canonici* Pii Pontificis Maximi iussu digestus, Benedicti Papae XV auctoritate promulgatus, Newman Book Shop, 1946. When the simple word *Codex* begins a footnote, it is to this book that reference is made. References will be given also to English translations or equivalent commentaries from: Bouscaren, T. Lincoln, S.J., and Ellis, Adam C., S.J., *Canon Law: A Text and Commentary,* Bruce Publishing Company, 1948, and/or Woywod, Rev. Stanislaus, O.F.M., L.L.B. and Smith, Rev. Callistus, O.F.M., J.C.L.: *A Practical Commentary on the Code of Canon Law.*

1. *Codex,* p. 5; cf. Bouscaren, *op. cit.,* pp. 34-35; Woywod, *op. cit.,* p. 14.
2. *Codex,* p. 164; cf. Bouscaren, *op. cit.,* pp. 232-3; Woywod, *op. cit.,* p. 206.
3. *Codex,* p. 198; cf. Bouscaren, *op. cit.,* p. 279; Woywod, *op. cit.,* p. 279.
4. *Codex,* p. 188; cf. Bouscaren, *op. cit.,* p. 265; Woywod, *op. cit.,* pp. 254-5.
5. *Codex,* p. 198; cf. Bouscaren, *op. cit.,* p. 280; Woywod, *op. cit.,* pp. 278-9.

6. *Codex,* pp. 198-9; cf. Bouscaren, *loc. cit.;* Woywod, *loc. cit.*
7. Bouscaren, *op. cit.,* pp. 229-30.
8. *Codex,* p. 201; cf. Bouscaren, p. 281.
9. *Codex,* p. 199; cf. Bouscaren, *op. cit.,* p. 279; Woywod, pp. 278-9.
10. *Codex,* p. 199; cf. Bouscaren, *op. cit.,* pp. 281-2; Woywod, *op. cit.,* p. 279.
11. *Codex,* p. 462; cf. Bouscaren, *op. cit.,* p. 697; Woywod, *op. cit.,* pp. 119-20.
12. *Codex,* p. 465; cf. Bouscaren, *op. cit.,* p. 698; Woywod, *op. cit.,* p. 123.
13. *Codex,* p. 466; cf. Bouscaren, *op. cit.,* pp. 698-9; Woywod, *op. cit.,* p. 123.
14. *Codex,* p. 468; cf. Bouscaren, *op. cit.,* pp. 700-1; Woywod, *op. cit.,* p. 134.
15. *AAS,* (16), 133; cf. T. Lincoln Bouscaren, *The Canon Law Digest,* I, 670.
16. *Codex,* p. 469; cf. Bouscaren, *loc. cit.;* Woywod, *op. cit.,* pp. 129-30.
17. *Codex,* p. 199; cf. Bouscaren, *loc. cit.*
18. *Codex,* p. 468; cf. Bouscaren, *op. cit.,* pp. 281-2; Woywod, *op. cit.,* p. 279.
19. *Codex,* p. 467; cf. Bouscaren, *op. cit.,* p. 700; Woywod, *op. cit.,* p. 126.
20. NCWC translation, p. 14.
21. *Canon Law Digest,* III, 551; I, 280, 644; III, 549; I, 662; II, 65.
22. *Canon Law Digest,* I, 664-665.
23. *Ibid.,* pp. 666-669.
24. *AAS,* (37), 173. *Canon Law Digest,* III, 545-549.

THE TRAINING AND EDUCATION OF PRIESTS AND MEN RELIGIOUS

The Reverend Charles Connors, C.S.Sp.
St. Mary's Seminary
Norwalk, Connecticut

As I understand my task, it is to point out the directives of the Church to be observed in the preparation of seminarians and men religious for their role in dispelling ignorance of the things that really count in life, particularly with a view to providing you with material for consideration in determining means and methods for more effectively fulfilling your role as religious and teachers in the same over-all task.

The primary source of such directives is the *Code of Canon Law.* In many instances the Code is very general in its legislation, and rightly so; for it is intended to be an enduring guide, although allowing of change, for the whole Latin rite. Consequently, it has been drawn up for application to a variety of conditions, in divers places, subject to different—in some instances, contrary—needs that frequently change with the times.

The absence of detailed legislation is especially noteworthy in the second part of Book Two of the Code, that part which deals with religious; and for obvious reasons. For some of the laws therein contained apply to all religious, some only to women and some exclusively to men, to cleric and lay. In addition, the Code is not meant to be the only directive for religious, for necessarily each institute has its own rules and constitutions; and these lay down more exact prescriptions, depending on the nature and end of the institute. In fact, the Code frequently "canonizes," as it were, these constitutions by explicitly decreeing in many matters that the way in which a universal law is to be fulfilled depends on them, even in so fundamental a matter as the vows themselves, which are taken in accordance with the respective rules and constitutions. Finally, the Code is not the last word from the point of view of time, for the Church always can and frequently does issue directives deemed necessary to attain more accurately the aim of religious life, to curb abuses, and to encourage adaptation to changing conditions.

The Code in Canon 487 clearly indicates in what the religious life essentially consists: the state of living in common by members of the Church who have taken the vows of poverty, chastity, and obedience. The same canon requires that this state be held in honor by all, since it is the way of perfection, the way of the evangelical counsels.

The general legislation in regard to the formation of religious is concerned chiefly with the spiritual life, since that is the element common to all who embrace the religious life. Thus Canon 565, Section 1, establishes as the purposes of the novitiate the spiritual formation of the subjects by the study of the respective constitutions, by prayer and meditation, by the understanding and the practice of the vows, and by the exercises required to root out vice and acquire virtue. Christian doctrine is to be taught to those in certain categories. As an indication that spiritual formation is to be the exclusive objective of the canonical year of the novitiate, the same canon forbids novices to engage in works of the ministry or in the study of letters, arts, or sciences or other activities that would interfere with this primary purpose.

It is not surprising if little is said about the intellectual training of religious—with one exception, to be considered shortly—because of the universal nature of the Code, for practically nothing in this field could be set down that applies equally to men and women, cleric and lay, contemplative and missionary, nursing and teaching Sister; because religious become such by reason of their public vows, not by reason of the purpose of their institute, and the Code treats of them as they are members of the Church in a particular state; because, finally, in the last analysis it is the particular rules and constitutions which establish particular objectives and means to those objectives. These rules require some ecclesiastical approbation, at the granting of which provision can be made that the aims and methods of the institute are consonant with the nature of religious life as fostered by the Church and are in accord with the policy of the Church in regard to religious institutes.

For example, if a new American foundation of priests to do foreign mission work sought approval of its rules, one of which was that its members should strive to Americanize all pagans whom they met, the approbation would not be forthcoming, for this is not the way of the Church in evangelizing pagans. As an example of how this works, we may note the present policy of the Holy See to require that in the constitutions submitted for its approval for institutes of women dedicated to nursing, articles must be inserted to provide for the attainment of a recognized degree and for the furtherance of professional knowledge by professed members. Constitutions for newly recognized institutes of women given to teaching demand of their members after profession an additional period of formation—spiritual and intellectual, including the attaining of an academic degree if it is at all possible. Thus, through the necessity of obtaining approbation, the constitutions are assured of providing effective means of achieving the objectives of the respective institute, without any change being made in the basic law.

Another mode of accomplishing the same effect is a general papal directive, since the Pope is the supreme superior of every religious institute. On March 31, 1954, in his letter to the Cardinal Prefect of the Sacred Congregation of Religious, on the subject of Institutes of Teaching Brothers, our Holy Father wrote of the importance of instructing young men "in the liberal arts and every type of discipline so that they may assume the direction not only of their private affairs but also of public matters." He then expresses the wish that the Teaching Brothers be "guided by those rules which their Founders have bequeathed to their respective institutes as a sacred inheritance . . ."; and "strive to imbue the youths confided to them with a doctrine that is not only certain and free from all error, but which also takes account of those special arts and processes which the present age has introduced into each of the disciplines." [1]

Again, speaking to the teaching Brothers of the Order of Discalced Carmelites on September 23, 1951, the same Pontiff pointed out that today, in view of the demands of the times, of the increased construction of schools, of the need for advancement in research and study, of the necessity of paying workers a just wage, a certain liberality in regard to the vow of poverty is required.[2] Just a year later Pope Pius echoed these words in addressing the Congress of Mothers General: "Be broad of vision. Whether it is a matter of education, pedagogy, care of the sick, of artistic activity . . . give them [the Sisters] the possibility of keeping their professional capacities up to date." [3]

Thus the supreme authority in the Church, within the present framework of canon law and particular constitutions, points out the need of broader interpretations in order to meet new problems. More marked departures from particular practices might require, of course, actual changes in the institute's rules; rarely would canon law itself have to be changed.

The one title in the treatment on religious in the Code which deals with studies is restricted in its application to those institutes whose members aspire to the priesthood. In substance this title requires of such aspirants and of the houses in which they study what is required of all seminarians and seminaries, with due allowances being made because of the difference in status. The exceptions to community observance which the Code allows for religious engaged in such studies are significant:

  1. They are not to engage in any activities that would interfere with their studies;

2. They may be excused from community exercises, including choir attendance, if the superior considers it necessary;

3. They may live out of community, if necessary, to attend schools other than those of their own institute.

From the exceptions it can be concluded that when there is an unavoidable conflict between the demands of religious life and the demands of a proper preparation for the priesthood, the latter take precedence, for the priesthood may be said to be the culminating step to the qualifications necessary for the religious cleric to carry out the work of his institute.

The general requirements for any seminary are that students have completed their courses in the classics before entrance, that they do two years of philosophy and four of theology. The time element itself, not merely the course content, is prescribed. At present there is some talk of extending the period of philosophy to three years because of the increasing philosophical errors of our times, or perhaps because of the need of a longer period of formation. The change has been adopted in some dioceses and has long been the practice in some institutes; but so far it is not a universal requirement.

The principal objective of a seminary is the spiritual, disciplinary, and intellectual formation of seminarians. In discussing this objective, a recommendation of the Sacred Congregation of Studies to the bishops of the United States on January 24, 1928, asserts: "Spiritual training does not consist merely in the acquisition of goodness and moral honesty; it embraces also all that group of virtues by which the priest ought to become a living image of our Saviour." [4]

In his encyclical on the sanctity of priestly life, *Menti Nostrae,* Pope Pius XII writes: "Particular attention must be paid to character formation in each boy by developing in him the sense of responsibility, the capacity to use his judgment concerning men and events, and the spirit of initiative." [5] He then goes on to point out the importance of gradual lightening of control and of assistance in accepting increased responsibility, the gradual and prudent establishment of contact "with the judgments and tastes of the people in order that when they receive Holy Orders and

begin their ministry they will not feel themselves disorientated—
a thing that would not only be harmful to souls but also injure
the efficacy of their work." [6]

As for the quality of the intellectual training, another quota-
tion from Pius XII's encyclical on the priesthood neatly summarizes the matter: "We urge that the literary and scientific
education of the future priests be at least not inferior to that of
laymen who take similar courses of study." [7] He gives one rather
unexpected reason for this: namely, so that a seminarian who is
undecided about going on for the priesthood will not feel compelled, like the unjust steward, to reason: 'To dig I am not able,
to beg I am ashamed,' but will feel confident of taking his place
in the world, his time spent in the seminary constituting no loss
to him. Perhaps, even, some young men hesitate to enter the seminary because they fear that if they change their minds about
being priests they will be useless for anything else; or at least
will have lost a great deal of time necessary to achieve another
objective.

Canon 1365, Section 3, requires that the student for the priesthood be given some practical exercises in such things as catechetics—what we might call practice teaching of catechism. Pope
Pius XI, writing on the teaching of pastoral theology, points out:
"In this connection special regard must be had to the times. For
the course of time has introduced many practices among the faithful which were unheard of in the days of our fathers. The priest
today must know these things so that he may find in the power
of Christ new remedies for new ills." [8]

Contrary to a fairly common belief, even amongst some of the
clergy, not every priest is qualified to teach every subject in the
field of education; indeed, not every subject in the seminary curriculum. Hence, seminary professors are to receive special training and are even urged, if teaching a sacred or allied science, to
have a graduate degree from a pontifical university. For other
subjects they may, of course, go to another university, which
should be Catholic. Canon 1379 gives the Ordinary the right to
decide when attendance at a secular college or university is justified for any Catholic, all the more for any cleric or religious. The
conclusion is obvious: permission of the Ordinary should be ob-

tained. You can well imagine the result if a bishop forbids all of his subjects to attend a certain institution of higher learning, only to have a priest or Brother from outside the diocese enroll in the same institution.

In the previously referred to recommendations of the Sacred Congregation of Studies to the hierarchy of the United States back in 1928, the bishops were urged to give consideration to an adequate and progressively increasing wage scale for seminary professors so that they will "not be unduly preoccupied by distractions of an economic nature." [9] One of the results of such an arrangement ought to be that the professors' "work itself will become more efficient." [10]

The religious seminary professor, enjoying the benefits of the vow of poverty, need not worry about salaries. But he must keep in mind the reason for the suggestion of the Sacred Congregation —to prevent unnecessary distractions of an economic nature, with which he, too, might be burdened if his institute does not provide adequate support, and thus be forced to engage in activities to increase the community's income, activities of such a nature and magnitude as to hinder his efficiency as a seminary professor. Incidentally, the present Roman Pontiff asks the question: "How can you expect fervent and energetic work from priests when they lack the necessities of life?" [11]

Since the seminary is meant to lay the foundations, the process of building the superstructure must go on after ordination. Hence, Canon 129 decrees that clerics—and clerical religious are included—should not abandon study, especially of the sacred sciences, after promotion to the priesthood. They are to be subjected to annual examinations for five years after ordination and are to assist at clerical conferences called several times a year by the Ordinary. Pope Pius XII has recently proposed that all young priests be gathered in special institutions, such as he has established in Rome, for several years after their ordination to prepare them gradually and prudently for the apostolate, to develop their piety and perfect them in sacred studies and put them on "the path toward that form of the ministry more closely corresponding to their temperament." [12] The spirit of novelty being diffused among some priests, "especially those less equipped with doctrine and of less strict lives" demands that some such steps be taken, since it is recognized that "the passage from the sheltered and tranquil life of the seminary to the active ministry may be dangerous for the priest who enters the open field of the apostolate if he has not been prudently prepared for the new life." [13]

Moreover, priest experts are to be trained for various positions in the diocese, including that of leaders in proclaiming and applying the Church's social teachings, a type of expert the training of which was particularly urged by Pope Pius XI in *Quadragesimo Anno*. As in the conducting of Catholic schools, as Pope Pius XII pointed out in his address on the Lay Apostolate of October 14, 1951, assistance rendered by the laity "is an indispensable necessity" since "the clergy must above all keep themselves free for the exercise of the sacred ministry proper to the sacerdotal state." [14]

*   *   *

Thus canon law is very general in its treatment of the training of men religious and priests, and fortunately so, for it thus remains flexible, allowing for new directives demanded by the times.

But there are some precepts even more fundamental than those of positive law; namely, those deriving directly from the virtue of justice. These deserve serious consideration from ecclesiastics who conduct schools of all levels. If they assert—and rightly so—that parents are obliged in conscience to send their children to Catholic schools, on their part they must make those schools fit to accept such a trust. When they accept students, they enter a contract to provide an adequate and truly Catholic education. The graduates of a Catholic school, by reason of its curriculum and the recognized qualifications of its faculty, ought to enjoy a status comparable to that of other schools of the same category.

Therefore those who conduct schools are obliged in justice to provide properly trained teachers; namely, teachers whose spiritual life and external works, as Pope Pius XII has put it, progress at an equal pace.[15] As long ago as 1878 Pope Leo XIII prescribed: "The more must you labour zealously to develop not only a good and solid method of education, but especially to make the teaching itself conformable in science and discipline to the Catholic faith. In particular is this true of philosophy, on which depends in a great degree the just direction of the other sciences." [16]

Since religious education, even more than instruction in other subjects, consists in much more than imparting learning, the teacher must be acquainted with methods of imparting the spirit of our faith and with the decrees of the Church governing the practice of religion. Such knowledge on the part of the teacher would prevent certain practices which, despite condemnation, are still found occasionally—such as requiring students to defame themselves publicly by admitting failure to assist at Mass on Sunday; reproaching children who do not participate in "general communion," a term which the Sacred Congregation of the Sacraments said "should either not be used at all or its meaning be carefully explained; namely, that all are invited to the Holy Table, but no one is obliged to approach" [17]; and other abuses of this nature. It is not surprising that Pope Pius XII reminded a group of teaching Brothers that to perform their task well they must follow the directives of the Church in matters philosophical and theological.[18]

Not every priest or religious will be called upon to be a school teacher; but those who are, in order to comply with the laws and directives of the Church and the obligations of justice, ought to be thoroughly prepared and well grounded in the matter they have to teach, ought to possess the intellectual and moral qualifications required by their important office.

By presenting you with these considerations I may have increased your problems. If so, I have lived up to the reputation canonists enjoy among their fellow priests—that of complicating simple problems and creating some where none existed. But I know that all of our problems can be reduced to one—to dispel the ignorance that keeps men from the God Who loves them.

FOOTNOTES

1. "The High Mission of the Teaching Brothers," *The Pope Speaks,* (Second Quarter, 1954), 125-126, *AAS* (1954), 202-205.
2. "Ad Docentes ex Ordine Fratrum Carmelitarum Discalcaetorum," *AAS,* 43 (1951), 734 ff.
3. "On Religious Vocations," *The Catholic Mind,* LI (June, 1953), 381, *AAS,* 44 (1952), 823 ff.

4. Canon Law Digest, ed. T. Lincoln Bouscaren, S.J. (Milwaukee: Bruce Publishing Company, 1943), II, 649-50.
5. Menti Nostrae, (N.C.W.C. translation, 1951), p. 31, AAS, 42 (1950).
6. Ibid., p. 32.
7. Ibid.
8. "Apostolic Letter, August 1, 1922," Canon Law Digest, 646.
9. Canon Law Digest, I, 655.
10. Ibid.
11. Menti Nostrae, p. 44.
12. Ibid., p. 39.
13. Ibid., p. 37.
14. "The Lay Apostolate," The Catholic Mind, L (February, 1952), 117, AAS, 43 (1951), 92.
15. See note 3 above.
16. Inscrutabili, Social Wellsprings. Fourteen Epochal Documents of Pope Leo XIII, ed. Joseph Husslein, S.J. (Milwaukee: Bruce Publishing Company, 1940), 10-11.
17. Decree of December 8, 1938. Sub, Cn. 857. Canon Law Digest, II, 213.
18. AAS, 43 (1951), 735. See note 2.

◦IV◦

SISTER EDUCATION FROM THE
VIEWPOINT OF THE
SUPERINTENDENT OF SCHOOLS

SOME NEEDS IN TEACHER PREPARATION

The Right Reverend Monsignor F. N. Pitt
Superintendent of Schools
Archdiocese of Louisville
Louisville, Kentucky

At the twenty-fourth meeting of the National Catholic Educational Association, held in Detroit, June, 1927, an important paper was read on teacher training by the Reverend Sylvester Schmitz, O.S.B. The title of the paper was "Trends in Teacher Training." It was important, because this paper and the discussion it aroused had considerable influence upon the objectives and methods of training our religious teachers. While not condemning a liberal arts education for our teachers, the writer would definitely discourage it for all but high school and college teachers. The plan advocated was two years of normal school training for the elementary teacher before entering the classroom. The necessary credits for a degree would then be gained in summer schools and extension courses, all of which should be professional training for specific levels of elementary education. As stated by Father Schmitz, "Teacher training should be differ-

91

entiated on the basis of future professional service in the elementary school." [1]

The general theme of the paper was in keeping with the trends of times twenty-seven years ago. At that time state normal schools were rapidly being transformed into teachers colleges and were operating, as most of them still do, four year specialized curricula leading to a Bachelor's degree. One of the discussions of the paper deplored the apparent necessity of limiting our teacher training program for elementary school teachers to two years and stated that the only alternative was to declare a two year moratorium on all teachers to permit all to receive a liberal arts degree before entering the classroom.

In quite recent years there has been a widespread reappraisement of teacher preparation in the nation's public schools. In July, 1946, The National Education Association created the National Commission on Teacher Education and Professional Standards. The purpose of the Commission was to establish an organized body of the teaching profession charged with the responsibility of guarding teaching standards, of elevating and upgrading them to a high professional level. This national Commission is highly organized. It now functions actively at the state level under the name of Teacher Education and Professional Standards Committee or Commission, usually referred to as TEPS.

The state and local TEPS have a wide range of functions which generally parallel those of the National Commission. To quote from the *Journal of Teacher Education,* for September, 1952:

"The state commissions have been instrumental in creating an awareness among teachers of the relationship between standards and teacher welfare. They have been instrumental in upgrading certification requirements within states. They have cooperated with institutions in the improvement of teacher-education programs. They have worked closely with advisory councils on teacher education in the . . . states in which such councils exist. They have stimulated the organizing and conducting of professional growth programs. They have been especially effective in developing statewide teacher-recruitment programs. They have sponsored studies of problems related to professional standards such as certification, teachers salaries, tenure, and retirement policies. The very heart of the Commission's program of activities is centered in the work of these parallel state committees and commissions and their cooperating local organizations.

"State TEPS Commissions serve primarily as media for the participation of every member of the teaching profession in a study of the need for and necessity of standards and the recommending of action programs to state education associations. In other words, the great function of the state commissions, insofar as they are related to advisory councils, is to mobilize every-member opinion and support behind the state legal authorities in the application of standards." [2]

From this we can see that one of the most significant properties of the NCTEPS is the dominant role in its activities given to classroom teachers. This is done on the assumption that unless the teachers themselves are convinced of the important link between standards and professional status, the public will not support objectives aimed at improving the profession. Public school teachers have become increasingly conscious of the lack of appreciation or consideration given by the public to the teaching profession. The democratic organization and functioning of TEPS have succeeded in arousing tremendous interest in standards among the rank and file of public school teachers.

The national organization through its state and local commission has made great progress in the eight years of its existence. Despite the shortage of teachers and the greatly increased enrollment, certification standards have been made and raised in most of the states. Research studies have been made and are being made in universities and a great number of conferences have been held by TEPS on what is a good teacher. In a word the NCTEPS has succeeded in a few short years in arousing the teaching profession to its own needs and status as a profession.

The whole program of teacher preparation was summed up by Dr. T. M. Stinnett, Executive Secretary of the National Commission, in his keynote address at the 1953 regional conference on Teacher Education and Professional Standards. I would like to refer to two points which I think are of interest to our Catholic teachers and teacher training institutions. The first is the fifth year program of teacher education:

"No area in teacher education at the moment is in greater ferment, is receiving more attention and study by the profession and by teacher-education institutions, or offers greater promise for the professional standards movement, than that of fifth-year and graduate programs for teachers. The growing trend of states to require completion of a fifth year of professional preparation following teaching experience, for full professional qualification and standard qualification, together with increasing trends towards salary differentials for a fifth-year of preparation, are resulting in increasing numbers of teachers completing fifth-year programs each year. This upsurge of clientele has compelled graduate schools and teacher-education institutions to examine critically the kinds of fifth-year programs which are needed and the appropriate content of such programs. Here is a major battleground in the current warring in teacher education.

"Is the best preparation for teaching a four-plus-one program with four years of liberal arts education and one year of professional work as an apex, either as a part of campus work, or divided between campus work and internship, superior? Is the five year continuous, sequential, and integrated teacher-education program superior to the completion of the four-year program, actual teaching experience, and then completion of the fifth year?" [3]

The second matter to which Dr. Stinnett referred is the rather bitter debate now going on between those who would emphasize academic training and those who would emphasize professional education. A writer in the *Journal of Teacher Education* for December, 1952, says:

"The major problem in teacher education of this mid-twentieth century is the bridging of the gap between the academic and professional minds. There is the ever-recurrent charge of concentration on methodology to the exclusion of essential subject matter. This point is made by Mortimer Smith in his latest book, *The Diminished Mind.*[4]

The question might well be asked: Do we find any such aroused interest in teacher education among our religious teaching communities and Catholic educators as is found among public school people? The answer is "yes," and it is so in an increasing degree. The literature on teacher education in our Catholic school system is not too voluminous. Sister Bertrande Meyers in her book on *The Education of Sisters* (1941) [5] lists only two books and eighteen articles devoted specifically to the education of our religious teachers. Until the last three years, practically nothing has been written about Catholic teacher training since 1941.

Out of the Atlantic City meeting of the NCEA in 1953 grew the idea of the Sister Formation Conference, which is now organized and recognized on the national and regional level. There is one striking resemblance of this organization to the TEPS of the public education. Both are composed of the rank and file of classroom teachers as well as leaders in the preparation of teachers. Both have the same general objective—to bring teacher education in this modern age to the highest possible level. The problems confronting the attainment of this objective are being explored, and means of solving them are being studied. My assignment is merely to point out some of the needs in our Catholic schools for better Sister training.

In doing this I am not referring to spiritual training. That part of our teacher training of religious is under the direction of the Church and canon law. It is the responsibility not of the superintendent but of the religious communities to see that the regulations of the Church are carried out. The superintendent, of course, is vitally concerned in the matter of the religious training of the Sisters teaching in his diocese, for he realizes how important it is for the teachers to be good religious. The religious communities are fully conscious of the vital need for strong and deep religious training for their subjects. They realize that this need is greater today than ever before. The needs I will point out will be the educational and cultural training of our teachers.

The first and most obvious need is for more teachers. When one talks with the superiors of religious communities and pastors of growing parishes, this problem of securing teachers assumes gigantic proportions. It is not merely to have more religious teachers but lay teachers also. There is in most communities in this country a growing shortage of teachers particularly on the elementary level. The NEA estimates the present need for new teachers is 173,000. The necessity for Catholic schools to employ more and more lay teachers is a factor in that shortage. But the real problem is how can our Catholic schools continue to meet this growing financial problem? A study of the increasing birth rate and a contemplation of the future hordes of children becoming ready for school each year is becoming a nightmare to all school administrators. Last year over four million babies were born in this country, and the first quarter of this year there were 30,000 more births than in the first quarter of 1953. The only answer I can see to this problem is prayer and a deep faith in Divine Providence. The Church in this country has overcome many a seemingly impossible difficulty, and I am confident she will find a way with God's help to give her little ones a religious education.

In the actual training of our teachers I would like to refer to three needs and to a way which I think might meet them. These three needs are 1) Better training of the mind; 2) A better understanding of modern life; and 3) The development of initiative. A probable answer to all is a broad liberal education for all teachers plus professional training for specific levels of teaching.

First, with regard to the training of the mind, our teachers should be taught and trained in the art of thinking, and this for two reasons. First of all, they themselves should have the ability to think, to judge, and to choose. Reason is a gift of God, a gift which God gave us to use to guide our own lives, to develop our personality and to help us do a better job in whatever position we find ourselves. It is through our reason we acquire wisdom. Moreover, the teacher has to teach the art of thinking, and that kind of teaching begins in the first grade. My old professor of education, the late Doctor Shields, told us many times that the child before the age of reason is a little animal with human potentialities and hence is to be trained under authority. But when reason dawns, external authority should gradually give way to reason. Then the child should be taught to use this gift of God, then he should be led step by step along the hard road of thinking, judging, and choosing for himself according to right principles. This is the task of the teacher. If she has not trained her own mind to think, to analyze, to judge, and to choose according to right principles, how can she teach her pupils to do so? It is absolutely necessary today for our people to learn this difficult art of thinking, for we are constantly exposed to a stream of propaganda through the daily press, the weekly magazines, the radio and the television. Our people are easy victims of the propagandists if they have not learned to be critical, not to accept at once on its face value everything they hear or read, to know how to use their reason, to analyze logically what they read and hear. Hence there is the need for emphasis on training of the mind in teacher education.

The second need to which I would refer is a need to know the modern world, its composition, its philosophy, and especially its needs. Our present Holy Father, Pope Pius XII, has pointed out this need in an Address to the Union of Italian Teachers, September 4, 1949:

> "Look then," he said, "with a sure eye to the times and the hour to learn the new needs and examine new remedies." [6]

In the same address the Holy Father also urged the preparation for leaders in the modern world:

> "The world will have nothing to regret if an ever increasing number of these Christians be placed in all sectors of public and private life. It is largely for you, the teachers, to arrange for this beneficial introduction by directing the minds of your disciples to discover the inexhaustible strength of Christianity for the improvement and the renewal of peoples.
>
> "Form strong men, train their minds to sound criticism, but at the same time imbue them with a sense of Christian humility, of just submission to the laws and the duty of mutual dependence among men." [7]

In order to be able to prepare our Catholic men and women to be leaders in their community, to understand the basic needs of the world, our city, state and country, our teachers must have a well rounded knowledge of the world in which we live. Our schools must also prepare our children for citizenship, active citizenship in their local, state and national communities. Hence our teachers must be given a training in civics, in the duties of citizens, and they must be informed in the working of our government on all levels. Above all, our teachers must possess a lively interest in these things before they can arouse interest in their pupils. They should give an example of good citizenship by keeping informed on the great and important questions of the day and by using their privilege as voters. To know the needs of the world, they must be educated in those needs and trained to keep abreast of the times.

The third need is for initiative. The dictionary says initiative means the right or power to introduce a new measure or course of action. The teacher needs to have originality, the ability to improvise, the knowledge to expatiate, and the understanding to avoid too much formalism in the classroom. Too much dependence upon groups and detailed teacher aids tends to blunt initiative and prevent the development of originality. Detailed courses of study and the demand for strict conformity to every detail also tends to stunt professional growth. Of all professions that of teaching is most likely to get in a rut, especially if the teacher works for years at the same level or with the same subjects. I know this from personal experience. A rut is a very comfortable place and sometimes it takes dynamite to get us out of it. Hence, in our teacher education every effort and method should be used to develop initiative in a teacher and a constant warning given of the danger of falling into a rut, of getting into a groove which will soon make her teaching formal, dry, uninteresting, and ineffective.

There are other needs, I am sure, which you could point out. Perhaps I have not touched upon some more important ones, but the three I have mentioned are the result of experience and observation over the years. The next question is how can these needs and others be met most efficiently? My answer would be by a broad liberal education leading to a Bachelor of Arts degree plus one year of professional training with practice teaching, for all teachers. And this should be given before entering the classroom to begin a teaching career. It seems to me the advantages and even the necessity of such a preparation would be obvious. I think they are to our teachers. There are educators and administrators and pastors who, under the pressure for teachers, would not consider this kind of preparation necessary, but all would hold it to be desirable. There may be some also who would not consider the fifth year necessary or even desirable under the present system of professional training periods of four years in our teachers' colleges. All now agree that at least a Bachelor's degree should be attained before a teacher is permitted to enter the classroom.

The Survey Report on Teacher Education revealed that thirty-seven communities now require four to six years pre-service training including the canonical year; a four year basic degree program including the novitiate is required in thirty-one communities. This shows that the four year basic pre-service training has been accepted as necessary and desirable by 217 religious communities. It takes real courage as well as educational opportunities for these communities to adopt such a course of training in these times when the demand for teachers is so overwhelming. In the long run our schools will gain by it and we will be carrying out the wishes of the Church and the Holy Father to make our schools the best possible.

FOOTNOTES

1. *N.C.E.A. Proceedings,* XXIV (1927), 357.
2. "Growing Up Professionally," *Journal of Teacher Education,* III (Sept., 1952), 223.
3. *Improving Standards for the Teaching Profession,* Report of the 1953 Series of Regional Conferences on Teacher Education and Professional Standards, National Education Association (1953), pp. 11-12.
4. Agnes Snyder, "Conflicting Points of View and Challenges in the Education of Teachers," *Journal of Teacher Education,* III (Dec., 1952), 244.
5. "Bibliography," pp. 235-241.
6. *Catholic Mind,* XLVII (Sept., 1950), 571.
7. *Ibid.,* p. 572.

INTELLECTUAL FORMATION OF SISTERS FROM THE VIEWPOINT OF THE SUPERINTENDENT OF SCHOOLS

The Right Reverend Monsignor Thomas. Cassidy
Diocesan Superintendent of Parochial Schools
Providence, Rhode Island

There has been in these United States a long and vigorous attempt to improve the quality of teaching in all schools. The pioneering efforts of Horace Mann and Henry Barnard did much to impress upon the public mind the great need for trained teachers in public schools. Very early, the Catholic Church in America saw the urgency of a personnel capable of undertaking the complete education of the child. At the Third Plenary Council of Baltimore, the bishops saw the necessity of fixing standards for classroom teachers. By recommending the appointment of a diocesan commission for examination of teachers in each diocese, by ordering the naming of a school commission for visiting, examining and reporting pupil achievement to the Ordinary of the diocese, much was done to improve the intellectual preparation of teachers in parochial schools. This formal attempt to meet a growing problem was seconded by the opening of many community normal schools, teachers colleges, and extension schools devoted to teacher-training. Certainly, a great step was made by the combined efforts of Bishop Shahan, Monsignor Pace, and Doctor Shields in the establishment of the Catholic Sisters College at Catholic University. Many of you are former students of this institution and recognize the importance that it has been in the training of teachers to train teachers.

In all of the undertakings that have tended to lift up the mental caliber of teachers, there has been the presence of opposition that may be classified as violent, mild, or just plain indifference. The first seems easy to meet and overcome because it is a positive thing. One may defeat it by an appeal to reason. The second may be broken by repeated attacks and presents no great problem to the enthusiast who glories in setting people on fire. But the spirit of indifference has haunted our splendid edifice of Catholic education and constant vigilance, united action, super-salesmanship are needed to alert us to our responsibilities in teacher-training.

For many years it was felt that a scanty preparation in the novitiate and a formal religious profession sufficed to ready a teacher for the classroom. Fortunately, we have moved far away from that day. This is evidenced by the recent decision of at least thirty-three communities of religious that have agreed not to send into the classroom those who have not earned a Bachelor's degree. This bold step has encouraged many other communities to increase the years of preparation for classroom teaching. So one has reason to be happy about a more widespread understanding of the need for giving our prospective teachers a better preparation through well-planned study under master teachers, by the opportunity for observing work in demonstration classes, and for actual teaching under supervision.

The reporter may write honestly that in a generation great advances have been made in the preparation of classroom teachers. But the work will not be done before we can feel that all teachers are receiving adequate preparation for effective classroom instruction.

May we continue with a look at the in-service training of our parochial school teachers. Here again there is some evidence of the spirit of indifference. This is observed on the part of superiors, of principals, and of teachers. Too often, the killing expression of opinion is heard: "She . . . you . . . I has or have my degree. So why worry about more training?" Now I am not recommending all teachers to enter courses leading to a Doctor's degree in education. But the talented teacher should be offered an opportunity for higher study. This does seem to be a matter for serious consideration in each religious community. Problems are involved, finances are required, sacrifices must be made. But the times call for experts in many fields. Each diocesan system needs trained people in curriculum-making, in the selection of textbooks, in guidance, in testing, and in supervision of instruction. Without this specialized training there are many gaps to be filled, if our schools are to render the kind of service that has been envisioned by His Holiness, Pope Pius XI in his memorable encyclical on the *Christian Education of Youth.*

Another hurtful influence in our schools may be called the spirit of self-satisfaction. The teacher who has taught phonetics, number combinations, or American history for thirty years by a method that dates her service is satisfied, content, happy, and undisturbed. There may even be a haunting fear that all new techniques are heresies.

Modern psychology has revealed some interesting facts in the learning process. What a pity for one to ignore or make light of the advances that have been made. There is no excuse for the teacher who stagnates. A medical man who failed to read his journals over a period of five years would fall back quickly in his practice. So, the teacher who does not read constantly in the science of pedagogy soon becomes antiquated in classroom work.

In a practical way, professional reading must be obtained or supplied to the classroom teacher, and time must be given in the crowded daily or weekly schedule for her to read and to discuss articles of interest, books of importance. The bibliography grows, and no one can read all professional publications. But one may be selective and keep alive in the field that comes close to daily duties. In this we recommend the purchase of standard texts in education and the use of public and college libraries. It goes without saying that if one desires to keep informed, there is always a way to find the valuable reading material.

From the evidence at hand, it is clear that our religious communities have responded to the crying demand for educating children in the way of truth. The history of our schools bristles with glorious examples of heroic self-sacrifice. But we are in a continuing process. We must answer the needs of a new generation. God will give the increase if we are alert in preparing our classroom teachers for their daily tasks of leading children to Christ by their example, their wisdom, and their adequate teaching methods and techniques.

THE INTELLECTUAL FORMATION OF SISTERS

The Right Reverend Patrick J. Dignan
Superintendent of Schools
Archdiocese of Los Angeles
Los Angeles, California

I think it was Emerson who said, "To speak adequately you should speak wildly." "Wildness," he said, "is the flower of the mind." I believe that he meant you should always speak imaginatively, but at any rate I can recall the first part of his statement and I hope that you will keep it in mind as I go along.

I hope that no enthusiast will get the idea that we must discontinue herewith sending any Sisters into any new schools for the next four years and let things become stagnant—let this tremendous number of young children pile up to flood in upon us even more four years from now. I think that Reverend Mother Regina's well balanced statement has already taken that into account.

We know that our curriculum is Christ-centered. We take due account of the subject-centered curriculum, the psychologically motivated curriculum, and the sociologically motivated curriculum, but we gather all those up into the Christ-centered curriculum, and we, therefore, can measure against that objective alone what should be the preparation of our teachers. I would like also to say that sometimes we exaggerate the opportunities that lay teachers get as compared with those that our Sisters get. Suppose that they do get four years' college and suppose that during that time they carry on their social life, their dating, and all the rest of it, sometimes looking for boarding rooms, and trying to keep up with the fashions and styles of the times, always having in mind the possibility of marriage. These things can take them away from a deep seated interest in their vocation. I can see that we should measure against that the advantages of the Sisters, even if they have to do most of their work in in-service training—the contact that they have with older teachers, the possibility of sharing experiences and the possibilities of getting help from other regions of the country where the same community is located, the possibility, for instance, being practical at the start, of building up, shall we say, professional libraries. By that I would mean first of all having on hand courses of study, teachers' manuals, and curriculum materials from all over the country in each convent just by the simple expedient of getting their Sisters who are scattered throughout the country to get the copies that are in use in their particular places.

Now, you see, I've made a plea—it isn't very subtle—for two things (or rather for one); namely, that you don't start cutting down the supply of Sisters for the Archdiocese of Los Angeles. That is what I've been working on so far.

Now to come to our subject matter directly. The fact that we have a Christ-centered curriculum means that the primacy of place must be given to the theological formation of Sisters. Certainly our Sisters can get to know the New Testament well. We know that there has been a tremendous revival of interest in theology. It is now not a matter of the Bible and tradition, you know; not the apologetical attitude with regard to Protestantism, but rather the Bible as the living word of God and the sustaining power of our spiritual life.

We must, of course, look into the other fields of theology. We are not thinking of specialized courses in theology. We have books like Adam's, *The Spirit of Catholicism;* we have books like Romano Guardini's and the works—many of them—of Von Hildebrand, which are dynamic and which are trying to do the things that we must do. We Catholics in our whole philosophy and theology concentrate on an extremely objective view, but we have to take into account the subjectivism of today. We have to incorporate, to get into our theological presentation what is good in it—to integrate the modern mind with eternal truth. These writers are doing this.

I am not making an attempt to be thorough or comprehensive, or profound in the slightest degree, but I will indicate that theology can be made dynamic. It does not have to be a technical course in the sense of the seminary course, but the Sisters need to get the basic outlines of dogmatic theology. Now moral theology, of course, must be presented too, for we know that Sisters run into serious problems. I think it is well to keep in mind that theological formation of the Sister is exceedingly important.

Now for the historical formation of the teacher. We need to be on our guard lest we lose our sense of tradition. We have said this before, but we sent out a questionnaire one time and the questionnaires were answered by our teachers. The survey was state-wide, incidentally. I want to protect ourselves because of the particular answer to which I refer. It didn't come from the Archdiocese of Los Angeles, although it could well have done so. The questionnaire asked what should be done in history curriculum. Someone put in this profound statement, "Isn't ancient and medieval history too ancient? Shouldn't we forget it and concentrate on the problems of our times?"

I think that reflects a dangerous development. You see, modern psychology and philosophy—there is no real philosophy—is anti-traditional. I say there is no real philosophy because philosophy has been reduced to the problem of knowledge and there is nothing but epistomology. This is true of positivism; that is why they have and can eliminate God, because they have eliminated metaphysics. This, of course, is a mighty good reason for keeping metaphysics in the philosophical preparation of Sisters.

It isn't enough to give them ethics, for instance, or logic, which we customarily do, because these things are not intelligible in themselves without an integration into the whole pattern in philosophy. Now we do not imply that they have to spend four years of philosophy. I think that every teacher needs to know that we are trying to impart the pattern of civilization, and you can't do that without the background and development of civilization. Every teacher needs to know and to appreciate that the barbarian tribes of Europe got their common background from the Church of God and from Christian civilization—plus, of course, that which the Christian civilization was making use of: namely, the traditions of Greece and Rome, especially the philosophical tradition, the natural law itself.

Now I do think that we have at least to work so that the Sister is so disposed that she will see the value of those things and want to study them. I think it was Pascal who said, "To know is to seek." We don't know anybody who has been in the exhausting,

challenging, and almost terrifying game of trying to keep up with
the progress of knowledge—such a person knows that it's never
finished—who does not realize that there is more to learn. That
attitude in the Sisters is a good one. This is just a little plea very
lamely made for appreciation of a good historical background
for the Sisters.

Concerning literature, we, of course, feel that Sisters can do a
lot by their own activities. After all, the formation of anybody is
intensive self-activity, and when we are able to read I think we
can do a lot to educate ourselves.

I'm not being reactionary. I believe that there are many cases
which need a lot of guidance, a lot of psychology, and psychiatry
even; but nevertheless, it is bad, it is going to be dead in a few
years, and we must not be caught up with things away beyond
our powers of keeping up with them from the point of view of
expense. And let us keep to our traditional philosophy.

What is this all about? It is a plea for sound liberal arts training for our teachers. There is the point that if we keep our philosophy and give our Sisters a good foundation in the traditional
subjects of the liberal arts, they will be prepared for the problems
of our present day world.

Now that is all very well perhaps in theory, but the highest
mother superior, the mother general, the provincial will say,
"How are we to get this in?" Let us try to make a few suggestions.
A convent should be a place where learning can go on, where in-
service training can go on. In every convent should be available
a certain amount of reference material for the teachers. Surely
it is false economy to deny our teachers that. You sometimes go
into convents and you see there a few ancient books—spiritual
books of ancient vintage; there may be a few more recent so-called
"good Catholic novels" of third rate authorship and a miscellany
of certain books—textbooks, a few workbooks—and you've about
exhausted the intellectual fodder and supply of that particular
institution. I feel sure if our Mothers' Club were approached—
and the pastor gives his benign consent—that a few hundred dollars could easily be put together which would enable every convent to be supplied with basic works of reference.

We should think at the beginning of the possibility of building up a good resource library of courses of study, of teachers manuals from all over the country because religious communities are so widespread. I know these things are very repetitious but sometimes they do have a few new ideas and there is no teacher—say of the third or fourth grade or any other grade—who will go to several courses of study which have been rather carefully planned for that grade who will not get from them some very good ideas, some stimulation, and some inspiration because, of course, it is a most essential factor, I think, in the whole process of teaching— the inspiration, the courage of the teacher.

It has been said well that just by making huge piles of bricks you are not erecting a great structure. It has also been said well that great teaching is not the result of the knowledge of methods. There is something infinitely more important—that is, personality and ideals. There is devotion, there is love, there is the utter dedication of self for the highest things a human being can be called upon to do apart from standing at the altar of God Himself and offering up the Clean Oblation, which is the sacred privilege of the priesthood alone. A teacher who knows the outstanding speeches of Shakespeare's dramas, who knows philosophy and theology will be an inspiring teacher and a self-confident teacher in the best and truly Catholic sense of that word.

In conclusion, then, let me sum up my remarks by saying that we hope it is not necessary to do anything revolutionary. To say that as of now we shall cease to send our Sisters for the next four years— "You will never get a Sister in the future who hasn't her A.B. and her credential all stowed away."

I think some of the house tasks—mopping the floors, and so on— might be postponed for some one day in the week. I don't know, but the washing and the rest of it—certainly it would be money well spent to get some one to do that. The poor Sisters oftentimes are burdened with unnecessary work that is really kind of slavish and certainly has very little (it may be good for humility, of course), but it hasn't much relationship to the great objective of the training of youth. If we have to resort to in-service preparation as much as we are, I think that these things could be looked into and that much more adequate budgeting of time could be done. Then, lastly, as already has been said, of course, the provisions of necessary materials so that the convent is a place of study where there can be that intense self-activity which is the essence of all good education.

Let us try to be as good as those who have gone before us; let us be as self-sacrificing. In keeping our eyes on the world and trying to adapt to it, let us never forget the high ideals of our founders, and I'm sure that in the providence of God it will go well with us, and we will be ready to do fruitfully the work of God under the guidance of the Holy Spirit.

THE NEEDS OF OUR SCHOOL SYSTEMS FOR BETTER SISTER EDUCATION

The Very Reverend Monsignor Edmund J. Goebel
Diocesan Superintendent of Schools
Milwaukee, Wisconsin

It was with a deep sense of privilege that I accepted the invitation to share with you some of my observations on teacher formation. As I stand here, however, I am well aware of the broad experience some of you have had in the field of teacher education. I recognize, too, that most of you hold important positions dealing with this problem in your convents. But we are not here to dwell on ourselves. We are here to focus our thinking and our planning on the preparation of Sisters for the all-important work of teaching. For the sake of clarification we call it teacher formation.

We might begin our discussion by accepting the rising tide in our school population as a part of God's plan. Of course, we cannot satisfy all the demands, but we can do much to meet them. In the first place we must try to increase the effectiveness of all available teachers. We cannot meet this situation by throwing up our hands and telling ourselves that we cannot do it. The fact is we have to teach them or reject the position of universal education. More than that, we are partners on the elementary or high school level; we cannot screen the select and shift the others to the public school. Our schools, to be truly Catholic, must enroll all educable children as they come to us. They are "all God's children" wherever they are, whatever their social or economic status might be.

They must all be taught. If we do not have enough qualified teachers, we must use unqualified ones, or we must find a way to use more effectively the teachers we have. If we do not teach them, some one else will. And that "someone" may be an enemy of the Church or of our country.

There are two ways that we should explore: first, we should examine the loss of teaching power in administration. There is a lot of energy wasted by performing tasks others could do as well or even better, such as filling out reports, calling parents, or checking absentees. Secondly, we must find ways of getting the most teaching out of the classroom teacher. This may call for Trained Teacher Assistants (T.T.A.'s). The work of the T.T.A. would be to supervise study, correct assignments, and such like tasks. T.T.A. should have special training in lesson planning, directed study techniques, and supervision of study. It is time for a full dress study of their possibilities. We might liken the status of the T.T.A. to that of the T.P.N.—the Trained Practical Nurse.

Up to this point, we have sought to provide a pattern for the present emergency. The answer for the future teaching Sister is quite different. I believe that every future teacher-Sister should have an adequate education before she is assigned to school duty. In this case the term "adequate" is somewhat relative. We could consider as adequate an education that would meet state and national requirements. In my own thinking, however, I would like to consider as adequate a complete college education.

If there is any one cause for the breakdown of young teachers in this crisis, it is the lack of adequate education. For the good and for the protection of our future teachers, it would be well for the convents to declare a moratorium on the acceptance of new schools until they have reached that goal. Whatever the loss might be at the present time would be more than repaid by the additional useful years given to each Sister's teaching life. The Sisters are actually committing slow suicide through summer school attendance. Certainly a program like this will not help in attracting vocations.

I want you to look at this from another point of view. With the present heavy teaching loads it is unfair to assign an unprepared teacher to a school staffed by adequately prepared teachers. Many of our teacher collapses can be traced to inadequate preparation. Such teachers have no resources to fall back on; they lack a teaching stockpile to draw from. They are like soldiers without ammunition. Though not every adequately educated teacher will make a good one, her chances of surviving under present day stress are much better than the chances of one who is inadequately prepared. Where professional training is lacking, confidence is quickly destroyed. We have seen teachers of this type give up completely; some have left religious life. I think, too, that this is an important factor in the assignment of teachers.

In other words, now is the time to focus our attention on the professional preparation of our future teachers. We have moved a long way, historically, from the time when any person could fill the classroom bill as long as she wore a religious garb. We need people who understand that the teacher must know something about children, child growth, and adolescent psychology. We need people grounded in this fundamental knowledge before they enter a classroom. To place Sisters in school today without this basic training is the equivalent of martyrdom.

The more professional the teacher is the easier it will be for her to meet these unusual conditions. She must not only know the needs of youth but must know also how to deal with youth. This calls for a well-rounded professional education. One or two years of college will not suffice. It calls for a full complement of college education. It calls for the best teacher-training program available. The better the beginner is prepared for her job, the more assurance we have of her ability to meet, head-on, the problem of "education for all."

The professional teacher is not produced solely by an academic degree. She must have certain inherent qualities of competency. She must be intelligent, have the will to work, the courage to face difficulties, and the willingness to take on a task where others have failed. Careful screening is necessary in the selection of those who are to be trained professionally.

The professional teacher will not only know techniques but she will be versed in their use. She will understand the quintessence of motivation and will see value in guidance when confronted with behavior problems. We cannot, as we have in the past, turn undesirable pupils over to the public schools. Such action is evidence of lack of professional integrity. We need to have courage and good education to adjust new problems ourselves.

Some of these inadequacies can be remedied by in-service training. This is highly to be desired, but the in-service program should be based on pertinent needs. Certainly, a course in English literature can hardly be taken as a substitute for guidance or behavior psychology. In-service training is another way of bridging the gap between the professionally trained teachers and those who are not. In this crisis we must engage in constructive thinking on the problem. In this very field we have much to share with one another.

If we look at our teaching ranks today, we can readily see that the inadequately trained teacher looks upon teaching as a chore, not as a challenge. Under the strain of chore, she is bound to wear out. Teachers of this kind are not only educationally illiterate but functionally as well. It is a sad situation. On the other hand, the professionally trained teacher will usually find a way to meet the challenge before her. To her teaching is not a chore but a summons for action.

These facts, known by and large to all of us, might well be considered the "ABC's" of our present day teacher education problem. They present, I believe, the root of much of our difficulty. The impact of present day enrollments and overcrowded classrooms seems totally unsolvable to the unprepared teacher. Her only resource is discipline, and discipline soon wears out. When it does, conduct becomes a tug-of-war with the teacher in the role of loser. There is no teacher living who is able to win in a tug-of-war against fifty, sixty, or seventy pupils.

It is axiomatic that a school is as strong as its staff. We might say, too, that a school is as strong as its weakest teacher. Knowing this, our plans for teacher formation should be built on the firm foundation of professional education. Against the background of actual experience, we see the necessity of completing the formal education of every Sister before she is assigned to teaching. We see, too, the necessity of calling upon the inventiveness and ingenuity of our master-minds to draw a blueprint for effective help in these critical days. Many questions about the means and objectives of teacher education, the function of educational institutions, and the content of educational curricula need to be clarified. This situation calls not for a committee to study the problem but for a "task-force."

Closely related to all this is the necessity of finding means to conserve teaching energy. We believe that this cannot be done adequately without a painstaking job analysis.

We must eliminate from the teacher's duties those tasks which can be performed by others. The T.T.A. (Trained Teacher Assistant) could save the energy of every classroom teacher for instruction only; a clerk could make the members of the administration available for supervision and for classroom teaching.

Your presence here gives evidence of your willingness to join forces in solving the teaching problems of the future. It is evidence, also, of your intense interest in teacher formation. With God's help we can do all this and even more.

IMPROVEMENT OF CLASSROOM PREPARATION OF SISTERS

The Reverend William Stone
Superintendent of Schools
Baker, Oregon

I must preface the observations which follow by noting that I have taken the liberty of conferring with several Catholic school superintendents before preparing this paper. Consequently, these ideas represent a general summary of the thinking of several men. I have done this for two reasons: first, because this subject is fraught with great peril, even for an expert; and secondly, because I have not even the most flimsy pretext for assuming the role of an expert.

I have divided the treatment of this subject into four general topics: professional competency, theological knowledge and instruction, counselling activities, and psychological preparedness.

Pope Pius XII, in his address to the Convention of Teaching Sisters in Rome in 1951, defined the minimum that may be expected of the teaching Sister by way of professional competency. It is evident from this that the Holy Father expects teachers in Catholic schools to have a scholastic background which is at least equal to that of the public school teachers. While it is true that some of the state Departments of Education do not demand that private schools meet all the requirements for standardization, it is to the advantage of the private school to maintain the highest level of instruction attainable. Considerable potential ground for argument against the private school is eliminated when all of its instructors qualify for and obtain the state teaching credential.

The parents who patronize the Catholic school have a right to properly prepared instructors for their children. In my opinion communities which find it expedient—even part of the testing of a vocation—to "try out," so to speak, a young Sister in the classroom before she is adequately prepared are acting unjustly towards the students. I will readily admit that diocesan superintendents and others often exert so much pressure on the community superior to produce teachers here and now that practically any device for relieving that pressure may seem justifiable. This sort of procedure, however, is not calculated to improve the level of teaching efficiency.

In the area of religious knowledge, the teaching Sister has a two-fold responsibility by which the adequacy of her knowledge of the principles of both dogmatic and moral theology is to be judged. She is committed by her vows to a lifetime of trying to become a perfect Christian, and at the same time she is professionally charged with the responsibility of teaching the principles of theology to others—immature people—who are not bound to tend to perfection as she is. It would seem that there is more involved here than merely need for a better knowledge of theological fact. It is also necessary that Sisters be convinced that they may not in justice teach as moral theology those things which are actually but counsels to perfection.

Increased factual knowledge of theology should be forthcoming both in pre-service and in-service training programs. Angels would undoubtedly fear to tread this ground, but I believe it should be covered. Priests who are assigned to the work of teaching theology in the novitiate should be both theologians and teachers—not merely men who are easily available because of conditions which render them incapable of other priestly occupations. In regard to in-service learning, it would seem to me that this area should receive increased attention from superiors in the planning of the program of the teaching Sister. Beyond this, though, there should be an improved program of the semi-monthly conferences in the individual convents. Is it not rather an obvious fact that there is here vast room for improvement, both with regard to long-range planning of the matter to be presented and the manner of preparation and presentation?

Closely related to the improvement of program and instruction in theology should be an effort to improve the competency of the teaching Sister in counselling and guidance. This effort should cover many areas.

There is needed a more realistic understanding of the problems which face the youth of today, including a trend away from the tendency of presuming that the problems of another generation can be identified with today's.

There is needed a more objective, reasonable, prayerful approach to the problem of encouraging religious vocations. Emphasis should be laid on avoiding the emotional, sentimental, and high-pressure tactics, which too frequently have resulted in concentrating on the wrong type of individuals and alienating fundamentally sound prospects for both seminary and convent.

There is need for emphasis on counselling for homemaking and the study of family relations. Failure in this area is the cause of a considerable amount of tension between home and school, and all too frequently it is based on the teacher's lack of understanding of the problems of the home. Often the religious teacher will have left home before becoming aware of the existence of these problems, or she will have come from a home where there never arose the problems which plague less fortunate children whom she teaches.

There is need for emphasis on preparation for group-work, such as choral groups, the Confraternity of Christian Doctrine, the Sodality, Legion of Mary, and the like. Properly handled, these activities can offer solid opportunity for influencing vocations. Altogether too frequently, for example, one will find a teacher instructing children diligently in the principles of the democratic process of government and parliamentary procedure and then scandalizing them by her failure to apply these principles to herself. To them this smacks of tyranny and bad sportsmanship and creates resentment.

Many of the problems cited above are due to a lack of understanding of the psychological nature of the children of various age groups. A certain amount of specialization is necessary in every profession; and teaching, even when done by religious, is no exception. It may be a proof of the divinity of the Church that the Holy Spirit has often made tremendous successes of people who possessed little or no natural talent for the work assigned to them; but it seems to be somewhat presumptive for a religious superior to make it an operating principle to assign subjects continually to jobs for which they have little or no aptitude. When a Sister has great success, for example, with a particular group of third-graders, it seems less logical to conclude that she will therefore continue to achieve that success by being "promoted" with those children until they finally graduate away from her by entering high school than it is to conclude that she would be even a greater success if she were permitted to specialize on third graders.

Have you not met the teacher who is bewildered because today's thirteen-year-old fails to react favorably to the same tricks of the trade which were so successful when he was only an eight-year-old? I see no reason, professionally at least, why a community may not successfully exploit the particular talents of its personnel with judicious and specialized appointments. There will be problems of supply, of course, which must prevent such an arrangement from becoming universal; but we speak here of the ideal, of cases where the talent is available.

Before concluding I should like to make one more point. In connection with the area of "professional competency" two Catholic school superintendents have made very specific suggestions which I wish to pass on to you.

One of these men considers that there is a lack of preparation in the language arts. He suggests that English courses should be offered in the houses of study in which the student religious would be required to work for at least six months on reading well-written essays and speeches and summarizing them, in order to develop a better understanding of the basic elements of sentence and paragraph construction. It is his opinion that too much stress is placed on the "mechanics," and too little on the "art of communication"; too much emphasis on learning the parts of language, too little on the development of an idea and the ability to express it verbally or in writing.

The second of these two men observed that teaching Sisters were weakest in the fields of science, physical education, and homemaking. He noted that many high schools are now introducing a course in homemaking, but that there seems to be considerable tendency to turn this course into another period of religion, perhaps, because of a lack of understanding of the practical methods of homemaking.

I have undertaken this assignment fearfully. I realize that there are many reasons for each of the failures or shortcomings listed in this paper, and that many individuals need to agree before much can be achieved by way of correction. But it is because I have been given to understand that the discussion of such weaknesses and the exchange of ideas is the aim of this group, that I have dared to present them. The recommendation of remedies belongs to experts and lies outside the scope of this paper.

THE NEED FOR BETTER TEACHER TRAINING
AS VIEWED BY THE SUPERINTENDENT OF SCHOOLS

The Very Reverend Monsignor John J. Endebrock
Superintendent of Schools
Diocese of Trenton, New Jersey

It is my task today to point out to this august gathering the need of better teacher training for those who staff our Catholic schools. Your committee has chosen a superintendent of schools to point out this need because he is the focal point of the school system, the liaison officer, if you will, between the bishop, the mother-house, and the state Department of Education.

One of my saddest recollections as a young superintendent over a decade ago was the vision of a young postulant teaching in a parochial school, and a white novice who looked out of place in the black veil and borrowed beads she was wearing for the occasion. That was twelve years ago, even before this tremendous influx of children was upon us. I am happy to say that much was done and is still being done to correct that unhealthy condition. But there is still much more to be done by way of better teacher training.

That we should provide the very best in preparation for our future teachers goes without saying. When Our Divine Saviour gave His Church the mandate to teach all nations, He certainly meant for us to do our very best in fulfilling that command. He never did anything halfheartedly Himself; neither was He satisfied with halfway measures.

The Church, following the mandate of its Holy Founder, obliges parents under pain of serious sin to give their children a Catholic education where such a religious education is available. Do we not commit a grave injustice to both parent and child, if we do not staff our schools with teachers who are adequately prepared for this tremendous task?

We all realize that the Catholic school system in America is the greatest bulwark of the faith. It is our greatest means of preserving and spreading the faith. What a terrible thing it would be to allow that school system to be weakened by inadequate preparation of the teachers who are the very heart and soul of the school.

We in America expect recognition of our schools on a par with public education. Must we not live up to that demand by keeping them on a par with or making them even better than the public school? A recent report from the National Commission on Teacher Education and Professional Standards reveals that thirty-five states either require or have set dates in the very near future when a Bachelor's degree will be necessary for any type of teacher certification.[1]

The Holy Father in 1951 and again in 1952 pointed out to the Congress of Teachers and the gathering of Mothers General his desire that our Sisters be as well or better prepared than the state would require them to be.

With this in mind, let us look at the picture of teacher training and see wherein lies the need of bettering that preparation, so that we can honestly and sincerely say that we are doing our best in living up to our obligations.

As my sources of information on a national scale, I am quoting from two major national surveys, both completed in 1952. This first is the survey on Teacher Preparation made by the section on Teacher Education of the N.C.E.A. through questionnaires sent to all general superiors of religious communities.[2] The second is *An Evaluation of Catholic Elementary School Teachers Preservice Education,* a Doctor's thesis by Sister M. Brideen Long, M.A., based upon questionnaires and personal interviews of some 1,800 elementary school Sisters.[3]

With regard to pre-service training programs in some 216 religious communities in the United States, the following was revealed:

Including the canonical year:

Four to six years was provided by 37 communities
Three years or less was provided by 179 communities (72 percent who answered)
Of these: a) 93 communities (37.9 percent) provided 3 years
　　　　 b) 26 communities (10.6 percent) provided 2½ years
　　　　 c) 60 communities (24.5 percent) provided 2 years or less

Obviously, the general period of pre-service education was too short to adequately prepare the Sisters for the task of teaching in the elementary schools—an average of two years, canonical year excluded. The increased enrollment in our parochial schools since 1947 has caused a consequent drop in the amount of pre-service education of Sisters at a time when their pre-service training should have been increased, if anything. Obviously, it takes a much better trained teacher to adequately instruct 60 pupils in a classroom than one who teaches in a classroom of only 30 or 35 pupils.

It was observed in both of the aforementioned studies that religious communities do not make a practice of having their elementary school teachers certified except where certification is required either by diocesan or state regulation. For example, only 37.7 percent of the 1,800 Sisters interviewed had any type of certification before starting to teach. Only 53.9 percent of these Sisters in service had any type of certification or degree, although 26 percent had at least three years of college completed.

I think all of us will agree that all of our teachers eventually receive the educational training that they need, that is, if they live long enough and do not die in the attempt. But that they all receive an adequate pre-service training is quite another story.

Furthermore, 124 communities sent out teachers with less than minimum state requirements!

The pre-service programs under study showed a definite weakness in the area of fundamentals of education. Scarcely half of the 1,800 Sisters had training in Catholic philosophy and only one-third in philosophy of education. Another weakness was manifest in the area of understanding the learner and the process of learning. Over half the Sisters did not have pre-service training in general psychology and only one-third had child psychology. Although the ratings on the value of these courses revealed that the Sisters did not noticeably miss these courses, their presence or absence made itself felt in instructional planning, classroom administration, and student appraisal. May I add from my own observation that the absence of such courses may well be the cause for many of the misunderstandings in teacher-pupil and teacher-parent relationships that crop up so often, and cause many a headache for principals, pastors, superintendents, and bishops alike.

In the field of guidance, administrators of teacher education in Catholic institutions have not always given sufficient attention to the interests and aptitudes of prospective teachers. For example, only half of the Sisters interviewed received formal guidance to determine their particular interests and aptitudes in the field of teaching. Just this week I spent considerable time helping a young woman prospective in the choice of a community. She is afraid to enter this or that community because she is afraid they will make her teach, and she doesn't want to be a teacher. Her interests are in nursing.

Without laboring the point of weakness in our teacher-training programs in general, I hasten to point out some of the major causes of these deficiencies. I do so, not with the idea of offering excuses for them, or of putting the blame on any particular persons, groups, or institutions; for all of us can strike our breasts in this regard. My purpose is to point them out as a means toward possible solution and correction.

Probably the major reason for deficiency is the fact that all too many teaching communities do not have the means of setting up an adequate teacher-training program, much as they would like to.

The N.C.E.A. Survey Report on Teacher Preparation reveals that, of the 217 religious communities reporting, only 31 had already established a four year basic degree. However, only 98 communities had adequate facilities for such a four year degree program; in 23 communities access to such facilities was possible, while 118 communities did not even have access to such facilities. The fact that such facilities are not available is due, I presume, to (1) lack of finance, (2) small size of the community. Both these problems should be solved.

The major obstacles impeding an adequate and more adequate educational program were listed by the motherhouses as follows:

a) Sister-shortage—232 communities
b) Lack of understanding of the need of secular teachers—129 communities
c) Finances—90 communities

Without going into the question of religious vocations or lay teachers, it is quite obvious that the increasing demand for Catholic education and the resultant demands made upon the mother-houses by pastors, superintendents, and bishops have practically forced communities to send out Sisters who are inadequately prepared for teaching. If Father demands two additional Sisters for his two new classrooms; if His Excellency insists that the community supply a faculty for his new school, what is Reverend Mother to do? You answer that one!

The fact of the matter is, are we really giving a Catholic education to the 50, 60, or 70 pupils we crowd into a room under the supervision of a sacrificing religious who is ill-prepared for the tremendous task? Are we giving them a Catholic education or are we merely putting them under the roof of a Catholic school building? At any rate this demand for Sisters has been one of the major causes of inadequate teacher training.

We hesitate to speak of money, but money, they say, is the root of all evils, and may well be the root of the difficulties we face in teacher training. The cost of maintenance of Sisters who are students is heavy, to say the least, and it is the main reason why communities have not been able to give proper professional preparation to their members. Obviously, it cannot be done on the present rate of remuneration paid the Sisters for their teaching services in our elementary schools.

What is the solution to these serious problems, these obstacles placed in the way of a more adequate teacher-training program? I, or anyone, would not dare to suggest a total, immediate solution, even if such a solution were known. Neither is it my task in this paper to give the solution, but rather, to place the accent on the need of such a solution.

However, I would like to make a few suggestions that are feasible in some instances, and I make them at the expense of receiving severe criticism.

Number one: The establishment of diocesan teachers' colleges in those areas where there are, within a reasonable distance, a number of motherhouses with their present normal schools in operation. The establishment of such diocesan colleges has solved many of the problems in the dioceses of St. Paul, Sante Fe, Brooklyn, Cincinnati, Cleveland, and Providence. By a diocesan teachers' college I mean an independent professional school of college rank, which is under the direct control of the bishop, which functions in an organic way with the parish school system, which is attended by members of the religious teaching communities and by secular candidates for positions in Catholic schools, which has a four year curriculum leading to a professional degree, which prepares chiefly, if not exclusively, for the elementary school field.

Secondly, those whose community is large should make a greater attempt, gradually, to add at least one year to their teacher-training program. This can be done only through greater use of lay teachers and an increase in the remuneration that is presently being paid to teaching Sisters. If all the pre-service programs of less than four years were increased by one year within the next decade, the increase in the amount of pre-service education that Catholic elementary school teachers would be receiving at the end of the decade would be approximately one hundred percent more than it is now. With the assistance of larger salaries and with at least temporary relief from demands by the use of lay teachers, smaller communities should further exploit the use of outside facilities of larger communities to augment their pre-service training programs.

In conclusion, may I remind you that practically all the material of this paper was gathered from the research of others more competent than myself. Personally, I would never have accepted the responsibility of preparing such a paper, unless such valuable information were available for our use. I have tried to confine myself to facts—facts gathered through research. In the application of these facts and suggested solutions to problems, we are all subject to human error.

In reviewing the weaknesses that occasion the need for better teacher training, I am condemning no one. I am pointing the finger of accusation at no one. I wish to offend no one. I have tried to point out the need, the great need of better teacher training.

We school people have a tremendous responsibility. Our mandate from Christ and the Church is clear. Our responsibility to child and parent and state is great. All of us, I feel, are doing and have been doing a good job, in spite of almost insurmountable difficulties. That we can do better—that we must do better—is all too clear to us. Let us all, Mothers Superior, pastors, supervisors, superintendents, and bishops who are at the head of this wonderful Catholic school system stretch our ingenuity a little further, sacrifice a little more generously. Only through such ingenuity and mutual sacrifice on the part of all concerned can we make possible a better training program, the best training program possible. Only then can we in conscience say that we are doing our very best to give our teachers the very best so that they in turn can give their very best in the best school system in America.

FOOTNOTES

1. W. Earl Armstrong and R. M. Stinnett, *A Manual on Certification Requirements for School Personnel in the United States.* 1955 edition. Washington, D.C.: National Education Association of the United States.
2. For an interpretation of the findings of this committee see Sister Mary Richardine Quirk, B.V.M., *Some Present-Day Problems in the Education of Teaching Sisters in the United States.* Marquette University Graduate School, 1953. M.A. Thesis, for private circulation only, with the permission of the author.
3. Washington, D.C.: Catholic University of America, 1952.

SISTER FORMATION FROM THE VIEWPOINT OF THE COLLEGE AND UNIVERSITY ADMINISTRATOR

THE EDUCATION OF SISTERS FROM THE VIEWPOINT OF A GRADUATE DEAN

The Reverend Robert J. Henle, S.J.
Dean of the Graduate School
St. Louis University
St. Louis, Missouri

When we are facing the problem of Sister formation today and facing it, as we are, in a new way, I think it well for a moment to recall one great fact: the achievement of the American Church in the last one hundred years. The tremendous network of churches, schools, high schools, colleges, orphanages, hospitals—centers of every kind of apostolic and charitable endeavor—all this vast upbuilding that has gone on in America in the Catholic Church in the last hundred years represents an achievement unparalleled in the history of Christianity—the growth from almost nothing to the tremendous assemblage of works we have today. This is a fact we must remember: that great achievement, particularly our parochial school system and our network of charitable institutions, is due in very large measure to the devotion of our Sisters. The fact that in America we have not lost the peo-

124

ple, that we have maintained a vigorous Catholic life, is, as a matter of fact, due very largely to the sacrifices of the Sisters who have gone before us, the Sisters who have achieved this with sacrifices that no man can tell, working frequently under the most extreme handicaps. And when we look to the future, it is always with a view of the past and a great respect for those who have gone before us. It is because of what they have done that we are able today to conceive and undertake a new program of Sister formation. They have given us the vocations we have today, the institutions, the organizations, congregations, traditions; and it is on these that we build.

Indeed, when I stand before you and realize the tremendous achievement that is represented here by the congregations in this auditorium, as a mere man, as a priest, as an educator, I face my task a humbled man.

As I see it, we are now discussing and thinking about a new and improved formation to meet new and greater challenges, and we are thinking now not merely of meeting accreditation or professional requirements but, as I understand your effort, you are thinking of a total and integrated formation to meet the needs of the individual religious, to produce high professional competence, and to develop educational and professional leadership.

What would it mean if this vast army of religious women were to increase its efficiency one percent? What a tremendous effect this would have not only on the Church but on American society! And this, I understand, is what you are thinking of—an increased efficiency based on improved training. After all, this is very sound, for the efficiency of any worker, above all of a person engaged in religious and professional work, is directly proportioned to the fundamental training of the worker.

The vision of possibilities which your movement holds up before us is breath-taking—and I am humbly and gratefully happy to have some small share in your enterprise. And as I watch your movement, it seems to me to bear the marks of a movement truly inspired by the Holy Ghost. This movement has appeared, almost independently in various forms and in different places, in Germany and Italy and France and America; everywhere there seems to be a fresh realization of the problem and an almost spontaneous effort to face and solve it. The movement has come up from the depths of the living Church. And simultaneous with this has been the active interest and strong encouragement of the Holy See in a remarkable series of directives and pronouncements. It seems to me that throughout history movements inspired by the Holy Spirit have shown these two marks.

This inspired movement is concerned with the integration of mature spirituality and cultural formation with the highest professional competence and indeed leadership. This brings me to my own proper point—for high competence and true leadership demands graduate education for large numbers of Sisters. There was a day when this sort of training was sought at the instigation of agencies outside the Church. Perhaps we had to be nudged into action by others. We often thought primarily of meeting educational certification and professional requirements quickly and painlessly. Your movement shows that we are beyond this; that we are now aiming at the substance of excellence because we realize the importance and intrinsic need for solid, thorough, and distinguished education of Sisters and nuns. And this movement will thereby establish our Sisters as leaders in their various fields of activity—education, nursing, social services, and so forth.

With regard, then, to the problem of the graduate training of nuns and Sisters, I have thought back over my own experience and have selected a certain number of points around which I should like to build my discussion. These are what we must consider in the preparation of a Sister for graduate work:

1) solid academic formation and general background,
2) maturity of personality,
3) Catholic intellectual outlook,
4) ability to organize and present materials in writing,
5) reading knowledge of foreign languages,
6) need of specialized prerequisites.

The first four of these are intimately connected, and they constitute the most important preparation for graduate work. The most important thing you can do to prepare your Sisters for graduate programs is not to give them the specific prerequisites immediately required for graduate work in some field or other, but to give them a sound academic formation—a general education, a liberal arts formation. This kind of formation requires a certain concentration. It cannot be done by piecemeal bits of education picked up—a smidgen here and there—over a long period of years. And it is the sort of thing that normally can be done only early in the religious life. Sisters can always pick up additional education courses, and the prerequisites for the specialties on the side, in part-time and summer work; but only by an early and concentrated effort can they obtain that fundamental formation—intellectual, academic, humanistic—that is the basis for any sound development in advanced educational and professional work and, above all, for graduate training of leaders.

And your concentrated program of training must allow time for personal study and independent development, specifically for wide reading and the preparation of papers and reports. It must not be merely a crowded curriculum of courses taught routinely and requiring only rote memory more or less at high school level. Otherwise, your Sisters will never have that rich background that reading and private study give, and that is essential for further growth, and they will be at a great disadvantage in graduate schools because of their inability to do independent papers.

Now, if this formation is carried out in a Catholic way, if it includes solid courses in English and literature, in social science, solid systematic and extended courses in philosophy, systematic and advanced courses in religion, the Sisters will come to the graduate school with a Catholic intellectual outlook. Perhaps you think I emphasize this without very solid reason. Well, I have seen transcripts of Sisters applying for graduate work in which there was little religion and no philosophy at all; sometimes a degree in education is presented where many of the courses were gotten in state institutions. Transcripts even from Sister-training institutions sometimes show little in advanced religion and often less in systematic philosophy. This I consider a great danger to a Sister, to the work she is to do, and to the community. A Sister should not go on in education, sociology, and so forth, without this Catholic intellectual formation. Otherwise, the resulting academic mind that is built will not be a Catholic mind, and the Sister herself will not know where the Catholic elements and

Catholic values lie. It is for this reason I emphatically say that, no matter what a Sister is going into, a sound formation that is simultaneously a formation in a Catholic intellectual outlook is essential. I am saying it is essential if she comes to Saint Louis University or to any Catholic university, though obviously it is even more important if the university is not Catholic.

If the fundamental formation is what it ought to be and is integrated with the spiritual, then we will have a mature personality. The Sister going into graduate work, because of the number of personal decisions to be made, the difficulties encountered, the adjustment to objective demands and to the realities of the new situation, must be a mature personality and, if she is that, then her presence in a graduate school becomes, besides, an apostolic mission. A Sister of this type is a welcome acquisition to a graduate school; the way she acts and her very presence there create an atmosphere of inspiring Christianity.

These are the four things that I think are most fundamental. It is possible always for a Sister to get up a reading knowledge of a foreign language and for a Sister to pick up in the summer and so forth the prerequisites necessary, but it is not possible for a Sister—or any individual—to pick up a good sound education in that way.

I have seen transcripts that are a genuine sorrow to me, transcripts stretching through a long period of years, courses picked up during one year in one city, and then in another, and ultimately adding up to an undergraduate degree, sometimes with various starts towards different majors and in different programs. When I look at such transcripts I think how much time and money went into this program; if all that money and time had been put together, there would have been less of both expended, and it would have been a much better program because this Sister who has picked up her education on the side would have had a thorough fundamental training many years before the time when she actually got her Bachelor's degree.

Experience with transcripts of this sort and with the Sisters whose education they outline has convinced me that such a procedure involves a frightening waste of time, money, and effort and that, if all this were concentrated into a basic planned formation, we would, in the long run, save time, money, and our most precious possessions—the Sisters themselves.

My dear Mothers and Sisters, I am going to be very frank in discussing my next point. Nothing, nothing at all, can be solidly achieved except on the basis of the most honest realism. In your planning of programs, be brutally realistic. It is possible to set down on paper a program of courses and credit hours which outline a good fundamental training and yet, as a matter of hard fact, not have such a program at all. Course names may merely mask substitutions which are not equivalents at all. To cite an extreme case, reading in the refectory as a novice is not an equivalent to Freshman English no matter what catalogue title you give it or what credits you allot it. Grades may not be, in any real sense, equivalent to the normal standards set for extern college students.

And the courses may be so squeezed into the timetable of community duties and pressures that there is no proportionate time for study, reading, and writing. This forces learning down to a minimum, hastily crammed and never truly digested. Such courses turn out again to be no equivalent to corresponding college courses. When you plan your program, estimate first how much time your Sisters really have for academic work and then assign courses according to a formula allowing (1) adequate private study time for each hour of class and (2) longer periods of study for thorough work, for writing and investigation. This may reduce the number of credit hours allotted to each semester, but these credit hours will be genuine ones.

It is a deep concern to me to find my departments coming to be sceptical about some, at least, of the transcripts presented by Sisters and nuns. Moreover, this sort of thing can be the cause of very serious mistakes in planning a graduate program—mistakes which place unfair and sometimes disastrous burdens on the Sisters themselves. Each graduate student is treated individually and every effort is made to plan the courses to fit the individual. In the case of Sisters, generally our most important source of information in advising is the transcript. If we assume that the transcript accurately represents the previous training of the Sister and, as a matter of fact, it really does not, serious mistakes can result. We have, to our sorrow, made such mistakes. In all these matters, for the honor of Catholic education and the good of our Sisters, let us be brutally realistic.

Permit me to make one more remark, a sort of confidential remark. Graduate work has many pressures, and those who have been through it know how trying it is to get a thesis in on time, a dissertation finished, an oral examination prepared for. When Sisters are in graduate work, be sympathetic with them and realize they are under severe pressure and tension just as all graduate students are. They need the encouragement of their superiors and the support of their communities.

Neither Jesuits nor Sisters can let subjects spend all their lives at graduate schools. But sometimes there is an excessive added pressure on Sisters because of a rigidly assigned time limit. Graduate schools have the responsibility of maintaining standards and must, therefore, make exacting demands on students. Many students cannot stand the added pressure of fixed deadlines or of a too demanding community expectancy of high grades and unusual achievement. If Sisters are put into graduate work, they need a certain latitude of leisure time and a certain degree of emotional security.

As has long been realized in communities of religious men, anyone in graduate studies needs a definite period each year which is a genuine release from duties and pressures—a real vacation. I often find it necessary, for example, to insist that, for their own sakes, Sisters do not go through both summer sessions.

My dear Mothers and Sisters, there is one thing we rarely have to worry about. Sisters work hard. They do energetically apply themselves to their studies, and I am happy to report to you that this is my uniform experience with them.

I want to tell you also that all the Catholic graduate deans of America are intensely interested in Sister formation and that we are all prepared to be of whatever service we can in your planning problems. I personally, our Graduate Office, and the entire University here at Saint Louis are anxious to be of assistance to your communities. It was the needs of the Sisterhoods that first prompted us to begin a summer session; and hundreds of Sisters have come to us both during the summer sessions and during the regular winter terms. Every Sister automatically receives a partial scholarship, and many of our fellowships are open to them. Recently the University appointed Father Bishop as a special adviser to Sisters in the University. And, once more, the Graduate Office is ready to help. Please feel free to call on us.

I congratulate you on the work you envision; I trust that, because of it, the Sisters will occupy a new position of leadership and will make possible another hundred years of unparalleled Catholic achievement.

Let me tell you again that I am very grateful for the opportunity to make any contribution to your movement.

THE TRAINING OF SISTERS FROM THE POINT OF VIEW OF THE COLLEGE ADMINISTRATOR

Brother Augustine Philip, F.S.C.
President, Manhattan College
New York, New York

For the purpose of suggesting an orderly discussion of the administrator's views about the Sisters' program, it seems that three areas ought to be examined: First, the content of the program in respect to the personalized goals to be achieved; Second, the program as a preparation for the vocational duties of the Sisters in the light of their respective Congregations' particular work; Third, the program, as the groundwork of the great and magnificent system of Catholic education which the Church in America has the unparalleled opportunity in history to promote and develop now and for years and years to come. The Sisters' Congregations are the task-forces to achieve this mission.

From the point of view of the personalized goals that a college education should achieve, a college administrator should see that what is set down for Sisters' education is at least equivalent to that drawn to prepare great minds in other walks of life. Students should be educed to manifest distinctive intellectual activity:

thinking clearly and clearly thinking, inspirationally communicative, avid for facts and knowledge, always assessing and demonstrating delicate evaluation of the moral and esthetic, the religious and the lay, the natural and the supernatural, the Divine and the human. The college administrator, really interested in the meaning of education, will hardly be satisfied unless students are alive and searching in the realms of knowledge, finding interesting relationships, and synthesizing their experiences into new forms. The well-conducted college program of the substance here implied will develop an essential quality of the teacher: love of knowledge and its constant quest as a lifetime work.

Inevitably this view of learning leads us to at least a passing reference to the virtues of the intellect: knowledge, understanding, and wisdom. Their perfection requires endless practice for any skill, and certainly for intellectual power, requires leisure. My return to the term leisure may suggest an unconscious yearning of the college administrator: the administrator usually is a person without leisure, busy about many things in order that the scholars and students may be concerned about the one thing necessary.

More specifically, what is one to do with leisure in order to become educated? He is to pursue fields of learning that will minister to his human dignity, his reason, his reflection in himself of God, whose image he is. We are reaching the fundamental issues respecting proper curriculum content for the end of knowledge. We should make at least passing reference to the disciplines.

In this assemblage no one questions that the basic spheres of learning are theology, philosophy, history, literature, science, and mathematics—all in the comprehensive sense. Neither do we have any doubt about our need for prolonged analytic and critical exercise in each area before we can claim any badge of learning. Greater distinction attends the student who forms new realizations and is inspired to do comprehensive thinking, at least in one or two of the fields. The knowing mind, however, does not hold such specialized insight in isolation. He knows his specialty in ordered relationship to the others. He has a composite view or vision, distinct from mere knowledge about things; he has a sense of an ordered whole, a perception of "marching to a single end from a single source." To the degree that a program of studies results in clarity of mind, sensitiveness of insight, comprehensiveness of interest, and universality of understanding, the program provides the intellect, the person, with learning worthy of human dignity.

I would think the college organization should provide, even respecting Sisters' education, for the personal application of learning and for following the leads of one's interests in co-curricular and extra-curricular activities. To what purpose should the vision of learning be revealed, if only to be laid to rest and forgotten? Education at college matures outside the classrooms, in forums, lectures, discussion groups, student publications, societies. This other world of associations opens the opportunity for student initiative in exploring some by-ways of interest in a formal subject. The variety of student associations answering to the social, cultural, intellectual, and spiritual forces moving them multiplies directly to the number of engaged leadership minds. Given the means of exercising their originality as part of student life—short of organizing proms, whooping up a team—Sisters, too, would gain by the development of their talents, the trial of their knowledge, and the chance to exercise organizing initiative. To attain these ends, again we are assuming leisure and the physical surroundings that will favor their pursuit.

Though I have set down as a second point for our discussion on Sisters' education the vocational duties that the various teaching communities exercise, I did not think of these duties being prepared for separately from the personal goals to guide the higher education of the Sisters. More pointedly, I do not intend to say anything about teacher training, specifically through courses in education. From what I have said of the disciplines essential to enriching the mind, you may infer that I regard courses in education as secondary under one of the disciplines— under history, if the course is about the history of education; under applied science or art, if it deals with the technical procedures and psychology of education; under philosophy, if it presents the principles of education.

Actually, my plea is for higher education in a comprehensive sense as the best preparation for our teaching Sisters. This view,

I would say, holds whether we are preparing teachers for elementary schools exclusively, high schools, or colleges. Whether the mission of a Sister is to be in one or other of these areas of education or in a succession of them, a deep and broad college preparation is imperative. The superstructure of specialized knowledge or know-how for special offices—kindergarten teacher, high-school science, principalship or other administrative office—can very effectively and efficiently be built on the strong foundation of fundamental education. I am sure the one unresolved issue about the amount of teacher-training and at what stage it be given in the Sisters' formation will long continue as a distracting question.

I would like to stress that the enrichment of the mind and widening the breadth of understanding are of vital concern and hence primary in the preparation for performing the vocational duties of a teacher. Whatever else of importance may be added, as one goes along, is all to the good. But first things should come first. Bluntly, the problem is to acquire a significant degree of education before attempting the office of educator. The teacher's function pertains to the learning process. Surely it is not arguable that the teacher should subjectively know the meaning of learning as the internal activity of his own mind in acquiring knowledge. How else than by one's personal experience of learning and properly discriminating among the fields of knowledge can a teacher have a true idea of his office? Without first-hand recognition in himself, how will he really educe the internal activity of other minds so that they become alert and clear, make valid assessments, demonstrate the faculty for analyzing, and finally synthesizing? To accomplish these tasks, even in the grades to the degree they can be achieved, requires the teacher's mind to be alive, flexible, and ever-growing.

The college administrator seems in his appropriate element if he speaks about buildings, physical facilities, and financing. To provide for the education of teachers as we have been thinking of it requires complete furnishing of classrooms and laboratories, libraries and all the necessary instruments in the great undertaking. A variety of ways exists for providing the educational setting: some communities operate a two-year program under the supervision of and in affiliation with a university; these two-year colleges send their Sister-students to a four-year college to complete degree requirements. This arrangement seems to provide only partially the well-ordered and comprehensive fields of learning for the training of the prospective teacher. It would seem that a four-year continued course under single auspices would effectively accomplish the ends in view. Two arrangements suggest themselves: one is conducting the education of Sisters at a regular college for women under the direction of a community; another is the establishment of a Sisters' college or a college for the education of religious teachers where many congregations may send their formation personnel. Administratively speaking, both of the latter arrangements seem best capable of providing the suitable framework for conducting a strong program directed toward the goal of the effective education of the Sisters.

One last point briefly. The religious teacher in formation prepares to play an essential role in a potentially mighty educational system. If the training is in respect to a Sister, she is preparing to join 87,288 other Sisters in our schools throughout America; if a priest, he will take his place with 8,153 other priests dedicated full-time to Catholic education; if a Brother, he will meet 3,637 confreres indentured to Christ in the classroom. The Sisters in Catholic education outnumber the priests by more than ten times, and the Brothers by nearly twenty-five times.

This surely is a wonder of our age in America. Nearly 100,000 priests and religious are conducting and guiding an educational system; all are imbued with singleness of purpose, holding basically the same views of their great office as teachers and of everything else that really matters, and all totally dedicated to the daily duties of the classroom for the welfare of Catholic youth.

The magnitude of the opportunity for perfecting the work of the Church in our age through the teaching priests and religious in our schools is hardly comprehensible. Our responsibility to secure the best education for all the thousands of other Sisters presently in training who will augment and replace the laborers now in the Lord's vineyard can be executed only if we have some sense of the proportions of the meaning of a Catholic system of education. Superlatives are not out of place in attempting to describe the greatness of the stakes.

To give Catholic education the force that it has within its grasp in our country is not the decision of any single individual, whether a Mother Superior, a college administrator, the reverend pastor or the Ordinary of a diocese or the superintendent of schools. The force I refer to is not describable by scattered numbers even if they add to thousands of teachers and millions of pupils. Catholic education will find its force in the consolidated action by the people engaged throughout the field who themselves have been thoroughly formed intellectually by the best schooling. Each must have a sense of his own part in the great cause. More, each must be consciously a member of the whole and act deliberately in concert with the totality; of course, the unifying structure of the Catholic system must emerge from the renewed intellectual growth. Shall not Catholic education then have new resources of power and leadership to challenge the gross materialism and secularism rampant in the schools across our land; new voices to speak out professionally of the true meaning of education, the rights of the family, the child, the Church, the school, the teacher, as well as the state; numerous alert minds given well-informed critical evaluation of the substance applied to the child's mind; multitudes of professionally trained, perceptive and inquiring, in subject areas, who will spot and oppose subverting action as it appears—such as Planned Parenthood's infiltration of the social sciences through family life courses, lectures, field trips to organizational headquarters. The power of Catholic education as a strongly interlocked system depends upon a well-defined over-all policy which must begin at the grass-root training of the religious teachers.

This implies heavy burdens of finances, and I suppose it is exactly at this point the college administrator is invited to take a vigorous role in the discussion. I am sure he has no prescription for magically turning up the great sums of money needed—millions of dollars. Certainly the Sisters themselves have no access to such resources. Some have thought the colleges through discounted tuitions to Sisters and religious generally might contribute greatly to the cause; if the colleges could get along without tuition charges they would be loathe to bill religious communities, all in as great a financial struggle as the colleges.

The necessary funds to carry on this program must be raised. It is inconceivable that among our wealthy Catholic philanthropists there are not men who could be inspired to dedicate their substance in perpetuity to that part of Catholic education that prepares the thousands of religious teachers annually entering Catholic school classrooms. By help of such kind could not our land be studded with semi-endowed colleges precisely for the purpose of giving young religious the thorough education needed to make them leaders of the teaching profession?

What I have been presenting are ideals. But unless they are stated, they will never become norms for judgments; not having them before us, we will never know how far short we fall of what we ought to aim at: whether in respect to the personalized goals of the education of our harvest of young religious teachers; fortifying the vocational duties of teaching Sisters; or magnifying the potentially splendid and influential structure of Catholic education.

THE FORMATION OF SISTERS AS TEACHERS

The Reverend Edward A. Doyle, S.J.
Dean, Loyola University
New Orleans, Louisiana

The religious Sister is unique as a professional teacher. Her religious obligations inherent in her divine calling to a supernatural vocation impose a serious personal responsibility, a philosophy of living, and a singular dedication far transcending the demands made of the lay teacher. On the other hand, the religious Sister retains the self-same responsibility to achieve that professional efficiency to be expected of all teachers, whether lay or religious. Consequently the total education of the religious teaching Sister involves a dual problem:

1) her development according to the ideals and constitutions peculiar to her Institute designed to facilitate her religious perfection and

2) her formation as a teacher equipped to discharge her teaching functions with professional efficiency.

It is not my intention to introduce into Sister formation an artificial dichotomy which neatly separates the Sister as a religious from the Sister as a teacher. On the contrary, my experience in the education of Sisters has convinced me that a realistic approach to this problem demands that the educator avoid the error of dissociating the spiritual formation of Sisters from the professional education of Sisters in any plan providing for the complete education of the teaching Sister. I would pose the problem thus: In an effort to provide for both the religious and teaching-education of Sisters we Catholic administrators, religious superiors, educators have tried to do too much, too soon, too fast. No wonder that hasty preparation of Sisters to achieve professional competency in teaching has often seriously impaired their proper religious development and by that very fact seriously harmed their total development as religious teaching Sisters.

In an effort to be practical I shall attempt to contain the problem of Sister-teacher formation within the limits of seven significant functions involved in the administration of a Sister-teacher formation program. These seven functions are: 1) planning; 2) organization, 3) staffing, 4) direction, 5) coordination, 6) research reporting, 7) budgeting.

Planning

Attempts to devise a plan for the professional formation of Sisters imply a recognition of the two-fold aspect of the Sisters' education. Different methods, techniques, resources, even aptitudes and interests are involved in the formation of a religious of high sanctity.

Sisters A, B, and C may be exemplary religious—solidly holy, observant, fervent, radiant additions to any community to which they may be assigned. It does not follow that they are thereby immediately equipped to step into the classroom and perform as expert teachers. It should be evident that even enviable advancement in holiness gives no clear title to proficiency in teaching elementary reading. Nor does successful completion of the novitiate qualify a Sister to parade as a competent teacher in any field the superior may designate, whether it be on the elementary, secondary, or collegiate level. Sisters A, B, and C may have shown great advances in religious perfection according to the measure of God's grace each has individually received; there may be marked divergences in their capabilities as professional teachers. Sister A may have shown exceptional aptitude for historical stud-- ies, the intelligence to master a special field, and the personality to impart this mastery to high school girls. Sister B may manifest no such qualities, but, on the other hand, may possess talent that Sister A does not include in her repertoire. Sister C's aptitudes and special talents may eclipse or, at least differ widely from, those of both Sister A and Sister B.

Here the fallacy of too much, too soon, too fast begins to operate in failing to plan the professional development of the three Sisters. Sisters A, B, C have hardly lost the shine from their novitiate dishpan hands when all three are thrust into a new school or an understaffed school; just temporarily, of course, because "we simply need three elementary school teachers immediately." Expedience rears its ugly head and frightens Reverend Mother into the comforting rationalization: "Now, don't you worry! These Sisters are such perfect religious that they can make any adjustment well; they'll do splendidly teaching anything." These three Sisters strive heroically for ten winters to teach as well as they can; for ten summers they travel the summer school circuit from Nebraska to Florida, and in their tenth summer retreat each breathes an innocent yet prayerful complaint: "Dear Lord, when, please when, am I *supposed to be prepared to teach?*" Has not too much been expected of these Sisters, too fast, and too soon in rushing them from novitiate duties to the quite different routine of teaching?

Heeding the persistent pleas for more teachers to be supplied as quickly as possible, unwisely opening new schools with skeleton staffs, and curtailing, and what is worse, eliminating special professional education for the qualified Sister are expedients foolishly short-sighted and fraught with disastrous consequences for the parochial school.

Prudent planning would dictate that the Sisters be well formed

according to the ascetical ideals of their institute. It is of primary
importance that as novices and as juniors professed they receive
correct instruction, expert guidance, and sufficient motivation to
provide that emotional and spiritual maturity which serves one
so well in effective teaching. It would not be amiss to utilize during this formative period those tests that reliably and validly report intelligence, aptitudes, both general and special, interests,
and personality traits, the data of which can be usefully applied
in the guidance of Sisters.

Alertness to the needs of the Sisters requires definite organization of the program, a staff competent to operate it, wise direction, and coordination of all the personnel involved.

Steps should be initiated to exclude from novitiate training
all teaching duties or professional preparation for teaching. As
junior professed the Sisters should begin their academic training
on the collegiate level, be thoroughly instructed in philosophy
and theology, the Catholic philosophy of education, and methods
of teaching. During this period provision should be made for student teaching under adequate supervision. No Sister should be
permitted to assume a teaching position before receiving the Baccalaureate degree and certification in her teaching field. Great
fortitude will be required to resist persistent pressure to yield to
the clamor for Catholic school teachers. It is wiser to withhold
twenty Sisters for four years of adequate preparation than to
thrust them untried and insecure into teaching positions that pre-
clude early completion of their degree work and entail the compromise of full-time teaching and part-time work in college.
Festina lente—hasten slowly—should be a practical watchword.
Better for the Sister to complete her four or five year program in
teaching education than to limp through almost interminable
summer sessions and Saturday classes.

Those institutes of Sisters who teach and train their own teachers can hold the line more consistently against external pressures.
An organized training program is underway in quite a few of the
institutes represented here today. Where such an organized program is not presently feasible, some arrangement demands coordination of the university program with the antecedent preparation, daily order, educational goals adopted by the Sisters.

Selection of staff for administration of such a program is of utmost importance. The Mother General operating through the provincials and councils would be the responsible agent in the enforcement of the teacher education program. Mistresses of novices, possessed of first-hand knowledge of teacher candidates under their direction, could ably serve in a consultative capacity. The Mistress or Prefect of Studies plays a key role in the direction and coordination of the teacher education program and should be immediately responsible for its administration. If her authority has been clearly delegated, properly defined, and universally promulgated, generous cooperation would smooth the way to administration of the plan devised. It would seem to be essential to the office of the Mistress or Prefect of Studies that she be free to assemble data relating to the general and special aptitudes of teacher candidates, their interests, personality traits, and all information pertinent to the educational preparation of teachers. Her duties would include conferences at specified times with teacher candidates with a view to supplementing objective data by information gathered through these personal interviews. Progress reports on teacher candidates serve well in establishing a cumulative record. The Mistress of Studies should have enough research experience to project the needs of the future, evaluate present progress, and present reliable data relating to the teacher education program for the benefit of all participants. Much planning will be utterly wasted unless there is an adequate follow-up to check results through coordinated research. Financial reports should be accessible to the Prefect of Studies; the outlay budgeted for teacher education may be a significant determinant of the total teacher education program. For that reason, close cooperation must exist between the treasurer of the council and the Prefect of Studies. Probably nowhere on the staff is more mutual understanding demanded than between these two offices.

Special efforts should be made by the Sisters to strengthen the quality of their public relations with diocesan superintendents of schools, with the administrators and teachers of those colleges where Sisters may be educated, with the hierarchy of the Church when direct communication is in order, with the parents of the children they instruct, with other religious institutes striving to achieve similar goals. By these means mutual understanding and cooperation can result when the publics we serve begin to appreciate the Sisters' consistent adherence to ideals, recognize the numerous obstacles in the path, and acknowledge the need of the moral, financial, and educational support the Sisters have merited.

The matchless dignity and influence of the competent Catholic teaching Sister require a formation effected by careful planning, organization, staffing, direction, coordination, research, and financing.

Let us refuse to compromise with mediocrity, accepting no substitute for the spiritually formed and professionally educated teaching Sister. Proper provision for the health, professional competence, and continuing happiness of our teaching Sisters should forbid our forcing upon them too much, too soon, too fast.

THE FORMATION OF SISTERS FROM THE VIEWPOINT OF THE GRADUATE DEAN OF STUDIES

Sister Mary Humiliata, I.H.M.
Graduate Dean
Immaculate Heart College
Los Angeles, California

In considering the subject of Sister formation for the graduate school, I think we must establish, first of all, the needs of Holy Mother Church in this regard. Then we can turn to the needs of the teaching Sisters themselves for graduate training if they are to fulfill their vocation.

The Church today needs what we alone, the teaching communities of America, can give her. She needs our wholehearted dedication to the work of the intellectual apostolate. Without it, without the development of a strong intellectual life within the consecrated ranks of her religious, without productive Catholic scholars in every field, the Church is powerless today to meet the challenges facing her—challenges, like those of Karl Marx or Jean-

Paul Sartre, rooted in the world of ideas. We in America have not had to face the horrors of persecution—indeed we have not felt the least privation or want—while our contemporaries in Europe and Asia have endured heroic sufferings and death. But do we realize that this fact constitutes not an exemption, but an obligation—that a special vocation in the Church devolves of necessity upon us, a vocation to assume the intellectual leadership for which the world looks to us.

Ask the Catholic student in any field of the liberal arts to name the American Catholic scholars in that area. Too often we find a pathetic lack of them—of men and women who have envisioned the power of the intellectual apostolate and who have burned out their lives for Christ in the quiet of the laboratory or the library.

In our religious communities we find a matchless opportunity for the development of such an intellectual apostolate. Here there is relief from material worries and an atmosphere of recollection which many a lay professor would envy. Why, then, do the names of our Sisters appear so rarely in the pages of learned journals, or on the programs of research groups—contributing the Catholic attitude on matters of intellectual controversy?

We can, of course, claim the demands of the active apostolate. But let us take warning that we fail the Church, and we fail the hungry minds of our own time, if we neglect the intellectual apostolate and neglect the intellectual perfection of those committed to our charge.

The blessed day has not yet come when religious communities will consider it a privilege to allow Sisters to devote themselves to higher learning or research instead of asking the inevitable: "When will you ever get that degree?" or "You have your degree —why are you studying *now?*"

But on the immediate and practical level, let us face today the problem of the ever-increasing need for advanced or graduate work on the part of teaching Sisters in the secondary or elementary schools. I am not referring to the special training demanded of the college teacher. We must, we know, face realistically a future in which religious teachers in our schools will be required to take graduate work for credentials, and most probably for advanced degrees. We know that many young religious have perceived their own incapacity to meet a classroom situation and have felt the need for further training. Perhaps far too often when Sister Innocentia, newly professed, has expressed this thought, she has been chided for her lack of trust in God. Or she has been cited the case of Sister Tenebrae, who in 1905 managed the boarding school, taught French conversation, advanced china painting, biology, needlework, and history, with music lessons from three to five. But let us be fair. Students of today are not those of fifty, twenty-five, or even fifteen years ago. Boys and girls of today sense immediately a teacher's lack of security in a certain field, and with their heightened awareness of themselves and the world around them, they will not hesitate to challenge her. Students are no longer willing to accept a statement as infallible because "Sister said so." Teachers who have an inadequate background bring discredit on themselves and their communities—and frequently this is not their fault.

We must acknowledge, too, that the parents of the youngsters we teach are, in growing numbers, college-bred. They demand a new proficiency from the teachers of their children. Trained, many of them, in education—or at least, acquainted with a vocabulary of educational and psychological terms through reading—they have become increasingly critical of deficiencies on the part of teaching Sisters. They are unsympathetic when they perceive inadequate or outdated teaching facilities. They deplore cultural poverty in their children's training.

Further, not only the young teaching religious, but the young administrator often feels her inadequacy when she realizes that comparable positions in the public school system demand advanced training and advanced degrees.

Thus the need and demand for further training are certainly apparent. It is inherent in the structure of our educational system and cannot be avoided. Nor is this prospect one to be dreaded if we take cognizance of it now, and if both superior and subjects are prepared to meet this aspect of twentieth century religious life in America. Certainly there will be new problems, and certainly new procedures must be adopted.

Now if it is admitted that graduate training is essential, at least for some of the Sisters, then an understanding of the intellectual apostolate and a respect for it must be built up among the superiors of a religious community and among the community at large. The young religious, to enter graduate school with the proper enthusiasm, and to continue her work with energy and perserverance, must be inspired with an appreciation for the apostolate of study and for its fruition in teaching. In other words, she must dedicate herself generously to the restoration of all things intellectual in Christ. She must see that the intellectual development can be truly unselfish in its aim and goal if it grows out of the great-hearted desire to serve Christ with the totality of one's being. Advanced study on the part of our Sisters cannot be viewed as activity snatched from the routine of conventual life and rather shame-facedly surrendered to the demands of secular agencies. This study cannot be huddled into a scant hour between the teaching of classes and prayers. If graduate study is done in an atmosphere of disapproval and viewed as unsanctified, somehow outside the round of true religious life, only needless conflicts and tensions can result for the graduate student.

Graduate study should bear fruit in religious teachers solidly prepared in their fields, joyous in the pursuit of knowledge and enthusiastic in bringing that joy to others, informed as to technique and dedicated to the passionate quest for truth. But the young religious must be shown that the Church today desperately needs the contribution which she in her role of scholar can bring her Mother. The work of the Catholic scholar is a work bearing the stamp of such great souls and disciplined minds as Thomas and Augustine, Catherine of Siena, Teresa of Avila, Anselm, Jerome, Francis de Sales and Thomas More. Graduate study for the religious with its attendant fatigue, loneliness, and lack of the consolations of the more active apostolate, deserves at least the encouragement of superiors who recognize the contribution of the student to her community, to her future students, and to the Church at large.

The graduate school has as its charge to set the eyes of the students upon the distant goal of intellectual perfection, but unless religious superiors are convinced of the nobility of that goal, there will be slipshod, careless, superficial work done by our religious on the pretext that "classes really don't matter—that's not why you entered." "When you come to die, what will such things count?" But why is it that a table carefully dusted is more evidence of sanctity than a term paper carefully documented? This attitude is shameful in the face of such selfless dedication to the intellectual apostolate of such contemporary Catholic laymen as Etienne Gilson and Jacques Maritain. Gilson, recognized and respected internationally for his work in philosophy, history, and literature, insists that piety—or religion—does not dispense with technique. And Maritain remarks: "It is impossible to imagine to what degree the Mother of the Incarnate Word cherishes the integrity of truth and abhors any stain on intelligence."

It is essential, then, that the ideals and goals of the graduate school be understood by superiors of religious communities. They must acknowledge the place of study and research as a valid and valuable part of the total offering made by their community to God and to His Holy Church. Unless the leaders of the community make a true evaluation of this exacting apostolate, the teaching orders of our time will fail to carry on the hallowed tradition of scholarship which is our responsibility. More, they will fail in their immediate apostolate for want of direction in their zeal.

While keeping before their communities the ideal of the intellectual apostolate, superiors must remember that the graduate student, to do her best work, must be released from a heavy teaching schedule, from innumerable extra-curricular activities, from clerical assistantship, and from household management. This will, of course, entail sacrifice on the part of the community, as those gifted for graduate study are likewise frequently those who serve best in a variety of other capacities. But it is only by affording this temporary release from pressures that superiors will allow students to pursue their work without undue strain on mind and body. Secular universities conscientiously limit the programs of graduate students in accordance with the amount of their outside employment. Yet we sometimes burden our religious, who carry far graver obligations, with more. Without doubt, religious communities devoted to educational work must acknowledge this problem and prepare to make the necessary sacrifices as a matter of course.

Recognizing the continuing trend toward graduate work, and seeing the part which understanding and inspiration play in producing the best results academically and apostolically we should next consider the imperative problem of preparing candidates for graduate school.

First, the necessity for long-range preparation: The finest candidates for advanced degrees are, of course, those who have a solid and sound undergraduate training. From the viewpoint of the graduate school the best preparation is one which is both broad and deep—broad in the sense that the student has received some training in each of the major disciplines in her general education program; deep in the sense that the undergraduate major is strong enough to hold graduate training without collapse from top-heaviness.

Doctor Martin McGuire, dean of the Graduate School of Arts and Sciences at the Catholic University of America, stated on this point:

> "The college graduate who wishes to enter graduate school should be able to write and speak English with correctness, if not even with reasonable facility. He should have some acquaintance with each of the major divisions of knowledge: the humanities, social studies, biological studies, and mathematics. There should also be a deeper acquaintance with some one subject or group of subjects . . . such as would constitute a reasonable undergraduate major, or preferably such as would be acquired in a program of concentration; but narrow specialization at the college level at least should be scrupulously avoided. He should have acquired a good reading knowledge of French or German, preferably both. His work in history, philosophy, and religion should have given unity and integration to his intellectual and moral training. Special attention should have been given throughout his undergraduate career to the development of orderly and critical powers of thinking. In other words, he should enter the graduate school as an educated man in the best sense of the term."

I should like to underline and supplement one statement made by Dean McGuire and that is the necessity of work in philosophy and religion—or theology—giving unity and integration to the intellectual training.

If the religious with an advanced degree is to be protected from the danger of becoming a mere specialist rather than a truly educated person—or worse, of becoming a philosopher, an artist, a chemist, a literary historian who happens also to be a religious—then training in theology must be central throughout the preparatory years of study.

For the religious, of course, training in theology is not merely a matter of formal courses, but the program of studies of a lifetime. Begun in the novitiate, continued by conferences, retreats, and spiritual reading, the theology of the religious is a living thing; the *lumen supernaturale* is the light which illumines at once both intellectual and spiritual life.

It might be remarked parenthetically that certainly we should stress the importance of training in Catholic graduate schools whenever and wherever this is humanly possible. Catholic colleges and universities on the West Coast, despite their youth, have been courageous in undertaking graduate programs so that the intellects of religious might be developed as Catholic intellects. The integration of theology and philosophy with the major field is the particular concern of these graduate schools; certainly the fine records they have established should make no one fear inadequacy in their programs.

If the candidate, on presenting herself to the graduate school, must report sketchy or superficial training in the undergraduate major, or in supplementary fields, superiors should not protest the period of additional training which the graduate school prescribes. Unless such time be allotted, the student will find herself frustrated and incompetent throughout her work for the advanced degree. It may be well to remark here that the frequent transfers from one undergraduate college to another, while no doubt an emergency measure on the part of the religious superiors, make the assembling of a solid undergraduate major preparation a difficult task. The major programs of various colleges differ just sufficiently to make the academic life of the transfer student, particularly in the junior and senior years, most difficult. I am not stating that the undergraduate program need be taken at the same college as the graduate work, but that transfers in the course of the undergraduate program often make the major preparation troublesome. Again, religious superiors should be on their guard against the fallacy of urging "quick degrees" or snap courses, especially for those of their subjects who show promise of special ability. Quite frankly, the most frequent complaint on the part of Sisters entering the graduate school is their lack of sufficient background in their chosen field. The causes for this are usually three: first, protracted undergraduate work so that the first courses are buried in antiquity before the last are completed; second, lack of sufficient challenge in undergraduate work—the misguided tendency on the part of certain professors never to fail a Sister; never to give a Sister D or even C; third, frequent changes in college and even in major field—the latter motivated by an immediate need on the part of the community for degrees. While no one doubts that religious superiors have innumerable and inexplicable reasons for the changes in plan they must at times make, the student of unusual promise must, if possible, be protected from such exigencies.

Now not every religious, even by virtue of her vocation to a teaching community, is a potential candidate for an advanced degree. What, then, are the characteristics of religious who show real promise as graduate students? The outstanding characteristic of the religious graduate student should be balance—and specifically balance between the spiritual and intellectual life. Without an objective evaluation of this factor, there will result disaster both for the religious and for her community. It helps a Sister very little to dismiss the problem lightly with a few words on the value of obedience or with the traditional jibes of retreat masters about the Ph.D. candidate's pretensions to wisdom. Practically speaking, there remains an area of inner conflict and even of destruction which religious superiors are unwise to ignore.

If the intellectual apostolate is seen as a valid religious obligation, a Sister will avoid the errors of one who studies and reads with guilty anxiety. The religious of intellectual gifts must realize humbly and simply that her talents and her training in intellectual pursuits will perforce demand from her a consistent generosity in her spiritual development. "To whom much has been given, of her much will be required."

Intellectually, how does the potential graduate stand out from her fellows in her classes? Presumably, of course, she is the student of unusual capability and talent, and is probably distinguished by her fine undergraduate record in certain fields. However, just as a successful high school record is not a necessary prediction of an outstanding college career, so the college record, or even a high score on the Graduate Record Examination, is no guarantee of ultimate success in the graduate field. The potential graduate student is the student of mature intellectual life. Her mind operates on a level no longer narrowly factual, although she does not scorn factual evidence. She is not confined to an intellectual area marked out by the limits of any single teacher. Rather, she can see relationships between various fields of learning or various aspects of one field. She shows facility in analytical critical thinking and in comparison of texts. She is gifted with originality in attacking a problem and creative imagination in solving it. She is discriminating in her reading materials, even those chosen for recreational purposes. Finally, she will voluntarily turn, even in her spare time, to independent, serious reading or scholarly pursuits.

With candidates thus carefully selected and their cooperative guidance by both the graduate school and by the religious superiors, the program of graduate study can proceed not without difficulties, but at least without major disaster. And what then? "Waitings which ripen hopes are not delays," a seventeenth century poet once wrote. Then religious superiors must be content to await the slow harvest. "First the blade, then the ear, then the perfect grain . . ." Having prepared the reapers for their task, you will witness the gathering of sheaves in gladness—rewards not graphable, nor calculable in terms of dollar signs or hours. But "when the fruit appears, then it is time to put in the sickle, because now the harvest is ripe"—a harvest, God willing, of souls grounded and established in Christ, Our Lord.

THE INTELLECTUAL FORMATION OF SISTERS AS SEEN FROM THE VIEWPOINT OF A DEAN

The Very Reverend Vincent C. Dore, O.P.

Academic Vice President
Providence College
Providence, Rhode Island

The general theme of last year's meeting of the National Catholic Educational Association held in Chicago was "Planning for Our Educational Needs." Among the many needs that call for immediate planning and holding a high priority rating on the agenda was the need for more and better prepared teachers on all levels. As the vast majority of Sisters are teachers, special attention was given to the intellectual formation of Sisters, or to be more exact, to the academic preparation and professional training of Sister teachers.

With the tidal wave of students that is already hitting the elementary schools but will not reach its crest in the first grade until 1960 and even higher crests to follow, American educators must find more than a million new teachers in addition to the 50,000 a year replacements. This means that for every three teachers now in the schools at least two more must be recruited to enter the teaching profession in the next six years. The burden of educating this unprecedented tidal wave of students will be far greater than anything we have ever been called upon to face. The increase is greater among Catholic families than the average for the total population. Consequently, the enlarging of parochial schools, high schools, and colleges places an almost overwhelming burden on Catholic education and calls for immediate planning for the recruitment and adequate training of teachers for these schools.

First, let me say that I have always maintained that the elementary school Sister-teacher should be trained in the Diocesan Catholic Teachers College. Elementary education and the preparation to teach in the grades is primarily the function of the Teachers College. They are better prepared and equipped to give this type of education and training than the Liberal Arts College. Men's and especially women's colleges can assist then by bringing the A.B. and B.S. graduates back to college for a year of professional education courses and practice teaching under a certified critic teacher. But with the already alarming shortage of public school teachers and the short six or eight weeks courses in teacher professional training for A.B. and B.S. graduates in states like Connecticut and Massachusetts and the lucrative starting salaries in the public schools, I do not think we can help very much unless a girl decides to enter the convent.

Last Wednesday night, I attended a meeting of the Rhode Island Board of Education, and I left that meeting more convinced than ever that we face a serious problem of attracting Catholic public school teachers to enter our system. Personally, I believe that public school teachers should be paid salaries commensurate with their effort and training and with comparable occupations and professions.

But where does that leave us in attracting college graduates to Catholic elementary and secondary education? My experience as dean for the past ten years leads me to conclude that very few of our graduates enter Catholic secondary and less in elementary education. The few that enter Catholic secondary education do so only to meet state certification requirements and enter public school education with its more attractive salaries as soon as they can. So the education of Catholic boys and girls falls on the shoulders of Brothers and Sisters and almost entirely on the Sisters in the elementary grades. Hence, the challenge of preparing good teachers for Catholic elementary schools, as well as girls high schools and women's colleges, must be met by the Sisterhoods. They need and want the help, the guidance and the assistance of all of us, especially of college and university administrators, and we cannot afford to overlook the Sisters. That is why we are here today.

The task before us calls for all the wisdom of Solomon. In fact, we must aim, in the intellectual formation of Sisters, to cultivate this highest of intellectual virtues—wisdom. Wisdom means a kind of knowledge which is in some way excellent. Whether in the university or elementary school, the Sister-teacher needs to know at least two things, the subject she is to teach and the art of teaching it. If she knows these two things, she has an excellent knowledge, a real wisdom. If we would prepare a wise teacher, we must see that she is provided with the following essentials:

1) A philosophical grasp of the subject she is to teach and excellent supervision and training in how to teach it.
2) A mastery of the liberal arts.
3) A solid introduction to
   a) Natural science
   b) Social science
   c) Theology all taught in a philosophic manner.

We should underline theology because the most excellent knowledge is the knowledge of God. Theology the queen, the keystone, and the summation of all knowledge shows us God as He reveals Himself and points out our sure way to Him. Hence, it is supreme both in the theoretical order and the practical order, the highest wisdom which man can acquire or teach.

The liberal arts should be particularly stressed since they are the primary tools of effective communication. Many professors are masters of their subjects but cannot communicate. The corrective is not a course in methods or a course in human development, although both have a place. What is needed in addition to theoretical psychological studies is practical psychology as developed in the art of rhetoric—psychology of the audience as ordered to the uses of communication. At Harvard, Cornell, Louisville, Arkansas, Gaucher, Peabody Teachers College, and Vanderbilt programs, sponsored by the Fund for the Advancement of Education, are being offered to liberal arts graduates in preparation for better teaching training in the elementary school. This program is based on the premise that the graduates of liberal arts colleges could be the best kind of teachers, because they are deeply conscious of the cultural heritage they transmit and the qualities of citizenship they must foster. This type of training calls for a four-year college program leading to an A.B. or B.S. degree plus a fifth year of professional education courses and well-supervised teacher training. It is an ideal situation, and we are fully conscious of all the difficulties that beset the American Catholic educational system. But here in a very small way we can see the ideal educational vision becoming a reality.

THE EDUCATION OF SISTERS FROM THE VIEWPOINT OF THE DEAN OF STUDIES

Sister Mary Rose Emmanuella, S.N.J.M.
Dean, College of the Holy Names
Oakland, California

Realizing how little by way of personal experience and accumulation of data I could bring to this assembly, I sent out a letter and brief questionnaire to the deans of fifty colleges for women listed as having institutional membership in the College and University Department of the National Catholic Educational Association. Those contacted were located in every part of the country. My purpose was to request information from those I thought might be engaged in the teaching of Sisters as well as of secular students from as many regions as possible. In some cases I found that the college had no religious among its students; but the amazing thing is that all but two responded; and my report today is based upon twelve detailed outlines of programs now being carried out, these having been generously sent to me with the answers to my questions.

Before coming to particular points, I should like, first, to note certain general discoveries I have made:

First of all, there is evidence of national effort and of national progress, both quantitatively and qualitatively, in the matter of developing programs of study for Sisters and in prolonging their time of formation before, during, and after entering upon the active works of their various communities.

Secondly, I have gained an almost overwhelming impression of all that is going forward throughout the land under the direction of our women religious. The numbers of their colleges, in addition to other institutions; the natural miracle of organization;

the manifold indications of the power of women to analyze their positions, needs, and corporate problems; and, as in such ways as that offered by this conference, to seek advice and efficient help in overcoming difficulties—all these things lead to sincere concurrence with the well-known slogan: "Never underestimate the power of a woman!"

Neither, on the other hand, let us overestimate her power—or ours.

We are not, as communities, as individuals, or even as deans, free agents, but secondary in ministering to the needs of the Church in assigned and regulated areas. Particularly, as deans, all express this recognition of official role as one of providing the means and machinery for students to go forward, as students, finding in the life of learning a means and way of learning Life. Even more is this true of attitudes towards Sister-students. Our ambitions and achievements in their regard must be measured against the needs of our own communities and of others sending their Sisters to us. Deans, as such, then, are liaison officers operating between the student and her future, in view of immediate standards; between her college and the state and other accrediting agencies; and between her college and the provincial or general administration of her own and other communities entrusting its Sisters to its academic program and little world of experience.

Particular situations in the various colleges differ, of course, in many ways. Some of the answers on the questionnaire, as a result, are widely at variance. By way of reduction, however, these are a few of the problems presented.

It would be helpful if directresses of study could discuss plans for their Sisters with the dean, or with someone within the college administration who could follow their academic program. A two-way road between the dean and directress would also help the dean resolve any difficulties found by Sisters in their individual classes, should they report these to the directress rather than to her.

Curricular difficulties have largely to do with lack of proper sequence and of lower-division preparation for some courses. Beginnings may be well made for a semester or a little longer by postulants; but often those of the canonical year are of a lofty character in theology, without the necessary philosophical foundation. Then, when young Sisters emerge as senior novices or professed Sisters, they sometimes must follow whatever courses are being offered at that time. In this case, advance requests from the directress might help the dean plan for their needs.

Many mention the difficulties of diverse kinds of preparation and ability found in any novitiate group. There is the double problem of making it possible for those with some or a great deal of college work completed to go forward; while, at the same time, very fundamental courses must be given to others—for example, in speech, written English, and even religion.

As for the major problem of time: Many bewail the expediency of simply "getting through units." This often dictates the taking of too many courses by young Sisters, perhaps just out of high school and with few established study habits or any profound interest in study. Now they want to do well, for God's sake; and strain may result. They may work too frantically, and consequently become over-anxious, nervous, discouraged, and hopeless about ever living up to such a vocation. On the other hand, a pious passivity may also set in. One may be prone to accept what she humbly assumes as limitations in ability as a permanent block to further intellectual advance; whereas the real reason is either one of inadequate time, age, preparation, or proper subject matter. In either case, there may be an early loss or prevention of any personal zest or ambition in study.

For the more highly endowed or advanced Sister, there are also problems: There may be a certain frustration in not being able any longer to fall automatically into old study habits. Faces, places, and events are all too different! Neither is she any longer in a position to create a new schedule for herself. She is subjected to a choppy time-schedule in which study is intermittently listed "in between fashion" like various strata in a new structure composed largely of community or religious duties, most of which— and especially, nowadays, the domestic—are entirely unfamiliar. All this may cause her to lose intellectual confidence and ambition also.

Then there are those others—the very religious ones—who had envisioned the whole life of a Sister as a prolonged retreat. Gladly would such a one have slipped off the yoke of *Econ. 2*, at least for a while; but during the postulate, here it is again!

Many deans in speaking of this item of time wrote of the need of it for Sister-students on all levels for *preparation* of class work. In the case of the young or of the poor student, it is all-important; but it is also essential if the more advanced and the good students are to do their best work and continue to advance. In view of the need of both to learn for themselves to harmonize the demands of heart, head, and spirit, and to taste the truths disclosed for them, there must be time for realization—for personal discovery.

Finally, if classes are attended with secular students, Sisters who lack adequate time feel very keenly the difficulty of the situation because of the generally recognized responsibility they have to do good, thorough, even professional work.

If ever habits of scholarship are to be developed, then the view of study and of class work must also be clarified. If they are honorable means of serving God, the time allowed for them should indicate this fact adequately.

As far as the content of study is concerned, the problems that arise are also complicated by disordered sequences. If one spends twenty summer sessions in acquiring a degree, the very facts of time, space, and human mortality destroy hope of any unity. The broken and uneven character of class offerings is bound to destroy interest also; and apathy is a natural consequent of interrupted spurts of progress. The same difficulty besets late afternoon or Saturday classes. "First things must come first," in the life of a Sister; and in such a case, it is the community assignment of the nurse, the teacher, or the social worker that must take precedence —while she also has a Saturday class. Furthermore, such class groups are never very permanent. After one semester or a year, "the Spirit breatheth where He listeth," and they are off—perhaps both teacher and students—in all directions. It is all in the best— if not better than—medieval manner. At least then there was something cohesive about student migration.

Another factor that disturbs deans in planning the sequence of courses is that among many Sisters, there is demand and real need for practical courses before the more theoretical or more generally liberal courses have been completed. Because of the very definite demands made in connection with a credential, for example, there is a tendency to include some education courses in the sophomore year, to introduce psychology into the freshman year; and so with other courses required in view of various professional works of a community.

A final group of questions related to whether it might be a good policy to demand the completion of a certain amount of college work before a subject entered a community where a degree would eventually be practically necessary. There were also recommendations from deans regarding houses of study for those leaving the novitiate. The recommendations varied according to the particular situations of the colleges; but the majority of deans see a separate house of studies for the junior professed as highly desirable, allowing a fuller experience of the community life of the order or congregation as lived after the novitiate, permitting some participation in the work of the community, perhaps; and m; cing necessary an independent ordering of her day of class and study by each of the student-Sisters.

Such, then, are some of the more common jottings from the c aestionnaires. The litany may make it appear that the lot of deans is even worse and much sadder than you had thought; but that thought I should not want to leave with you. The deans who ans ered wrote in such a way that I judge deans to be quite a dauntless lot.

Let us not underestimate the power of a woman: her power to analyze, formulate, and accept her problem; her power to employ practical means in its solution; and to realize the need of pooling experience and effort.

Neither let us underestimate her power of winning help from those who can foster the effort she is making by giving her more theoretical knowledge, by inventing better techniques, by applying stronger methods of organization and implementation than those at her disposal.

And never let us forget the power of that Woman who presided over the education of Him in Whom we are Sisters. Under her direction we must be busy about filling up the water-pots— some busy as Mothers general or provincial; some as mistresses of novices; some as deans, counsellors, registrars, house-mothers, teachers, refectorians, treasurers, secretaries, nurses, receptionists, case-workers, and as students.

We do not underestimate her power with Him to see that the wine will never fail.

EDUCATION OF SISTERS FROM THE VIEWPOINT OF THE UNDERGRADUATE DEAN

The Reverend Joseph S. McGrath, C.S.C.
Dean of the Faculties
University of Portland
Portland, Oregon

I feel that the education of a Sister is no different from the education of anyone else. Sisters should start their college training early, before any teaching assignments are given them, and they should be free to pursue their studies. I do not believe that lay students should have to be employed during college; neither should Sisters. Canon law forbids it for seminarians. Everyone does not agree with me, but that is the subject for another conference.

Sisters cannot earn their degrees in summer sessions only. One dean recently pointed out that a certain Sister would need forty years to get her Bachelor's degree. I did not ask the age of the Sister applicant. But let us say that a Sister could earn annually the maximum of ten hours credit. She would need thirteen years to complete her work; and in the meantime her interests have changed and also her superiors.

If Sister education is delayed, it has little purpose. If it is interrupted or sparingly given, superiors change, and the young are changed from place to place and become discouraged. These things we see.

Special classes on Saturday or at odd times in the convent are no remedy. The student must have the full college experience in order to become an effective teacher. These odd classes for one or two produce little or no results. Sisters should not be asked to study in fields in which they have no interest. Superiors should not demand A grades as a basis of continued study. Sisters should go away to school. There should be varied experience within the community: regimentation kills initiative, leads to mediocrity, gives no incentive, no competition. Sisters must meet the public in learned societies, and similar groups. Sisters should take part in some extra-curricular activities because they in turn must direct their students in these same activities.

Karl Stern has a line which I should like to quote, albeit a bit out of context:

"The Catholic Church is a church of the multitude. Consequently the outsider, approaching her, faces a thick layer of mediocrity. . . . The misdeeds of one member are more broadcast than the sanctity of a hundred others." [1]

Again, in a recent issue of *Time* in the section on religion, Gordon C. Zahn of Loyola, Chicago, states that Roman Catholics have not moved forward so far or so fast as many Catholics and Protestants think.[2]

Likewise, John D. Kane of Notre Dame says that the Catholics tend to educate their children less well, are less successful in business, concentrate in fields that sacrifice prestige for security:

"Catholics creep forward rather than stride forward in American society, and the position of American Catholics in mid-20th century is better, but not so much better, than it was a century ago." [3]

I offer no easy solution to the difficulties I raise. This Conference cannot solve your problem. It is your problem, individually —that is, as an individual community. We can point out the sore spots. We can indicate general remedies. You must select and act.

FOOTNOTES

1. The Pillar of Fire (New York: Harcourt, Brace and Company), pp. 247-248.
2. *Time* (January 10, 1955).
3. *Ibid.*, p. 62.

SISTER FORMATION FROM THE VIEWPOINT
OF THE GRADUATE DEAN

The Very Reverend A. A. Lemieux, S.J.

President of Seattle University
Seattle, Washington

In this paper we should like to discuss the nature of graduate work; to outline the qualifications of those who should be encouraged to do graduate work, or who are capable of graduate work; and to present some practical directives in regard to graduate work which might be helpful to directresses of studies as well as to the individual student teacher.

First of all, the nature of graduate work. What are the aims or objectives of graduate work? (Here we might pause to note that graduate work may be either directed to the M.A. and terminated here, or it may be directed through the M.A. to the Doctorate. Our remarks will be made primarily about the fifth year or M.A. program.) The objectives of the strictly graduate M.A. program are the following: (1) To give the student some practice in and some knowledge of the technics of research. This is a basic preparation for any student who wishes to go on to a Doctorate, and it is an essential preparation for any student who is to do any sort of writing. (2) To give some knowledge of and some practical work in the sources of information and material in a subject area. A teacher should know source materials; what has been written; where it is to be found; who are masters; how to use them. (3) To develop the ability to work and to think on one's own with guidance and direction.

In an article appearing in the second issue of the *Sister Formation Bulletin,* Sister Mary Emil summarizes very aptly the objectives or aims of graduate work on the first level in the following words:

"Sister formation looks to the forming of a woman who can think for herself, who is able to continue her education independently, through reading and study, and who has a love and appreciation of the things of the mind. To put it in another way, it aims at training a Sister who has the philosophical and theological background to understand the principles of asceticism which are part of the spiritual-formation program, who has enough general culture to meet and converse with professional people on their own level, and to recreate herself and her Sisters on an intellectual plane, and finally, who has such a mastery of both the subject matter she teaches and the techniques of instruction as will satisfy her obligations in justice to her pupils and do credit to the Catholic educational system. Sister formation, finally, is the combination of spiritual and intellectual training in such a way that they positively reinforce one another; and leave in the mind of the Sister no false impression of tension or incompatibility between the general and specific ends of her congregation."

Now, who are eligible to do graduate work on the M.A. level? To be admitted to graduate programs, there are two basic or major qualifications which must be met: (1) A student cannot be admitted to the graduate school to do graduate work in any teaching area or subject area unless he or she has completed undergraduate work in that particular area. Graduate work is a continuance of work for which one has prepared herself on the undergraduate level. Oftentimes graduate students fail on the graduate level because they lack the background, foundation, or the proper preparation on the undergraduate level to carry on work in that area on the graduate level. It is important to be clear on this point.

Planning for graduate work must be done in the early stages of the B.A. work. Education is a continuous and developing process. Plan on an undergraduate level what you hope to take on a graduate level. Shifting always lengthens the educational program.

The second general requirement for graduate work is the proved ability to carry on work on the graduate level. Students who do A or B work on the undergraduate level are presumed to meet this qualification. Students who do C work, however, are presumed not to have the ability. The reason for the stress on this qualification is the basic aim of graduate work, namely, developing students with the ability to work on their own, with guidance and direction. Graduate work should not be simply a matter of lecture work and of assignments. Its aim is to develop individual thinking: ability to read and develop a subject on one's own resources.

Now we pose a practical problem: Should elementary and secondary teachers be directed toward the Master's program, at least as an ideal? To this I would say: All those who have the proved ability and the proper preparation should be given this opportunity. Or, at least, this is something which we should work for. Surely our teachers in our own Catholic and secondary schools should not have less training than those in the public schools. Secondly, our schools require administrators. As a minimum, the administrators of our schools should have the Master's degree. And, in regard to the preparation of administrators, it would appear more feasible to direct them towards the Master's in Education than the Master of Arts. At the present time in the State of Washington, a principal's credentials requires only twelve hours of specific courses in administration, supervision, and organization, plus the teacher's credentials. Those communities are blessed, indeed, who have some nuns with Doctorate training— even those communities who do not support collegiate training.

However, we must face up very realistically to the fact that there are some, even in religious life, who do not have the ability required to do graduate work. There may be very wonderful people, excellent religious, with an important place in our school system, but their undergraduate work clearly shows that graduate work would be much too rigorous and demanding for them. In fairness to these Sisters we should not impose upon them a burden which they cannot carry, or saddle them with frustration. It seems to me that the requirements for teacher certification very clearly recognize the existence of such people, both within and without religion, and nevertheless consider it a group who could profit from further help, study, and knowledge in their subject areas. The present certification program in the State of Washington on the A.B. level is too thin in subject matter areas and perhaps overloaded in techniques and teaching methods. Hence, the State of Washington requires a fifth year of training—that is, a year beyond the Bachelor's degree in which this training in subject areas may be secured, but it does not require that this be done in a graduate school or on the graduate level. It requires, merely, that fifty percent of the work be done on a graduate level or in upper-division work.

What about the length of the graduate program? Upon applying for admission to graduate schools, most graduate students are anxious, not only to have their program roughly outlined for them, which is proper, but they are quite determined that the dean of the graduate school will assure them that they will complete their graduate work within a year plus a summer, or within a year and a half or two years of work. This assurance cannot be given to any student. The student is only told of the general requirements and will not be given any assurance as to how long it will take. The student may be told how long it normally takes various groups of students to complete their M.A. Graduate schools want some look at the student and the quality of work done before formally approving the student for graduate work even though the student has been accepted in graduate school. Hence, Sisters should expect as normal this vagueness as to the time it will take them to complete their requirements.

Now some practical problems with regard to Sister formation and graduate work. If you set a five-year program as an ideal, then, of course, you are faced with a serious consideration of whether or not this long program can be effectively accomplished only through summer sessions, or largely through summer sessions and/or through partial addition of the burden of carrying a university course with a heavy and already full day of teaching activities. If you attempt to work toward this ideal only through summer sessions, then you face the prospect of completing your undergraduate work at best in twelve summer sessions and your graduate work in a minimum of five summer sessions—a total of seventeen summer sessions. Are you not then setting up a very discouraging and disheartening program of education for your Sisters?

What effect does this not have on the spiritual life of Sisters? Upon morale? Upon the inspiring appeal of the vocation to teach God's children? And can you neglect the impression made upon young girls, potential vocations, by the picture of a vocation to a life which is overburdened during the year and made wearisome from summer sessions piled upon summer sessions?

There are, indeed, problems with regard to the shortage of teachers at present in our parochial school system, and any practical solution must move slowly. But are you not faced with moving toward a general pattern of giving your young nuns the opportunity of completing their entire undergraduate program, or at least the major part of it, before they are placed into a teaching situation? In the instances where Sisters shall have already completed their A.B. work before the first teaching assignment, then the prospect of doing their fifth or M.A. work during summer sessions is a very reasonable one.

Personally, I am very much concerned with the readiness of some superiors to urge attendance at university courses in addition to a heavy teaching program during the year. It has always seemed to me that if one is to be an effective teacher, and to teach with energy and enthusiasm and prepare classes, teaching is itself a full job, particularly when one has the addition of community and spiritual exercises. In those instances in which attendance at university classes should be deemed necessary, attendance should be countenanced only on condition the teacher does not carry a full teaching load; and on condition that the reason for a reduced teaching load is clearly understood and accepted in the community. Many of our young Sisters are of a comparable age of university students. Universities throughout the country consider that a student has a full load with seventeen hours of work; and they discourage the student from outside work if effective study is really to be effected.

There are problems here which certainly need careful consideration. It is not my place to attempt to give you any solution. It is only my office to show you the complete picture of a professional training which includes a fifth year, and what it involves if this is the ideal toward which you are working. Personally, I am strongly in sympathy with the ideal. Our parochial schools should not suffer in comparison with the public schools in the amount of training and the quality of training insisted upon in the preparation of teachers. Secondly, if young girls are to enter a teaching order, they should be able to look for the opportunity for the same training and under comparable conditions that their young high school friends who remain in secular life and who enter the teaching profession definitely will consider minimum training and preparation. The potential vocation should have the right to look forward to the same training and with the additional hope that this training will be imbued with the greater and higher ideal of service to the honor and glory of God. Finally, there is no question that those communities which have professed better prepared and trained Sisters will be much more efficient instruments for God's kingdom. Entrance into such communities, living and working in such communities, will be a blessing and privilege for young girls who desire to devote their lives to teaching—directed and inspired as it will be by administrators formed to the highest professional and spiritual ideals.

It seems to me that the communities of Sisters are very much in a comparable position to that of communities of men who operated colleges were some twenty years ago. These found themselves in a position where they had very few people with graduate training—either on the Masters or Doctorate level. They had lagged far behind. They were faced with either finding a way to upgrade the preparation of their staffs or face loss of confidence in their schools as institutions of higher learning. They found that there were no short-cuts. Sacrifices had to be made, some programs delayed; but the administrators who preceded us had the courage and vision to carry through a program which they saw was necessary for the good of Catholic higher education. We know that our Sisterhoods, under the leadership and direction of the hierarchy, will have the same vision; and we can expect them to have the same courage in tackling their own problems. May God give direction and His blessing to their efforts which set forth for His honor and from deep love of Him.

·VI·

SPECIAL TOPICS

**THE DIOCESAN SUBSIDY PROGRAM FOR THE
EDUCATION OF RELIGIOUS AND THE PRO DEO
ASSOCIATION**

The Right Reverend Monsignor John J. Voight
*Secretary of Education
Archdiocese of New York*

I have been asked to present briefly two projects initiated by the Archdiocese of New York to help assist religious communities stationed in our schools with their teacher-training programs. I know this audience will find these projects both interesting and challenging since they represent positive and concrete ways in which diocesan authorities can lend a helping and encouraging hand to aid our Sisterhoods towards the realization of higher standards in the field of teacher education.

Before I describe the major objectives of these two programs, I would have you keep in mind that I do not intend to imply that what we have done and are doing here in New York should be duplicated in or introduced by all other dioceses of the country; nor do I wish to infer that our way of approaching the problem of improving teacher-training programs should serve as the model for any and all future solutions for this involved and complex problem. After many and varied contacts through the years with the superintendents of schools from every section in the

United States, I am fully aware of the tremendous differences in material and personnel resources which one finds in surveying the one hundred and thirty-five dioceses which go to make up America. The major premise which I do wish to stress this afternoon is that there can and should be cooperation of the very highest order on the part of all concerned with the religious and professional improvement of our teaching Sisterhoods. Since bishops, superintendents of schools, pastors, parents, Mothers General, and Sisters themselves have vital and important roles to play in the expansion and improvement of our Catholic school system, it stands to reason that among these respective groups there should exist at all times and in all places maximum cooperation and mutual understanding together with the appreciation of the problems faced by one another.

As a firm believer in the value of discussion and analysis of our strong and weak points in Catholic education, I am more than ever convinced that we should make better use of these important techniques in much the same manner we follow in making our particular examination of conscience. This we do to obtain a better and deeper knowledge of our character, not as an end in itself but rather as a means to remedy defects and to strengthen what is desirable and beneficial for the total well-being of our character and personality.

This meeting today, together with the significant fact that there are here in this audience some three hundred representatives from one hundred communities with motherhouses in New York, New Jersey, Pennsylvania, Delaware, and the District of Columbia, represents a marvelous beginning indeed. When one considers also that two other regional meetings are taking place over this weekend and that three additional meetings of a similar nature will have been held in other sections of the United States before this year is finished, there is added reason for us all to be greatly encouraged by the remarkable progress achieved to date by the Sister Formation Movement. How well do I remember the first meeting attended by a few Sisters and school superintendents held in Kansas City some three years ago to discuss the important problem of doing something, no matter how little, to improve the professional and religious formation of the Sisterhoods. Today I marvel to think that as an outcome of that small meeting this great and influential audience has been assembled. If any here today should have any doubts about the future of the Sister Formation Movement, I strongly would urge a renewal of faith in God's Goodness and Power, since He through His Providence has made this remarkable and incredible progress in the short space of three years.

Today and tomorrow you will have the opportunity of discussing your common problems and of seeking out new ways and means of improving your noble and heroic apostolate of leading others to the knowledge, love, and service of God. It is heartening to realize that when the proceedings of this Conference and of all the other regional meetings are compiled and published we shall then have in our hands a veritable treasure of helpful and challenging materials which, I am sure, will give us new and valuable insights into our present problems and perplexities and will at the same time reveal any number of untried ways and means of resolving them.

The first project I would like to discuss this afternoon is that known as the "Diocesan Subsidy Plan for the Education of Religious Teachers." Initiated in June, 1952 in cooperation with the Fordham School of Education, this program is designed to render financial assistance by the archdiocese to all religious teachers in the elementary schools who enroll at Fordham for courses leading to the B.S. degree in education. Thus, any Sister or Brother who teaches in the elementary grades may register at Fordham for afternoon, Saturday, or summer programs and have sixty percent of the tuition costs paid by the archdiocese. The religious community is responsible only for the remaining forty percent. Where communities find it possible to release some of their Sisters for full-time work at Fordham (sixteen to eighteen credits a semester), the archdiocese also pays sixty percent of all tuition charges. During the seven semesters that have elapsed since the program began in the Summer of 1952, a total of approximately 3500 religious teachers have benefited by the diocesan subsidy; each semester about 500 teachers participate in the program. In terms of cost to date for the archdiocese, approximately $100,000 has been expended.

At this point it might be well to review briefly some of the basic reasons which led to the development of the Diocesan Subsidy Program. Among these were the following:

1) In 1952 the recommendation of the Superintendent of Schools that the requirements for teacher certification be advanced to a higher level was approved by the Diocesan Council. Regulations were then issued making it necessary for all religious teachers in the elementary schools to meet the new requirements for permanent certification by the Fall of 1957 and for all to have a Bachelor's degree by the Fall of 1960. Since the archdiocese was responsible for advancing the requirements for teaching, it thought it could best assist the religious communities to attain the objective by helping them defray the major part of tuition costs incurred by teachers. The action of the archdiocese in this matter is a recognition of the principle that cooperation and when possible assistance on the part of diocesan officials should be extended to religious communities in encouraging them toward improving and advancing their teacher-training programs. Prior to 1952 many religious superiors complained that they could not afford to send their Sisters to Fordham, even though the University charged the Sister $10.00 a point instead of the usual fee of $16.00 per credit. A year or so ago Fordham found it necessary to increase the fee for Sisters to $12.00 a point and as a result of the increase the archdiocese now pays $7.20 for each credit with the community paying the remaining $4.80.

2) Since Fordham is the only Catholic institution in the archdiocese with a School of Education, it was a logical and natural choice for this cooperative enterprise. It was thought, moreover, that Fordham was exceptionally well staffed to provide the guidance and direction in organizing programs of instruction suited to the individual background and experience of teachers from fifty-three different religious communities teaching in the elementary schools of the archdiocese. The many and great differences found among religious communities with reference to both the type and scope of their teacher-training programs made it more than ever necessary for the archdiocese to work closely together with an approved and recognized educational institution.

3) Prior to the adoption of the Subsidy Plan, some consideration was given to the possibility of establishing a Diocesan Teachers College. This was judged unfeasible since such an institution

would be in effect in direct competition with the Fordham School of Education. The Subsidy Plan offered the opportunity of assisting not only the communities but Fordham as well.

4) The archdiocese in its teacher-training program with the Fordham School of Education does not imply that it prefers to have its Sisters obtain the B.S. in Education degree rather than the B.A. Existing teacher-training regulations now in force recognize both degrees as qualifying for the permanent teacher certificate. Thus, communities which prefer to have their Sisters take the liberal arts program with a minimum of sixteen credits in professional subjects are at liberty to do so. In this way the freedom which religious communities should have in preparing their subjects for their college degrees is preserved and maintained.

5) The Diocesan Subsidy Plan includes all religious teachers employed in the elementary schools of the diocese. No assistance under the Program is extended to religious teaching in high schools or to those studying for higher degrees.

The second project I have been asked to discuss is the Pro Deo Association organized in the Spring of this year to provide opportunities for the librarians and deans of our six junior colleges with teacher-training programs to meet regularly in order to discuss their common problems and exchange ideas concerning the development and improvement of their respective programs.

In the Fall of 1953 I had discussed with Father Harrington, librarian of our major seminary at Dunwoodie, the possibility of working out some program whereby our junior college librarians could be directed and guided in the purchase of books and in organizing special book collections which could be utilized by the other colleges. Father Harrington was most enthusiastic about the possibilities involved, and as a result of our discussion the librarians of our junior colleges were invited to attend a meeting in the superintendent's office on December 15, 1953. Those who attended gave hearty approval to the proposal to pool their efforts and resources and unanimously agreed to hold another meeting within a few weeks in order to discuss this matter at greater length. At the close of the December 15 meeting two deans who accompanied their librarians suggested to me it would be a wonderful idea if the deans of the junior colleges involved could be organized along the same lines as the librarians. Thus, it came about that instead of having just the librarians organized as a group we also had the deans interested in forming their own organization.

In the year that has elapsed four meetings attended by both librarians and deans in their respective groups have taken place, and I am very much pleased to report that remarkable and incredible progress has been made in this short span of time. Last spring the name Pro Deo Association was unanimously agreed upon as the name for the organization, and at present by-laws are in the process of being formulated outlining the purpose and scope of the librarian and dean sections.

The Pro Deo Association is thus but another example of the cooperation that should exist between the diocese and the teaching communities. The fact that the librarians in six junior colleges were called together by a diocesan representative to discuss the possibility of their pooling resources indicates that religious communities are ready and willing to work together on their common problems if the opportunity is presented to them. It might well be that if the librarians were not invited to come together there would be no Pro Deo Association in existence at this time and that each librarian and each dean would be working more or less alone without the guidance and assistance from her co-worker in other communities. I sincerely hope that as time goes on there will be a welcomed increase in cooperative enterprises and undertakings among our Sisterhoods carried on in much the same zealous spirit which has moved you to be present here today.

I sincerely hope and pray that you will remain firm in your high resolve to initiate some action or program to advance the religious and professional formation of the Sisters under your charge. No one can afford to delay action on this vital and important matter nor should anyone permit herself to be beguiled by the false hope that somehow, someway all will one day be remedied without hard work, hard prayer, and great sacrifices. Strongly do I feel that if we miss the wonderful opportunities now afforded us and fail thereby to come to grips with this problem, well might another fifty years come and go before we seriously consider it again. I am frankly afraid that by then we shall be entirely too late.

COOPERATION OF COMMUNITIES IN PROBLEMS OF SISTER FORMATION

The Reverend Brother Bonaventure Thomas, F.S.C.
President, College and University Department, N.C.E.A.
La Salle College, Philadelphia, Pennsylvania

At the Executive Committee meeting of the College and University Department of N.C.E.A. held in Chicago recently, it was unanimously agreed that a new committee be appointed and designated as the "Committee on Sister Formation." In this way, official recognition was given to a project prepared for by a group of Sisters who had already spent several years in thought and work before submitting their proposed plan of action to this Department of the Association.

Besides recognition, it was obviously the consensus of the members of the Executive Committee that practical help is imperative if the teaching Sisterhoods are to be expected to continue making their invaluable contribution to Catholic education. This help, it is evident, should be in the form of improving the present situation in reference to the availability of higher education for young Sisters in their years of formation; and when necessary, their "in-service" education work, to assure its *completion* within the shortest time possible after their assignment to teaching positions.

The pioneers in this project are a group of devoted, self-effacing Sisters who have had the advantage of intelligent and prudent leadership. Their successful groundwork has merited and received general and favorable recognition, and it is to be ardently desired that this will issue in effective help by all who can assist them in the realization of their commendable aims and objectives as soon as is reasonably possible. But first, it may be well to consider some of the impelling considerations generating this Sister Formation movement and the reasonableness of its appeal.

The importance of having adequately prepared Sister-teachers for our parochial and diocesan grammar schools, high schools, and colleges has always been recognized by religious superiors. Community pride, and the good name of their schools, the individual's desire to improve in professional competence, the standards set by accrediting agencies, justice to the pupils who attend—these are among the motives which inspire the increasing demand for improved advanced education for our teaching Sisters. The enormous increase in Catholic school attendance in recent years, and the criticisms expressed by those school people who are feeling the rivalry and fearing the spread of Catholic power in this country are other reasons stimulating the congregations to provide their younger members with better and better preparation for their school work.

The Sister Formation Group

Organizations form and individuals unite to work toward the attainment of goals because of felt needs and in the knowledge that unified efforts will be more effective; in this case, such cooperative work among the Sisters themselves will also be more likely to attract favorable attention to their Cause from those in positions to assist them. This latter effect of the Sister Formation group, though subordinate to their own efforts, becomes essential to the success of their endeavor. For some of the means which must be taken to assure progress depend for implementation on the activity of those who are apart from their membership.

Thus the Committee on Sister Formation will find themselves in a helpless position to effect very much progress unless efficacious aid is forthcoming to enable them to realize their plans and objectives. Their own commendable, harmonious, and cooperative work towards the achievement of these objectives should inspire a similar cooperative spirit in those who can help them to help themselves.

It may be superfluous to remark, except by way of compliment to the Sisters, that the kind of cooperation for which we appeal is surely not needed on the inspirational side, for the Sisters are well aware of their needs and vigorous in their efforts to meet them. The "extra-community" help they require is chiefly the material means of attaining their objectives. Those who can help must realize that the Sisters' educational preparation to meet even minimum requirements has resulted from a nearly superhuman struggle against adverse conditions—not the least of which has been financial limitations. Their prevailing difficulties have been generally *aggravated* for the Sisters and paradoxically made more *complacently acceptable* by others because of the effective pressure brought to bear on the Sisters' communities to provide teaching Sisters before they have had time to complete their collegiate and professional courses.

Cooperation—By Whom and How?

It would seem, then, that an imperative procedure is first: to work out a plan by which a compromise will be accepted in this regard on the sound theory that an "ideal" solution of the admitted, great need of more nuns in the classroom will have to await the time when the additional nuns will have had sufficient time in which to pursue their educational formation. Meanwhile, the practice of securing supplementary teachers among qualified lay men and women should be adopted or increased, regarding the number of lay teachers presently employed.

This, it would seem, is the first step which must be taken by those in determining positions; but it is by no means the only action necessary. To facilitate the educational programs in the Sisters' scholasticates or houses of study, which should be developed to include a full college curriculum, it may be necessary in many cases to provide additional financial resources to help the Sisters to realize such a project. And from this point and beyond, a cooperative educational-financial program among the various communities, congregations, or religious Orders of both men and women would assist invaluably in securing desired results.

Suggestions relative to detailed action would be worse than useless in the present setting. Undoubtedly, in many cases nearly all possible has been *well* done to meet a situation long since recognized; but the Sisters' Formation group referred to would not have "clamored" for creation and appealed for a hearing were it not necessary to initiate much-needed improvement in many geographical areas. In an effort to explore the field and to initiate ways and means of improving conditions by the best utilization of first their own resources, the Chairman and other selected Sisters of the Sister Formation Committee have accomplished much in the few months since their appointment. They have visited and appealed to many Mothers General and others who, by their position and academic and administrative ability, can supplement their own efforts. I know they would have me say how grateful they are for the gracious receptions they have been given at the several regional preliminary meetings they held during the summer of 1954 in localities from Los Angeles to New York, and New Orleans to Oregon. The subsequent meetings, such as today's, for which the planning meetings prepared, augur well for the attainment of gratifying results and considerable progress in their brief, but intensive "crusade." It is to be devoutly hoped that these good results will be followed generally by the kind of practical action which has already started the Sisters in some large archdioceses and smaller dioceses on the high-road towards ideal conditions, as regards their intellectual and professional formation. As all will admit, this formation is a necessary complement to their religious preparation in their respective novitiates, which is universally and rightly considered by all concerned as of primary importance in the Sisters' formation.

Cooperation for Sisters' Communities with Inadequate Houses of Study

The desirable goal as stated is to assure the Sisters of a four-year college program in the scholasticates of their houses of formation after they have completed their novitiate, as set forth by the Sisters at the recent Cleveland convention, when they adopted the four-year college program as their basic aim with a fifth year as "ideal" preparation.

While the Sisters are working towards this ideal situation, a high degree of cooperation to facilitate and expedite their in-service education must be forthcoming from religious communities of both men and women. This aid should come in the form of educational and financial help adequate to achieve results. I refer here to religious Orders of both men and women conducting colleges or universities accessible for fairly convenient attendance by Sisters.

One of the most important areas on which certainly a favorable situation would have to be carefully worked out is the financial one, so as to meet the limited income of the Sisters—entirely inadequate to pay full tuition for even the nuns who are now pursuing courses. This number will be increased manyfold by reason of the stimulus which the present Sister Formation Movement will effect. The matter of tuition charges should definitely be an effort towards not merely an arbitrary sort of "discount" granted by the administration of the college in the hope that it will be "covered" by other income.

In considering tuition from Sisters, a sort of "cost-price" tuition plan should be adopted, with an *assurance* that determining calculations will result in a figure (perhaps on a sliding scale) in favor of the *Sisters* and *not* the *college*. Finally, careful plans for the adjustment of schedules, daily timetables, summer sessions, and Saturday classes and so on, must needs be fully considered, and as many reasonable adjustments as possible should be made in favor of the Sisters, without an unrealistic leniency which would have disastrously baneful consequences.

"Sisters' College Center"—A Suggestion

In geographical areas not having the size or type of Catholic college or university treated above, or when despite best efforts on the part of all concerned a practicable plan cannot be worked out with a conveniently-located large Catholic college, another method or plan might be tried. Perhaps the best over-all description of such a plan is an Extension Division of a given college or university, though, as may readily be concluded, this ("Extension") designation may not be entirely accurate.

Conclusion: Cooperating with those already cooperating— Papal wishes:

The activities of the Sister Formation Conferences reveal the admirable efforts of the Sisters towards attaining the mutual help

178   THE REVEREND BROTHER BONAVENTURE THOMAS, F.S.C.

which is available among their own congregations and communities, and which can be increasingly facilitated through the purposeful work of the Sister Formation Committee. Some of the attainable benefits have been mentioned. Other sequential results, too numerous to treat in this setting, may well be expected as gradually the best means, wisely enacted, attain their objectives. All familiar with the Catholic educational scene know of the invaluable contribution made by the teaching Sisters. It is obvious that even greater opportunity for the salutary influence of these apostles of truth and virtue is imperative in the present world crisis, to combat the purveyors of irreligion and immorality.

The International Congress of the Sisters Superiors-General, held in Rome in 1952, indicated that this type of united action now sought by the Sister Formation Conferences, is ardently desired by Our Holy Father and the Congregation of Religious. So besides assuring practical beneficial results, it is evident that the Sisters engaged in this movement have the assurance of the highest ecclesiastical approval. This sanction is reflected on the domestic scene by the cordial encouragement of the members of our own hierarchy. For this and other evidence of hierarchical approval and encouragement, needless to say, the Sisters and all who are striving to help them are sincerely grateful.

·VII·

FORMATION PROGRAMS OF
RELIGIOUS COMMUNITIES OF MEN

ASSUMPTIONIST FATHERS

The Reverend Oliver Blanchette, A.A.
Assumption College
Worcester, Massachusetts

Since I am not sufficiently informed to speak authoritatively about the entire seminary program at Assumption I am sure that it will prove more beneficial if I spend most of the time allotted talking about that which I know best, the program of our American philosophy house of study, of which I happen to be the spiritual prefect.

First, though, let me give you a brief picture of our entire program culling my information from the chapter of our constitutions on studies. The opening words of this chapter remind us that the Assumptionist must become and remain all his life a man of study and a man of doctrine. The congregation, we are then told, has no other doctrine than that of the Church. In philosophy and in theology we will be religiously faithful to Saint Augustine and to the Angelic Doctor.

The spirit and the governing principles of our studies determined, the constitutions then enter into the program of study as such. Classical studies—here in America this means a liberal arts education up to and including the sophomore year of college—

normally precede entrance to the novitiate. Studies will be in accordance with the requirements of the Holy See and include sacred sciences and even profane sciences, in conformity with the particular needs of our apostolate.

Three years of study will follow immediately upon termination of the novitiate. They will be employed in the study of scholastic philosophy and in complementary literary studies. These literary studies may be spread out over the three years of philosophy, or one year may be devoted to them and the others to philosophy alone.

The theology studies, lasting four years and following immediately upon the course in philosophy, contain the ordinary subject matter: dogma and moral theology, Holy Scripture, Church history, canon law, patrology, liturgy, pastoral theology, sacred eloquence, and liturgical chant. It is worth noting that our General Chapters try to see to it that these studies are kept up to date and in conformity with the actual wishes of the Church.

This is what our constitutions have to say about the program of studies; they then consider the spiritual formation of the students. Superiors, we are told, will make sure that during all the course of studies the religious formation of the students be continued, and that all the rules relative to piety be perfectly observed. They will warn young intelligences of the danger of intellectual pride, or simply of the danger of loving science for its own sake. To attend to this spiritual formation of the brothers a spiritual prefect will be named, endowed with the same qualities as the master of novices.

It seems fair to conclude that the objective of the seminary program is therefore twofold: the intellectual and the spiritual formation of the student-brothers. The intellectual aspect itself is also twofold. First, at the house of philosophy, the general formation of the student is completed by means of philosophy and complementary literary studies. Then in theology the specialized intellectual training of the priest is given.

During all these years the spiritual formation of the religious, the monk-apostle, is continued and that of the future priest is intensified as the years fly by.

How is this program actually working out in our American

house of study? Some remarks in reply to this question should be of particular interest to this audience for the simple reason that we are still in the pioneer stages not yet capable of having a completely independent house of study. One good way of knowing a thing is to watch it grow.

We have but very recently become an independent province here in America. Until the last World War our student brothers spent the usual six or seven years of study in our European houses. The war made this impossible. It was then decided that the best place and the most obvious one for our Brothers to pursue their philosophical studies was right at our own Assumption College in Worcester. This they did for a few years with their only real superior the superior of the whole community, the president of the college, and with a program of their own as good as could be found at the moment. But they were to a considerable extent lost in the larger community of religious and lay students.

The Brothers are still at Assumption, but the picture is slowly changing, evolving constantly toward a separate house of studies. They have their own home, their own chapel, their own refectory and recreation hall. To a very great extent they therefore pray, study, and play as a separate community. They still, though, must attend classes with the lay students of our college for we are not yet prepared for a separate faculty.

I mention this genesis of our present house simply because I think that I can say that this change that has taken place under our very eyes has been for the better. It is a change that the Church would encourage; it is a very modest confirmation of her wisdom in wanting separate houses for student Brothers.

Since we do not have our own faculty, we must accept the program of studies that the college offers lay students. This arrangement permits us, however, to give the Brothers a sound, general though perhaps a bit brief, view of Thomistic philosophy. The individual aptitudes and tastes of the student Brothers as well as the needs of the province are also taken into consideration as much as possible. Thus, one Brother is offered as much of the sciences as is reasonable, another absorbs a good deal of English literature, still another quite a bit of Gregorian chant, and so on. The emphasis is kept, nevertheless, as much as possible on philosophy. We have obtained permission to have but two years of study for our philosophy students, as we are not prepared to offer the customary third year.

The next important question is how do we integrate studies and spirituality? First of all, by seeing to it that the students are faithful to all their regular spiritual exercises. A day that starts with Prime, meditation and Mass and ends with community as well as private prayers has a good chance to be spiritually integrated.

A spiritual prefect who himself has achieved this integration is a valuable asset; here, too, example is better than words. But words can help. Thus spiritual conferences, and short exhortations, "pep talks" now and then are valuable. I remind the Brothers of such simple truths as these, for example: knowledge normally leads to God; study is their duty of state and therefore very agreeable to God; study is a preparation for their apostolate. Or again, study at Assumption is to be one of our chief forms of obedience, mortification, and reparation; study can help one to avoid sentimentality in the spiritual life and offers substantial food for meditation. Confession and spiritual direction by men who understand this problem can help a great deal too. The regular monthly meeting with the spiritual prefect is also a precious aid in individual adjustment.

This integration of the spiritual and the intellectual is not always an easy matter, especially for the student fresh from the novitiate; but it can be realized a little more each day if all concerned cooperate intelligently and charitably.

BENEDICTINE FATHERS

The Right Reverend Raphael Heider, O.S.B.
Abbot, St. Martin's Abbey
Olympia, Washington

Spiritual formation is primarily the objective of this group, trying to weave the spiritual formation into the intellectual formation of teachers. We have then a kind of dual purpose, I think:
first of all to form members of our particular Order, congregation,
or society on the one hand; and on the other hand, and at the
same time, to make them monk teachers or religious teachers.
Now as to the formation of Benedictines, primarily that seems
to be the purpose of my being here. Certainly I would not ven-
ture to say that I could give you a complete scheme of things.

Formation of a religious or any character, I suppose, is a matter
of the rules specific to each congregation or group. It is all the
canon law that we have in respect to men's religious Orders; it is
all the reading that one does while he is being trained up to ordination and afterwards; it is the conferences which are held in
religious communities, theological conferences, and in ours the
culpa conference, which is a weekly affair; it is all the people
who make up the community, or it is the common life. Then it
is the work in which we are engaged. Certainly, all of this goes
into formation. Now that takes place, of course, only after one is
admitted into religion. With us, and I think quite generally, it
begins somewhat earlier if our candidates for the Order are attending our schools. Then we have some control over the situation in high school and in college at least for the first two years.
We receive candidates, generally speaking, after the sophomore
year. They make the novitiate, and after the novitiate they finish
two years of college with a major in philosophy; then they go on
to theology for four years and are ordained.

After ordination comes the problem of intellectual formation
for a teaching career. With us, where we have both colleges and
high schools, it is hard sometimes to determine whether an individual monk is going to be a high school teacher or college

teacher and to channel the efforts of intellectual development. It becomes a problem also because of all the requirements of certification. A young man after ordination, if he has the capabilities for graduate work, is chosen or selected or advised to follow a certain pattern of studies for degrees. If he is not a prospective college teacher, he probably has to go through the formation of a high school teacher, which includes the methodology and education courses required for the high school teacher. To us sometimes it seems a little bit frustrating to find that a man who has earned his A.B., has gone through a year of novitiate, and put four years of theology on top of his A.B., is then not able to teach in high school, nor has any more than a junior standing in his speciality. We feel, of course, that he should be able to teach in the high school, but actually he is not certified. It gives us trouble sometimes to determine what program to set up for an individual as to high school or college teaching.

Let us get back to the formation as a religious. We would like to control that situation a little more in the high school and college than we are able to do or have been able to do in the past years. We find this particularly true now in facing up with new state regulations in regard to what people are going to have to get out of high school. There has been some fuss in our state now about a course which became mandatory on protection against firearms. There is also driver-training. Then there is the trend toward a course for boys which parallels domestic science for girls. This is not an authoritative interpretation, but the course is probably something in the way of fixing flatirons, electric plugs, push buttons, and the like. Useful things in the home are all well and good, of course, but are they educational subjects? Looking toward that kind of development of a high school curriculum, we face the problem of what we are going to do to reform people who have learned to fix light plugs. Now we wish they had mathematics, English, languages, sciences, history, and so on. What the future candidate for religious life is going to have in the way of secondary preparation remains the question. We would like very much to have high school students all through high school to take five solid subjects through the whole course plus some physical education and so on. In college, we would like to get a program which is thoroughly liberal, but it is a question whether we can hold to such a program in the face of the drift which is taking place in these days.

Let us say that this man has come to us now, has applied, and has been accepted into the novitiate. In the novitiate he does not get anything except spiritual formation. He is engaged principally in matters which pertain to Benedictine life, which, of course, for the work of God, are the psalms and the Office which he needs to know. He has every day lessons on behavior in the religious life and in our particular community as such. There is much spiritual reading: two hours of reading broken up into four half-hour periods plus, of course, the community reading at table totaling another two half-hours at dinner and supper. In addition, there is monastic history in which the men write some papers. But all their work in the novitiate is based on the aim of gaining the spirit of religious life basically, and Benedictine life particularly. That is the program for one year.

After the novitiate there is the clericate of two years during which the young men complete their philosophy. They do not engage in any teaching during the clericate except in a few rare instances of catechetical instruction, but they are not engaged in manning the school as such. In the pioneering days, of course, when a man would get out of the novitiate, he would immediately be assigned to prefecting and probably teaching a couple of classes, and even sandwich his theology and philosophy in between his other jobs. Actually the men religious groups have struggled with this problem for a number of years. Now we have freed our clerics altogether from extra-curricular activity. According to the code they are released for the purpose of the studies in which they are engaged at the moment. That is the ideal situation, and we have achieved it almost totally.

As for the theology, of course, it is the regular theological course prescribed by canon law. In all of this, certainly canon law is the controlling factor. I might indicate that the idea of noviti-ate, of course, was something which came out of the rule of Saint Benedict.

As to the formation, I do not think I can give very many specifics. The fact is that the Benedictine life as such is not specific.

It was not an Order founded for a specific objective other than the personal sanctification of the individual and the glorification of God through the recitation of the psalms, or the breviary, in common. Of course, out of that grow all the things that have happened since Saint Benedict wrote his rule. Out of the adoration of God through the Office develops the liturgy, an interest in the things that grow around the glorification of God in divine service. Out of the liturgy grows the development in the field of the arts because it is a natural concomitant with the edifice which is built for God's glory and in which are sung the hymns of praise for God's glory.

Then, of course, this business of education attached itself to the monasteries rather than the monasteries going out and putting up a school. If you recall anything of Benedictine history, remember how Saint Benedict's reputation got around and back to Rome, and Tertullius brought his son and put him in the care of the monks at Monte Cassino. That was the way the monastery schools originated. And then, by and large, education became a task which was quite congenial to monastic living. It did not take the monks away from their monastery; rather the monastery school was attached, and the staff could go from monastery to school and back without any great interference with monastic routine. Again, Benedictines are not specialists in anything, let us say hospital work or education. They are just for the service of the Church wherever they possibly might be useful and do the most good so long as the work is congenial to the monastic way of life and the sanctification of the individual.

Now basically, I suppose we could say that the end result of Benedictine formation is contemplation on the one hand, but not taken too strictly. Even the eremitics or the hermits, while that is their sole objective, are not living on the mystical life level twenty-four hours a day for a lifetime. It is humanly impossible to maintain that constant contact with God. But all of us are aiming at contemplation, and we are aiming also at intellectual development. Probably this is what we could say about the end result of religious formation: that we become, first of all, good religious; that we become educated if we are going to be in edu-

cational work; and that out of that combination, religious formation should result in contemplation, which should go out to the
students whom we teach. That is what we would hope is the end
result of our way of life.

BENEDICTINE FATHERS

Very Reverend Theodore Heck, O.S.B.
St. Meinrad Seminary
St. Meinrad, Indiana

The training of Benedictines as herein described is limited to the
specific program used at St. Meinrad Seminary for the preparation of young men for the priesthood and for teaching on the
secondary level. Other Benedictine abbeys are concerned with a
similar problem and undoubtedly have found procedures for
carrying out their objectives to their own satisfaction. From the
perusal of several catalogues of Benedictine colleges and seminaries, it would seem that the plan described here may apply fairly
well to Benedictine training schools throughout the United States.
Exceptions, however, must be allowed, depending on the size of
the community, facilities at hand, and customs peculiar to the
Benedictine congregations with which the abbeys are affiliated.

In general, such a training will take on a three-fold aspect,
namely, the spiritual formation, the intellectual preparation, and
the specific task of teacher training.

Besides the general requirements of canon law for aspirants to
the novitiate, the Benedictine tradition does not admit one to the
clerical novitiate until he has completed high school and two
years of college work, or what is generally known as the six-year
minor seminary course. The novitiate is of one-year duration and
is followed by six years of clerical studies in philosophy and theology. At the close of the third year of theology the Benedictine
cleric is ordained to the priesthood, but continues his studies another year, residing during this period with the clerics. Neither

the clerics nor the newly ordained priests are assigned to any teaching or prefecting positions during these years of studies.

The chief scholastic preparation for teaching is obtained through the seminary program of studies set up in accordance with canon law and the statutes of affiliation with The Catholic University of America. This program as found in the six years of the minor seminary and six years of the major seminary comprises a four-year academic high school course, a four-year liberal arts course, and a four-year theological course.

The high school section of the minor seminary comprises the following subjects: English four units, Latin four units, social studies three units, mathematics two units, science two units, religion one unit, Greek one unit, physical education, health and safety one unit, and music one unit.

The program of general education is coextensive with the offerings of the junior college section of the minor seminary and provides courses in the following subjects: religion, English, speech, Latin, Greek, modern languages (French and German), history, science, mathematics and fine arts (history of art, music appreciation and Gregorian chant). Electives are permitted in the fields of modern languages, advanced Greek, history, science, and mathematics.

The major seminary curriculum supplies the two years of upper division college with concentration on philosophy and collateral courses in the social sciences (history, sociology, economics, cultural history, education), in science and mathematics (physiology and electives in other sciences and mathematics), in language arts (English, Greek, Hebrew) and in the fine arts (art appreciation, classical music and Gregorian chant).

To these are added the four years of professional theological studies embracing Sacred Scripture, dogmatic theology, moral theology, canon law, ecclesiastical history, Oriental theology, ascetical theology, sacred liturgy, homiletics, pastoral theology, catechetics, Gregorian chant, and education. Elective courses are provided in the arts, sciences, and education.

A teacher training program is secondary to the work entrusted to the seminary, yet because of the growing need that men who have profited by seminary training be enlisted in the work of teaching, it has become a matter of concern to seminary authorities to provide the essential elements of secondary and higher teacher training for its alumni. Seminarians as well as Benedictine clerics may take advantage of this program. Students who find that their time is taken up entirely with the basic courses in philosophy and theology are urged not to apply for the program in its entirety, but they may take the required courses at this time and complete the work in summer sessions at other institutions later on. A few have followed this plan, especially when they wish to major in mathematics or the sciences which normally take more time.

St. Meinrad Seminary is accredited by the Indiana State Department of Public Instruction for the training of high school teachers in specific areas. The general pattern that applies to the Seminary toward the Provisional Certificate for high school teachers is drawn from the four-year liberal arts curriculum and from courses, required and elective, offered in the theological curriculum. Students who have completed the liberal arts course with an average mark of "C" or better and have written the thesis required in the major field are entitled to a Bachelor of Arts degree.

Requirements of general education are drawn from the work of the lower division of the college whereas the major portion of the professional preparation is carried out in the upper division of the college and completed during the years of theology. Thus, the courses in the history of education, educational psychology and philosophy of education are offered in the upper division of the college and are required of all students. General methods, methods of teaching religion are required of all theology students, whereas special methods in the various subject fields, educational guidance, school administration and practice teaching are elective and are offered during the last two years of theology.

Student teaching is carried out under approved critic teachers who are members of the high school section of the Minor Seminary. Classes in the Minor Seminary high school section and the upper grades of the local town school are used for observation and practice teaching.

Training of the faculty is not limited to the preparation offered by the seminary. Faculty preparation includes additional work on the graduate level in various universities and institutions both in America and abroad. For example, during the past scholastic year men preparing for the faculty of St. Meinrad Seminary were in residence at the Pontifical Institute of Christian Archaeology, the Pontifical Institute of Biblical Studies and the Pontifical College of San Anselmo in Rome, at the University of Paris, at The Catholic University of America, and at the University of Notre Dame. During the summer sessions as many as ten to twelve priests are regularly in residence at different universities in the United States and Canada.

While such a program has its limitations, it does fill an immediate need and has done it fairly well. The number of students using the facilities has been somewhat small, from three to ten each year. However, if those who do carry out the program and earn their teacher's certificate were to be assigned to teaching in the Catholic high schools throughout the dioceses (this applies to the diocesan seminarians primarily) it would help to staff the schools and relieve the pressing shortage of teachers a little. Some students who have taken part of their teacher training work in the seminary and have afterwards discontinued their seminary studies have continued their preparation for teaching elsewhere and are entering the teaching field as Catholic laymen. There is a place for the seminary in the teacher training field, and its possibilities should not be overlooked in the preparation of priest teachers for the Catholic schools of America.

THE DIOCESAN PRIESTHOOD

The Very Reverend J. Cyril Dukehart, S.S.
Superior, St. Edward's Minor Seminary
Kenmore, Washington

For nearly four centuries, it has been and is the mind of the Church, repeatedly and clearly expressed in canon law, papal documents, provincial councils and diocesan synods, that the training of boys and young men who show signs of a vocation to the priesthood take place in what have come to be called minor and major seminaries. A seminary, minor or major, is a school the only essential purpose of which is to train to a truly spiritual and supernatural life those to whom God has made known, and who desire to accept, His invitation to a share in the Eternal Priesthood of Jesus Christ. There may be other aims and ends, but they are subsidiary to this. If intellectual development, for example, were allowed to obscure this essential purpose, the seminary would have no right to exist. The seminary, minor or major, must have a clear idea of the spiritual perfection that is to be learned in it and of the standard of life that must constantly be placed before the aspirant to the priesthood.

It is the mind of the Church that this training toward perfection begin as soon as possible, and this is the reason why she insists on minor seminaries. It is our purpose this afternoon to outline some of the means taken in Sulpician minor seminaries for the formation of the diocesan priest.

When a boy or young man enters the minor seminary, he is not given a picture of what he ought to be and then nagged into becoming so. He is hardly aware of the efforts made to transform him. His education is in the hands of priests whose sole work in the Church is the training of young men for the diocesan priesthood. Each one of them feels a personal responsibility for the full training of each and all the students, the full responsibility of seeing that they are directed and helped by his personal efforts. Hence, they are with the seminarian not merely in the classroom and chapel but in the study hall, dormitories, and recreation grounds, not so much to be the surveillants of his conduct and policemen of his activities but, leading his life as much as they can, they embody the law he is to keep and exemplify the spirit in which it is to be lived. A particular priest is assigned to each student, or offered to his choice, to be his confessor and guide on the spiritual path he is to walk, to be his confidant and mentor, in whom he may rely with implicit trust that he will never betray him, who stands to him as a visible guardian angel, as one of the twelve, as Christ. This is one of the most important means in the formation of seminarians young and old, but particularly the

young. Our Sulpician system of spiritual guidance calls for each
priest-confessor to be at the same time a spiritual director and
confessor to a number of individual students. The students are
constantly reminded that they may change confessors at any time,
that the director may say nothing about his penitent, good or
bad, in any faculty meeting, that his director is the best friend he
has in the seminary.

The rule of the seminary is designed by the Church to form
boys and young men to prompt and ready obedience, especially
in matters that cost them a good deal. To rise promptly at a fairly
early hour; to be ready for definite duties whether of prayer,
study, classes, recreation, or meals punctually; to devote attention
to subjects of study, for some of which there is no natural attraction; to observe minute rules of dress; to keep silence at certain
times; to ask permissions for exemptions and the like—these
things, conscientiously carried out, render a man capable of accomplishing work efficiently, either as a subordinate or as one
holding authority, in matters where an untrained man would
fail lamentably. Habits of will and prompt acquiescence to duty,
even when nature rebels, will carry a priest over many a difficult
obstacle, especially when he has been trained to them from his
early youth.

Again, to live day by day with other boys of different ages and
habits, with individual characters more or less mutually attractive;
to practice kindness, forbearance, consideration in such surroundings; to build up on a supernatural foundation the great natural
virtues of honor, truthfulness, courtesy; correcting and overcoming any shortcomings that may be self-perceived or pointed out in
these matters of extreme importance—herein is another far-reaching field of training invaluable to the future priest.

Need we speak here of the formation which comes from direct
daily contact with our Blessed Lord and His Mother through the
daily spiritual exercises? You know them well: meditation suited
to the age and development of the boy, Holy Mass, Communion,
rosary, Confession, retreats, days of recollection, visits to the
Blessed Sacrament; the liturgy carried out in all its detail and
splendor in the recurring feasts of Christ and His saints, the
Gregorian chant—who can measure the influence of all these

things in the moulding of the priestly character in the boys whose good fortune it is to say: I will go unto the altar of God, to God Who gives joy to my youth? How wise the Church is in providing all this for the boy who, early in his life, senses the promptings of grace to become a priest!

In our Sulpician seminaries there is a daily exercise which has a far-reaching influence on the formation of seminarians. It is called spiritual reading. However, it is seldom a reading and not always spiritual in the restricted sense of the word. Each day, in the early evening, the students gather in one of the larger rooms for fifteen minutes (one half hour in the major seminary). The superior presides at this assembly. The period begins and ends with prayer and is considered a spiritual exercise, but its efficacy lies in its very simplicity, freedom, and elasticity. It is the superior's opportunity to make himself the guiding spirit of the community, which he should be, and to discharge his duty of governing the community effectively. The superior makes use of this opportunity to give notice of coming events, changes in schedule, and so on. He calls attention to laxity in observance of points of the rule, thus avoiding in most cases any need for individual correction; or he may commend the students on some job of work well done, such as success in studies, games, and special projects. On the eve of great festivals an exhortation is given for the fitting celebration of the feast. In this way he comes in close daily contact with the life of the community.

When the above subjects do not arise or have been dealt with, spiritual reading is devoted to its main object. At the beginning of each scholastic year, the rule of the seminary is explained in detail with the reasons and motives which underlie it. Out of this explanation come forth naturally careful instructions on mental prayer, the Mass, Holy Communion, examination of conscience, Confession; methods of study, use of time, good manners, and the like. This commentary on the rule takes a couple of months. When it is finished, talks are given on various aspects of the spiritual life, and readings from books will illustrate the points to be driven home. Thus, unity and earnestness are maintained in the community.

While the emphasis in the seminary must be on the future

priest's spiritual formation, his intellectual development is far from neglected. It is never lost sight of that the minor seminarian must prepare for higher studies where thinking and application must prevail. Philosophy and theology, canon law, Scriptural background and interpretation call for judgment and appreciation. The student must be prepared and accustomed to think. Hence, it is taken for granted that high school is the time and place to acquire mastery of intellectual tools. In the languages, form, syntax and composition are acquired by relentless drill; ability to grasp the sense of a foreign text and to ferret out carefully the nuances of subtle distinctions is developed with painstaking care; power to convey one's own thoughts with facility and clearness is unfolded through precept and practice. The accuracy and logic of translation—inestimable aid to promote habits of correct thinking—is complemented by insistence on mathematics and the sciences. In these branches of thought the most rigid precision is necessitated, the realm of abstract reality is opened, and the student is initiated into contact with mental paths he must trail when he studies notions like being, essence, beauty, truth, and knowledge. In the study of history and literature the student encounters the same insistence, the same seriousness of application, the same motive urging to the very best of capacity. He is separated from the distractions of social life, and the order of the day sends him to the study hall where silence and supervision assure that atmosphere of quiet and isolation which a scholar must have and where the rigorous demands of the classroom are normally and properly provided for, and haphazard preparation rendered unthinkable and impossible. This regime is extended over a period of six years and, in view of the purpose, is not the regime justified?

The modern preparatory seminary provides recreational facilities ample enough to allow full participation by all the students, and the daily schedule allows a minimum of two consecutive hours of recreation besides the normal number of holidays. The policy of *mens sana in corpore sano* receives a balanced stress throughout the day and year. No student is allowed to be a hermit or a bookworm. In the recreational program, there is a discipline and character formation that is not lost sight of, and sports and related activities are given their rightful place in the routine of seminary life and make a real contribution in the overall formation of the student.

The library has ample material in the way of magazines, papers, and periodicals to keep the student in touch with the fast-moving pace of modern life. The limited use of radio and television is permitted also to keep the student in touch with the outside world.

Without going into a mass of detail, I have tried to give an indication of some of the important means taken in our minor seminaries for the formation of the diocesan priest, in keeping with the prescriptions and mind of the Council of Trent.

DOMINICAN FATHERS

The Very Reverend Philip E. Mulhern, O.P., S.T.M.
Regent of Studies and Dean of Faculty of Theology
College of the Immaculate Conception
Washington, D.C.

We Dominicans train our own teachers only in the Sacred Sciences. For preparation in other fields, we send out students to other teachers. I will, therefore, consider only our program of study in the sacred sciences, its objectives, the means to its objectives, and its relation to spiritual formation.

The aim of our course of studies is to form in the student habits which he will be able to use all his life, in order to grow in the knowledge of theology and the other sacred sciences. This, the immediate object of our studies, is further ordered to the spiritual perfection of the individual and his exercise of the ministry. It has been well said that a Dominican who is not a theologian is nothing. The Dominican curriculum is set up to produce theologians; the constitutions of the Order insist on it; the work of the Order requires it.

This is the objective of our training. What of the means? As the constitutions set the goal, so, too, they decide the means, and most precisely. Over one hundred canons of our law consider in detail the obligations of study, the doctrine to be taught, the method to be followed, the examinations to be given, and so forth.

In the first three years of his course, the Dominican cleric is taught philosophy and the auxiliary sciences by professors who have taken an oath not to depart from the solid doctrine of St. Thomas. These years are intended to lay the foundation for the more important work of theology. As a philosophy student, the young Dominican begins to learn the alphabet of theology; he becomes familiar with its terms; he begins to practice its method of argumentation. And, in the four years of formal theological study, every student uses as a textbook the *Summa Theologica* of St. Thomas. In some places, perhaps, theology may be studied for a particular purpose, for solutions to problems of conscience, for apt sermon material, and so on. For a Dominican, theology can never be a mere tool for use in a particular objective only. His mind, his conscience, his habits of thinking and acting are to be dominated by it. He is to be its tool. To its service—as to the Queen it is—he is to be dedicated in whatever type of work he has to do.

How is this program carried out in concrete detail? With the text of the *Summa* before him, the student—guided by the professor—becomes familiar with the structure of St. Thomas' work, the relation of reason to revelation, of part to part, of article of faith to article of faith. By daily practice, by analysing the arguments, by reducing articles to their core, he begins to adopt the method, to work it into his own thinking. He begins to do the work of theology, to study the sources of revelation, to reason—as man can—about what God has revealed, to apply the findings of reason about God to every realm of human conduct.

At stated intervals, to make them articulate in theology, the students must play the teacher. The old scholastic disputation is kept alive, week by week, in every Dominican Studium. One by one, each student must expose and defend against the objections of his peers some question in theology. Student conducted seminars are held bi-weekly. Two, sometimes three, students, collaborate on the presentation of a theological problem, the application of principles to modern questions. Students in the House of Theology write and edit a magazine, *Dominicana*. The aim of this, again, is to promote the habit of theological thinking. Writing for the magazine demands the expression in simple words of truths learned in technical terminology. Further, each year, the student preaches six to eight times, before his companions and a professor. The aim here is to foster in them the preaching of theology without the marks of the theology classroom on it.

The integration of the spiritual and intellectual formation in the training program is found in the very nature of theology. It has been noted that a Dominican who is not a theologian is nothing, but theology without at least attempted sanctity is dead.

At the very head of our constitutions, study is sanctified as one of the means necessary for the realization of the Dominican vocation. From the day he receives the habit until he dies, the Dominican sees the intellectual life as inseparable from his vocation. And the very nature of the material studied lends itself to the integration of the intellectual and the spiritual. Fullness of knowledge leads to intensity of love, and so the study of sacred truth leads to the love of divine goodness. With learning and holiness so intimately related neither need be an obstacle to the other. Theology, in itself, is neither speculative nor practical. It is above such division and is eminently both. It is at once concerned with the highest object of contemplation and with the most intense activity for a particular goal. A truly sanctified theologian prays at his desk and studies at his *prie-dieu*. This is the integration offered the Dominican student.

This, I believe, is a fair expression of our program. It embodies high aims, but we constantly try to improve their achievement. St. Dominic aimed at giving the Church sanctified theologians; St. Thomas was one of the many the Dominican system made. The young Dominicans we are making today may not come up to the sanctified learning, or the learned sanctity, of Dominic and Thomas, but they aim at it.

DOMINICAN FATHERS

The Reverend Thomas A. Hennessy, O.P.
Professor of Ascetical Theology
Dominican House of Studies
Washington, D.C.

The Dominican Order was founded for the salvation of souls. However, its specific purpose is to impart the truth of God so that its members might be, as Pope Innocent III prophesied they would be, "the champions of the faith and the true lights of the world." The purpose, therefore, of the education of Dominicans is to prepare them so that they may teach and defend the truths of Catholic faith.

The whole notion of the aim of the education of a Dominican can be summed up in the phrase: "Fidelity to the absolute Truth." It is obvious that there is no fidelity where a single principle or consequence of truth is cast aside. We are bound to truth in its highest principles and in its ultimate consequences. And we arrive at the absolute Truth only through faith. As St. Thomas Aquinas so beautifully puts it: "Faith assimilates us to divine knowledge, inasmuch as through faith we adhere to the supreme Truth for its own sake, and so, upheld by divine knowledge, we see everything as if through the eye of God."

The primary end of our Dominican study and contemplation is to enable us to get a glimpse of absolute Truth, just as the end of all ascetic and moral discipline is to enable us to have a foretaste of absolute Good. The faith of which we are the champions, by which we live day by day and which we have to spread abroad, is the faith that sees all things as God sees them.

In educating our future Dominican teachers to try to see things as God sees them, we insist that all their teaching must flow from an abundance of contemplation. They are to contemplate and then go forth to give the fruits of their contemplation to others. For the attainment of this end the means set forth are, besides the three solemn vows of obedience, chastity and poverty, regular life with its monastic observances, the solemn recitation of the divine office and the assiduous study of sacred truth. All these means are ordered to a single purpose—the contemplation of God; and the contemplation of the supreme Good in God is impossible without some emotion of the heart. For us, whose doctrines have always affirmed the subordination of the will to the intellect, it is a special duty to let the luminous principles of divine science produce in our souls both warmth and strength. For that we must open and unfold the receptive faculties of our minds to the pure light of these principles. The sense of intellectual light and the love of absolute beauty need developing. Generally, they imply training and involve persistent effort. The perfect law is to seek intensity through appreciation, to go to love through light. So, if appreciative charity seems to some too cold, or if some are inclined to consider it unworthy of God, it is either because they have never, in real earnestness, applied their minds to the idea and contemplation of the Supreme Good, or because, on the contrary, they have studied the divine truths as they would any ordinary subject and through such irreverent familiarity have been refused the grace to find in divine science the fuel of divine love.

The regular course of studies for a Dominican is limited to the sacred sciences and philosophy. At the end of his novitiate the future Dominican teacher begins a three year course which embraces philosophy, history of philosophy, apologetics, sacred eloquence, and biblical Greek and Hebrew. At the completion of this course he moves on to the *studium* of theology. Here day by day for four years he studies article by article the *Summa Theologiae* of Saint Thomas Aquinas. He also pursues the study of Sacred Scripture, pastoral theology, ascetical theology, patrology, Oriental theology, canon law, liturgy, Church history, the history of dogmas, and homiletics.

The approach to all these subjects is the scientific one. Dominicans are interested in the natures of things. They realize that in order to understand how and why things act as they do is determined by what they are. Moreover, they realize that a true knowledge of things depends upon an understanding of their relations to other things. That is why a characteristic note of Dominican pedagogy is an insistence upon the essential definitions and divisions of things. To arrive at such truth we utilize the best resources and the most expert ability available. Solutions, decisions, and plans of operation are derived from thorough investigation and mature deliberation.

So that no shadow of error will contaminate the sacredness of divine truth all courses in philosophy and theology are taught in Latin. Moreover, the works studied are those of the Angelic Doctor; and this is in complete accord with the canon law of the Church which insists that in all seminaries philosophy and theology be taught according to the method, doctrine, and principles of Saint Thomas. The Dominicans go a step further and study the very text of Saint Thomas, and the constitutions prescribe that, in so far as it is possible, the student commit to memory the very words of the articles of the *Summa*.

While every Dominican teacher uses the scientific method in teaching, each does not teach in exactly the same way. The natural gifts of the teacher and the capabilities of his students will give his method of teaching a character of its own. Not every Dominican is permitted to teach in our seminaries but only those who have the degree Lector of Sacred Theology. Before one is elevated to this honor he must have given evidence of his excellence throughout his course of studies and at the completion of it in a prolonged oral examination by five master theologians. He must also have written a scientific theological thesis. What is more important, only those are chosen to be lectors who are well known for their prudence and stability. Moreover, before they begin to teach lectors must take an oath not to depart from the pure and solid doctrine of Saint Thomas Aquinas.

Since the very ideal of Dominican life is the attainment of sanctity through the study of truth, there is no great problem in integrating the scholastic and spiritual phases of the lives of our future teachers. Where truth is regarded as sacred, a close relationship exists between learning and sanctity. The history of the Dominican Order brings this out. Its saints are scholars, its scholars saints. Saint Dominic deliberately set out to make saints through the study of sacred truth. His action threw together the two greatest forces in human life, learning and holiness. It was a masterpiece of supernatural genius. The anticipated result would logically be personal perfection of the highest type. The facts bore out such expectation. From this simple stroke of divine strategy came the mighty intellectual friar movement that brought the medieval universities to their heights of greatness and glory.

It is this same spirit of Saint Dominic that today characterizes the education of future Dominican teachers.

DOMINICAN FATHERS

The Reverend Martin M. Donnelly, O.P.

Portland, Oregon

The Dominican Order has been dedicated by St. Dominic, not only to Truth that is embodied in the articles of belief and the moral law, but to the very metaphysical idea of truth. It is based in God the Fundament of Christian life and revelation, the Source of all moral law and holiness in the Church as the fundamental source of her activity.

The Order aims in general: to present every object of teaching as true. There is no science, whether secular or sacred, that does not fall into the orbit of its interest. The secondary characteristic is that it is democratic. This idea has always been one of its greatest crosses and at the same time one of its greatest blessings. It was a revolutionary idea in its time in the fourteenth century. It has sometimes hampered the Order because of the weakness that is inherent in any man. But as Bede Jarrett, the provincial of England, once put it: "Autocratic government, no matter how great, does not bring out the best in man because man of his nature is independent both as a person and as a subject with regard to his position in society." Man is naturally subject to authority, but according to the Dominican doctrine of grace he has to operate freely and he is moved freely. Hence, the methods and the emphasis in the Order are based on those two ideas. Nowhere in the Order do we have what we call a "pat" system or an unchangeable *ratio studiorum.* All of the houses of study throughout the Order submit to the master general and his council their plan of studies. It behooves them, and it behooves the local superior, to fit the men to meet the particular crises of their own particular locale.

The primary thing that the Order has been founded for, of course, with regard to truth, is sacred doctrine or theology. Before accepting a member for the Order, we prefer that the man have completed his university work. We do accept men at the end of their second year of college, but no sooner than that.

With regard to boys who feel the Dominican vocation in the earlier and tenderer years, we entrust them to the care of our Benedictine or Sulpician fathers where we believe that they get adequate training in the right concept of the priestly life. They are sometimes sent to our own apostolic schools where these exist. The truly Dominican stamp will come later when they can, and when their faculties, intellectual faculties primarily, are judged mature enough to take it.

I think that the best idea or example that I could give would be the idea of Truth. Saint Thomas stated that Truth is where we find it. He based his whole life in dealing with heretics, in dealing with the pagan, in dealing with men who did not agree with him, on the one idea that the light came unto all men, in the words of Saint John. And that is why Thomas, under the discipline of the great Saint Albert, did not hesitate to bring into the western world the oriental works of Avicenna and Averroes, the Arabian philosophers, and the works of Plato and Aristotle. And believe it or not, Thomas was excommunicated and condemned by more than one bishop at the time, many of whom were Dominicans. To make mention of one, the Cardinal Archbishop of Westminster, Cardinal Kilwardby said that any man who would follow the works of Saint Thomas would be excommunicated, in this his own particular realm, and all the works condemned. Leo XIII maintained that that was the reason for the Reformation and the failure of so much of the Church. Saint Thomas had never been accepted, especially in the northern regions.

With regard, then, to the particular methods we use after a man has had his university training: he enters the canonical novitiate where the emphasis is on spiritual development of the man according to Saint Thomas. After the novitiate we have at least three years of philosophy followed by four or five years of theology. The work of the Order is not given over, let us say, as is the work of the society of the Fathers of the Holy Cross, to any particular field of education. That is why we emphasize that a man finish his university training before he comes to us, so that if he has any particular bent in one of the secular sciences, we will know of it. He is to be encouraged, never in any way to be limited.

The Order does not take upon itself the administration or founding of colleges, except as they exist. The future policy of the Order is merely to teach where it is called to teach. Part of the emphasis in the training of the Dominican, according to the aim of Saint Dominic in founding the Order, is on the fact that the Order is an auxiliary to the bishop. It is always the desire of the Order to accommodate itself to the will of the local ordinary.

With regard to the Sisters, I will say this. Saint Dominic first founded the Order among Sisters. The Order of Preachers, the teaching Order of Sisters, was the first thing that he founded in the south of France, primarily to educate young women.

In conclusion, and I address particularly the Sisters of Saint Dominic: If you have neglected to prepare your congregation for the work of teaching, if you have neglected to set aside time for study, then you cannot be said to be truly Dominican. The only important rule that we have is contained in the canon you find in the Church that gives superiors such tremendous freedom with regard to study. There is no means in a religious Order, at least Dominican, more important than the study of truth. Even our liturgy is subordinate to that in the constitutions. Christ is the Truth. The Sisters, of course, upon whom falls the major portion of education, especially the education of youth as far as the Dominican Order goes, are expected to follow the rule of Saint Dominic there, and to put aside for each subject the adequate time for necessary preparation as they find it necessary for each locale. Thus, those Sisters can meet the needs of the bishops and be ever ready to answer their call when that call comes.

204 THE REVEREND JEROME M. BOYLE, C.S.C.

HOLY CROSS FATHERS

The Reverend Jerome M. Boyle, C.S.C.
Head, Department of Philosophy
University of Portland
Portland, Oregon

The Holy Cross Fathers are priests of the Congregation of Holy
Cross which has as its general aim the glory of God and the sanctification of its members. In the houses of formation the primary
objective is to provide a solid spiritual formation. As in all religious communities, the spiritual occupies the first place in the
hierarchy of values. As an active community engaged in the ecclesiastical ministry and the apostolate of Christian education,
particularly in colleges and universities, the members must have
a solid ecclesiastical and general education. The program of studies in the minor and major seminaries is directed immediately
to the formation of priests. The aim of the seminary training program, in conformity with all the directives and papal pronouncements on the formation of seminarians, is to produce a learned
clergy.

After high school the seminarian follows a four-year liberal
arts program leading to the A.B. degree. His studies include the
classical and traditional liberal arts subjects along with the social
and positive sciences. The major subject is Thomistic philosophy.[1]

After college four more years are devoted to theological studies: dogma, moral, canon law, Scriptures, Church history, liturgy,
and so on.

As the seminarian goes through his years of formation before
ordination, he may not be conscious of receiving any special
preparation for a university teaching career. Those with a special
interest and aptitude for a certain field of studies may take extra
courses in that field during their college years. Others may not
be interested in teaching or may not have decided on any particular field for future specialization. Yet the philosophical and
theological training is the best possible preparation for the
teacher. It does not dispense with the necessity of specialized

training in the particular academic subject which he may later teach; and consequently after ordination he will pursue studies leading to advanced degrees. The priests selected for graduate work are sent to various universities in America and Europe for higher studies.

A priest who is to teach English, history, or physics must receive a thorough training in the subject, but he will never be a good teacher unless he looks upon the work of Christian education as an apostolate. He must know the end and purpose of education and understand its principle of unity. Only theology and philosophy can give the teacher the total view of reality so necessary for effective teaching.

The training program of the Congregation of Holy Cross helps the priest-professor to understand the meaning of the apostolate of Catholic education. The Catholic Church maintains centers of study and encourages them in the degree that they serve the apostolate. It is not the simple search for truth itself, but the search for truth in the service of souls that interests the Church. The apostolate of Catholic education does not aim at knowledge itself, but seeks to make Christian truth shine more brightly so that souls may be attracted to truth. Knowledge for knowledge's sake has meaning only in reference to the explicit search for the Truth, the final end of man which is God Himself. The Church's apostolate of education has no other end or purpose than to render explicit man's implicit appetite for the Absolute. The search for truth must tend to a possession by which man accomplishes his purpose, the perfection of his own being. Education must be God-centered; and even the secular sciences are our legitimate concern inasmuch as they are related to the end of man and the science of divine things.

These principles are not vague generalities, but they have a depth of meaning only to one with a background of Catholic philosophy and theology. Only one who knows the end can adapt means to reach it. One who is properly equipped to teach—and this implies more than a knowledge of his own specialty—is able to show how the various academic subjects, all different aspects of the study of reality, contribute to the seizure of the Ultimate or Total Reality in which all participate, each one showing different aspects of the procession of the multiplicity toward unity.

Once the apostolate of teaching is properly understood, there is really no problem of achieving an integration of the spiritual and intellectual formation. The religious state is called the state of perfection. It embodies in a concrete way the achievement, as far as any achievement is possible here on earth, of the end of a Christian education, the perfection of the human person, union with God. The life of the religious becomes necessarily a life of contemplation as it is dedicated wholly to the love of God. This means more than personal holiness as the life of contemplation finds its prolongation in the active life of teaching. St. Thomas tells us that teaching comes from the plentitude of contemplation. It is not something added to it, but is its expansion. Teaching finds its source in the contemplation of Truth itself. Prompted by an act of love, the communication of truth to others entails a life of contemplation as its indispensable condition. By reason of his special union with Christ, the religious must be instrumental in bringing about the unity of reality, of guiding and regulating the activity of the children of God. This is the work of education.

Holy Cross houses of formation do not directly train the members of the community to be teachers. Courses in methods and techniques are unimportant. Rather the objective is to train and develop the human person, his spiritual faculties of intelligence and will. This purpose is accomplished through the liberal arts and the philosophical and theological disciplines. The goal of the formation program is nothing more nor less than the goal of Catholic education in all its fullness. This is, I believe, the best foundation for the advanced studies leading to a college teaching career.

FOOTNOTE

1. Pius XI in his encyclical on the Catholic priesthood gives the reasons for the emphasis on philosophy: "It will help him to a thorough understanding of dogma. It will effectively forearm him against modern errors of whatever sort. It will sharpen his mind to distinguish truth from falsehood. It will form him to habits of intellectual clearness, so necessary in any studies or problems of the future. It will give him a great superiority over others, whose mere erudition, perhaps, is wider but who lack philosophical training." *Ad Catholici Sacerdotii* (N.C.W.C. translation), p. 44.

SOCIETY OF JESUS

The Reverend Joseph Glose, S.J.
Regional Director of Higher Education
The Society of Jesus
New York, New York

The primary and more general purpose of the Jesuit teacher program is formation rather than adjustment. This concept is not unique in education. It is traditional in all Catholic education and of particular importance to priests and teachers because they are the moulders of men, and as such should experience in their own educational training genuine processes of spiritual and intellectual formation. To follow a program of training based on adjustment alone would not prepare them to inculcate either the character discipline or the cultural values essential to a man living in a world where he must make daily effort to do battle with the effects of original sin. This primary purpose is sometimes expressed in other ways, but basic to any of the ways of expression is the notion of formation rather than simple adjustment to life experiences or living environment.

The secondary or more specific objective of the teacher training program in the Society of Jesus is twofold. First, the program aims to ground the student in the traditional liberal principles which are the foundation of Catholic theology. Secondly, it endeavors to impart the specific learning and pedagogical techniques which are pertinent in the teaching profession.

The structure of the program in its main outlines follows a pattern moulded on the Colleges of the University of Paris and on the years of formation required by the Constitutions of the Society of Jesus. This structure divides itself into three phases.

On his admission to the Society of Jesus, the student begins a period of two years of study that is largely ascetical, and, therefore, non-academic in character. In order to keep up his intellectual interests, however, class and study periods are assigned for Latin, Greek, speech, religion, and modern languages. A further educational feature for this period of the novice's formation is that he is then initiated into the spirit of the Order, which is that of Christian humanism. He studies from many facets the part which his predecessors have sustained in the religious and cultural history of Europe, America, and the mission countries since the Renaissance.

At the end of this period of initiation the student begins a five-year course in the liberal arts. The first stage of this course, covering a period of two years, is devoted primarily to literature and particularly to the ancient classics under their aspect of the moulders of the European literary tradition. English and one other living literature are taught as supplementary and illustrative of this tradition. History and mathematics are also taken in conformity with the general American practice. Along with the skills in critical thought and expression which are the natural derivatives of literary study, the future teacher also learns the elements of library science and bibliography, the technique of study, and the fundamental processes of research.

The second and final stage of this course is a three-year period devoted to logic, philosophy, psychology, the sciences, social studies, and electives. Formal courses in educational subjects based on and integrated with these branches are now begun. These courses are recognized as of particular importance at this phase of the student's training, since he will, directly upon the completion of this final stage, enter upon a two or three year term of teaching.

This structure has its functional aspect. Since the program especially aims to awaken the student's awareness of the problem of human existence arising from man's nature, his place in the universe, his aspirations and his destiny, every effort is made to awaken a scholarly appreciation of the liberal arts and sciences which illuminate these problems. As the students are also to be teachers, it is insisted that their knowledge be not inert and inarticulate but communicable in vital form and that it have as far as possible a social orientation. This is one of the legacies inherited from the Renaissance. It is a determining motive for the importance given to oral examination, research papers, repetition, "circles," and seminars. No student is approved—no matter what his proficiency in memorization or mastery of laboratory problems—if he cannot express his ideas in correct, concise, and easily intelligible language.

It is further in keeping with the professional aim of the course that stress is laid upon the study of the *Ratio Studiorum*—the method of teaching which is traditional in the Jesuit Order.

From this brief analysis of the structural and functional aspects of the program, it is evident that there is a continual integration of contemplation and action, of spiritual and intellectual formation. The master of this integration is the teacher who combines these aspects in his life and his methods. The student is also an integrator of these aspects of formation. He acts as an integrator by exercising the capacities of his soul which is one and active in integrating through study and asceticism.

SOCIETY OF JESUS

The Reverend George P. Klubertanz, S.J.
Dean, College of Philosophy and Letters
St. Louis University
St. Louis, Missouri

In view of the purpose of this Conference on the one hand, and of the religious devotion and dedicated service of the Sisterhoods of the United States on the other, it would be superfluous and irrelevant to do anything more than to present the training program developed by the Society of Jesus for its members, and to point out problems and solutions as they appear to me.

The present training program of the Society of Jesus in the United States has been developed over a period of years and in view of many different needs.

The entire program can be considered as having four aspects: the religious, the general academic, the general professional, and the specialized differentiated programs for advanced training. Briefly again, the scope and purpose of these four aspects can be considered.

The religious aspect of the training is the first to begin. At the start is a two-year novitiate; the training is continued through annual retreats, tridua, days of recollection, instructions, and personal conferences, and is climaxed by the "third probation." The purpose of all these exercises is ultimately sanctity in the full, traditional Christian sense: an intense supernatural love of God coupled with an advanced state of prayer, based on a well-rounded and grounded Christian character. Character, we all know, is not merely information about the spiritual life; much less is it sentimentalism and the superficial practice of "devotions." It is an integrated possession of the habits and virtues proper to moral maturity, resting on sound intellectual knowledge.

The second aspect, namely, the general academic or intellectual training, aims at a full possession of Christian culture. As conceived in the Society of Jesus, this consists of three mutually related phases: liberal arts, philosophy, and a rational understanding of the faith. Specialization or professional requirements narrowly conceived should never be allowed to interfere with these basic necessities.

As far as the liberal arts are concerned, their part in the program admits of no effective substitute. The liberal arts provide an education on both intellectual and sensory levels, and are directed toward emotions and feelings as well as knowledge. Such humanistic training has always been a part of Christian education, and by and large the Saints and Doctors of the Church have given it full approval. The precise amount and emphasis of this part of the academic program will be governed in general by the work of a particular religious institute. Its value lies not only in its utility for communicating with other educated people, but also, and principally, in its development and unification of the multiple facets of the human personality.

The training in philosophy is similarly conceived as part of Christian culture, and as a broad general background for all later work whatsoever. In the Society of Jesus, where the young philosophers are also candidates for the priesthood, philosophy is professionally necessary and is enjoined by the Church. But its professional function is not its only one. The course in philosophy produces a level of understanding of one's self and his world which can be reached in no other way. It gives an over-all appreciation of the order of reality and provides a firm and enlightened basis of judgment. As a by-product it brings about an enlargement and openness of attitude and a care in thinking that are very worthwhile. To achieve all these ends, philosophical thinking must be conducted according to its own rational exigencies. Here the same rule holds as in the literary, humanistic studies. Just as the works to be read during liberal arts studies must measure up to the proper standards of good literature, as well as not offend against revealed dogma and good morals, so the philosophy must be true to its own character as a rational discipline as well as be in harmony with the faith. Ineptness and error can never be useful tools for the attainment of supernatural ends.

The general training of a religious must include a developed understanding of the faith itself. Here again it is not possible to state *a priori* and in an absolutely universal manner the precise mode and degree of this understanding. But a general principle can be stated: a religious (indeed every Catholic) should have a developed understanding of his faith that corresponds with his abilities, the general level of his attainment in other fields, and the character of the work he is to do. Certainly anyone who has gone to the master's or doctor's level in an academic field cannot be content with a simple knowledge of the catechism. Likewise a person who has charge of advanced spiritual guidance ought to have a developed understanding of the faith. Often, particularly in the latter case, formal training in theology strictly so called will be the ideal—provided that proper preparation has been made to undertake this study seriously.

The third aspect of the training in the Society of Jesus is the professional. There is first of all the professional training necessary for the priest as such: knowledge of Latin, a certain kind and level of knowledge of philosophy and theology. The requirements here are specified by the Sacred Congregation of Seminaries. Since most Jesuits in America are engaged in teaching, there are also specific courses in education, usually the ones specified by the accrediting agencies, by state requirements, and the like. All that need be noted is that a merely nominal fulfillment of requirements will not ensure good results.

The fourth aspect of the training is that of specialization, and this part is to a very great extent to be adjusted to individual needs and capacities. This consideration is very important, for individual capacities differ greatly, and obedience will not ordinarily supply when capacity is lacking. Moreover, specialized training should be gone into seriously; it is not really worthwhile over the long haul to get a "cheap" degree or a certification that does not rest on achievement. Finally, the specialized training given should be sufficient for the work assigned. It would be cruel and unfair to put an inadequately trained person in an exacting position and expect good results.

This program is complex in itself. Under normal conditions, it cannot be administered by one person; many people—teachers, directors, superiors—are involved in it. So it is easy to see what the basic problem will be: how to produce integration in the face of this diversity. The solution is twofold: in terms of the people engaged in the formation of religious and in terms of the program itself. The first and most important element in the solution is the harmony of the people. Each teacher, and so forth, must be conscious that there are other parts to the training; that each part has its own purpose and value, and that each part has to cooperate with others. It is not enough not to deny the other parts explicitly. Since fundamental attitudes are here involved, it is well to remember that attitudes are communicated even in spite of explicit declarations to the contrary. To illustrate: if a spiritual director should be convinced that all academic training is useless or evil for a religious, those who are trained under him will have great difficulties later on, and their studies or their later religious life may suffer; they may even suffer a mental breakdown. And, of course, an open lack of cooperation will cause even more difficulty. Hence, it is absolutely necessary that all those engaged in the formation of religious have a high esteem of all aspects of that formation and have an integrated ideal in mind.

Furthermore, each part of the program itself should be in harmony with each other and with the over-all purpose of the religious institute. To illustrate again: the details of the spiritual formation of a congregation engaged in social works should not be based on an ascetical ideal of hermit-like retirement; those engaged in works of charity should not be trained in many daily hours of vocal prayer; those who are to take up advanced academic training should have a spiritual formation that is not based merely on simplicity. There should be no difficulty in finding solid, authentically Christian ascetical doctrines and practices that are properly appropriate to a particular kind of life and work; we need but remember the variety of saints like St. Thomas, St. Bonaventure, St. Francis de Sales, St. Ignatius. Similarly, the liberal studies should be Christian (to harmonize with the religious ideal) and on the other, open to the further development of philosophy and theology. The philosophy in turn should not be narrowly technical; it should not be exclusivist (pretending to give all the answers to all known problems), and it must be completely and intrinsically Christian in tone. Wisely, the Church has suggested the philosophy of St. Thomas as a safe norm. Finally, the rational understanding of the faith should be different for those who are priests and those who are not; it should build upon all that has gone before, but not rashly assume that all are capable of and need the full course in technical theology as it is taught in the seminary.

I have tried to stress the point that there is no one detailed program that is suitable for all alike. Yet it remains true that there are basic similarities in all, and I hope that these remarks will point up some fundamental considerations. I consider it a great privilege to have taken part in so important an event as these Conferences.

SOCIETY OF JESUS

The Reverend William M. Weller, S.J.
Prefect of Studies
Oregon Province
Portland, Oregon

Objectives of the Jesuit Program: What are the objectives of this fifteen to twenty-year program, three of which, however, are given wholly to spiritual formation. One objective is to prepare some who will devote their whole lives, or at least a major part of them, to the pursuit of learning and become writers, lecturers, or research scholars for the good of civil society, the honor of the Church, and the greater glory of God. Another aim is to supply our universities and our high schools with adequate teachers. And lest some be misinformed on this I would like to stress the point that our regular rather lengthy program was not designed for university professors only. It was set up that way for high school teachers also. In fact, the Jesuit schools in Europe, although called colleges, are only university preparatory schools, and their main courses are the classical languages. My point is this: the *Ratio Studiorum,* the Method of Jesuit Studies, aimed this entire program even for the high school teacher of today. Its underlying principle is that the teacher in a Jesuit high school should not only be a master of his own tongue as well as of Greek and Latin, but should also be liberally educated through the natural sciences, philosophy, and theology.

Contents and Methods which are specifically Jesuit: Now what in all this is specifically Jesuit? As to content, it seems to me that only two features stand out. And even these two are not really specifically Jesuit except for the special emphasis we give them.

The first feature is the special emphasis we place on the mastery of language and the special importance we give to the ancient classics. Many educational systems are humanistic, but there are various ways of humanizing. The traditional Jesuit system has been to use the fountains of Western culture, Greek and Roman thought, as the means for humanizing her own members as well as those who come to her schools. Even today, therefore, the core of our high school training is the study of Latin, Greek, and English.

Of course, the humanizing effect of these literatures is not the only reason for their choice. The Jesuit *Ratio* holds that the mastery of the language arts, the skills of gaining knowledge and passing it on, that is, the intellectual skills of observing, reading, listening, writing, and speaking are the best formation for anyone who intends to go on for higher education. And we who have had any experience in college work can surely see the soundness of this theory. Give the university a student who can read, listen, observe, write, and speak, and the professors can really educate him. But without these skills it is useless for him to go to college. These skills are the Jesuit answer to that whole problem of formation instead of information.

The second special feature of the Jesuit program is the extra year of philosophy. Most programs call for only two years while ours calls for three. The reason for this is that the Society wants to make doubly sure that all her subjects who go on for higher studies, especially in the secular fields, get a solid grounding in philosophy, the integrating science on the natural level, of all the other arts and sciences.

As to methods which seem to be specifically Jesuit I might mention one which I think has some merit especially in a teacher-training program, and that is the examination system in the Society of Jesus. During the entire intellectual formation program the Jesuit is subjected to the oral examination before four or five examiners. The grading system is such that the mark given by each examiner specifies whether the examinee has sufficient mastery of his subject matter so that he would be a worthy teacher of that subject. This means that the examiner is supposed to question the student in such a way that he will find out not only whether the student knows the matter but whether or not he knows it well enough to explain it clearly to others and answer adequately all the objections which might be thrown to him. And since the student has to do this under fire, it is a real proof of his mastery of the matter: not only mastery of his matter, but also mastery of self-expression in Latin and in English. For the juniorate orals are in English; the philosophy and theology orals are in Latin. In other words, the Jesuit system of oral examination points up the whole system and aims it towards the goal of teaching. It wants her subjects to keep this in mind and to study and to learn with a view of becoming masters, that is, teachers.

Intellectual and Spiritual Integration: Our last question: What means do Jesuits use for intellectual integration and spiritual integration? The only answer I can find to that question is—knowledge. Knowledge is the one and ultimate integrating force of the mind, and the will, and the whole person. But by knowledge I mean truth. Truth alone integrates a person with reality. God's reality is integrated.

To put this same thing another way, let me say that disintegration, intellectual or spiritual, is due to ignorance or error. Those are the only two causes of disintegration.

To explain my point let me give a few examples. That person who has only one piece of knowledge in his mind—let us say, 2 + 2 is equal to 4—is intellectually integrated because he has the truth. If he has only one piece of knowledge—2 + 2 is equal to 5—he is intellectually disintegrated because he has error: he is not integrated with reality. Or if the person has two pieces of knowledge, 2 + 2 is equal to 4 and 5 + 3 is equal to 7—that person has one truth and one error. These two are in conflict. This person is intellectually disintegrated.

But how about spiritual disintegration? Let us take an example of a person who is doing penance because he wants to please God. Penance pleases God. But this person's penance interferes with the work his superior has given him, namely to teach geometry to sophomores. So his superior is chiding him. Now the subject is in conflict. He wants to love God. He thinks God wants penance. His superior wants geometry. That person is spiritually disintegrated. He is in conflict. But why? Not because he lacks good will. He sincerely loves God and sincerely thinks he is pleasing God. What is his trouble? He is ignorant of how to please God. He is in error in thinking that he is pleasing God by doing penance rather than teaching geometry. Nobody pleases God except by doing His Divine Will. The superior's will is God's Will.

The Jesuit program achieves this integration by its emphasis on the virtue of obedience. Obedience means submission to God's Will. Obedience brings us the knowledge of what God's Will is. All the Jesuit has to do is love God and to obey.

———————

SOCIETY OF JESUS

The Reverend John A. O'Brien, S.J.
Professor of Philosophy
Fairfield University
Fairfield, Conn.

Some Problems of a Special Studies Program

If my vague recollections of St. Albert the Great, Bishop and Doctor of the Church are correct, he was not a man who was averse to new ideas. An idea, then, such as this conference would appeal to him and his blessing must be upon it, as it convenes in a college dedicated to his memory.

The function of us panelists seems to me to be a simple one. We are, as I understand the assignment, to describe summarily of course and perhaps to comment briefly on the academic and spiritual formation programs of our communities and to note any special methods of integrating both. It is expected—not vainly, I trust,—that this process will shed some light on Sister formation programs and problems.

The idea is an excellent one. Its originator deserves commendation. I hope, however, that lurking beneath it, there is no male superiority complex which assumes that the religious Orders of men have solved all formation problems and that the good Sisters have solved none. Such an assumption would be far from the truth. That both groups, religious men and women, can profit greatly and be of mutual assistance to each other by an exchange of experiences and opinions on formation problems and programs is most assuredly certain; and from a conference such as this, these advantages should be gained.

The Sisters should console themselves that at least in one important element of the problem—the time element—their task is simpler than that of the cleric religious Orders. The aims of a Sister formation program would be, I should think, three in number. First, the Sisters should be trained to be cultured, educated women in the glorious tradition of Christian humanism. Secondly, they must be religious women, carefully trained in the truths and practices of the spiritual life. Thirdly, they must have the special training needed for whatever educational work in whatever capacity and at whatever level they will undertake. In this last element, they must have at least equal training as lay women engaged in equivalent tasks.

The religious Orders of priests must train their members for these three attainments. Moreover, the canonical four years of theology must also be added to their training program. Their members must also be ministers of the Sacraments, liturgists, exact rubricists, brave if discordant singers of Gregorian chant, wise confessors, spiritual advisers, skillful retreat masters, eloquent preachers, and profound theologians. Four years is all too little time for the achievement of these aims.

The Jesuits, I believe, further complicate the problem. We require three rather than the usual two years of philosophy. A three-year teaching period between philosophy and theology is considered desirable, and after theology we have a required year of tertianship—a third year of novitiate. To add to these years of training the years necessary for the acquirement of the ever-elusive Ph.D. and to expect that it will be acquired before the candidate has completed the Biblical three-score and ten or at least before the age of necessary retirement is indeed a difficult problem. The three-year teaching period or at least part of it is now used for study for those selected for special studies, and usually the work is completed after tertianship.

Not infrequently, however, as is probably true in most religious Orders, the rugged individual who has survived the long years of training and is now an educated man, a religious, a priest, and a Ph.D. in chemistry, political science, economics, or some other highly specialized field becomes a bursar, dean, or university president. He must gamble in the stock market or learn how to evaluate transcripts or organize and spearhead a drive for X millions of dollars. A modern efficiency expert after a study of the process would probably be aghast at its low rate of productivity and efficiency.

However, despite all this, our special studies program, quite recent in origin, is producing satisfactory results. My knowledge about it is gathered from only indirect and somewhat remote experience with it. My remarks about it, then, have many limitations. Any program of this kind seems to me to present three difficult problems: (1) The man-power problem. How many individuals can be spared for it in the face of the urgent need of active workers? (2) The allocation problem, I shall call it for lack of a more accurate name. This problem presents such questions as these: Who will be selected for it? How much time for special study can be granted to them? Where will they study? In what fields is there the greatest need for them and how provide that they will be used for that work after they have been prepared? (3) The administrative problem. Who will administer the program? And how? And under this heading also, the ever-present financial problem—how much will it cost? And what will we use for money?

Our special studies program is on a province basis, and there are eight provinces in the United States. We have a National Jesuit Educational Association. Our Fathers Provincials are its board of governors, our province deans of studies its executive committee. It has a full time executive director who also is editor of a quarterly publication. There is then exchange of ideas and some exchange of personnel between the provinces. Each special studies program, however, is proper to each province. Within the province it is administered by a director, and the province treasurer pays the bills of the student. They must be considerable.

The following figures will give some idea of its scope. In 1952-53, there were 173 full time graduate students in the entire American Assistancy. This represented a decline from the peak year of 1949-50 when there were 254. Of the 173, 140 were priests and 33 scholastics; 119 were candidates for a Ph.D.; 6 for another type of doctorate and the others for other types of degrees.

Of the 173, 27 were from the province of New England, and in numbers the New England Province ranked third after Chicago and New York. The 27 New England students were studying in 15 different fields and in 12 different universities. This wide variety helps to the achievement of three aims: (1) the aim of having a Jesuit Ph.D. in each department of the province's colleges and universities; (2) to have them trained in the best uni-

220

THE VERY REVEREND JAMES FITZGERALD, S.S.E.

versities; and (3) what is very important—to keep abreast of what other universities are doing and thus avoid the danger of complacent "inbreeding" and "ostrich-head in the sand" deception.

As part of the Special Studies program, I should also add that our New England House of Studies (and that I believe is true also for those of the other provinces) is a Pontifical Institute. At the conclusion of their theology, in addition to the M.A. that is received from Boston College, a Licentiate or Doctorate in Sacred Theology is also granted to our priests.

Let me end as I began, with St. Albert. In his day, he helped to win an intellectual victory for the faith in its conflict with the Arabian interpreters of Aristotle. In our day, in our own land, the faith is engaged in an even more critical intellectual conflict with its enemies. The faith, if it is to survive, must win this victory. To win it, champions girded with the armor of truth must be trained in every field of specialized knowledge. They must come from our Catholic colleges and universities. Conferences such as this can help us to learn how to obtain them. To participate then in such a conference is indeed a privilege.

SOCIETY OF ST. EDMUND

The Very Reverend James Fitzgerald, S.S.E.
St. Edmund's Seminary
Burlington, Vermont

In outlining the intellectual and spiritual formation of the seminarians of our community, I trust that I may shed a little light on your problems concerning the formation of the members of your various communities for the important task that is theirs in directing Catholic youth toward their goals in life. The future lies in their hands.

The candidates for our community are accepted for the novitiate after two years of college work. Following the novitiate of one year, they complete their college work at St. Michael's College, Winooski, Vermont. They follow the same classes as the regular students with particular insistence upon the work of philosophy and the courses best fitted to their calling as priests. Their religious formation is safeguarded by residence in a special house of study where the master of scholastics is charged with their formation and fidelity to the details of their religious rule. A special chapel is provided for the Mass and other religious exercises.

When the required work for the academic degree (B.A.) is completed the scholastics are assigned to St. Edmund's Seminary located in Burlington, Vermont. Here they devote themselves during four years to the theological studies and the practice of the religious rule. The goal is the learning and sanctity that will assure the candidate that he is a worthy instrument for the work of mediation between God and men.

The course of studies is regulated by the law of the Church: theology, Scripture, history, canon law, liturgy, ecclesiastical chant, catechetics and homiletics. Courses in dogmatic and moral theology are held five times a week in each matter, and in my opinion do much to enrich the individual life of the religious and give deeper meaning and purpose to all he does. The concentration on the particular dogmas, the teachings on how man must live in conformity with the dignity of his nature and the grace of God, help the young man in his struggle for religious maturity.

The course in Scripture is held three times a week during the four years. Two years are devoted to the Old Testament and two years to the New Testament. This course should likewise be directed to the formation of the religious according to the Word of God addressed to His children far from their heavenly home. Two years are devoted to the history of the Church and one to patrology, which is greatly aided at present by the availability in English translations of the writings of the Fathers of the Church. The course in liturgy embraces the origin and development of the Mass and the breviary as well as the rubrics of the same. Needless to say, a good understanding of the liturgical year is an incentive to devotion and an aid in following the directives of the Church in her various rites and devotions.

In homiletics the training is mainly practical. A layman teaches the techniques of good speech. The sermons given each year during Advent and Lent are under the supervision of the Fathers.

The scholastics aid the neighboring parishes in the teaching of catechism and the training of the children in the music of the Church. They likewise help in the summer schools of Christian doctrine in parishes where there are no parochial schools.

Because a good part of our scholastics will be engaged in the teaching field, six weeks of the summer are spent at college doing advanced work in other branches of learning. Thus they may gain credits towards their Master's degree.

Together with the intellectual training, the religious and moral formation of the candidate for Holy Orders is fully as important. Their studies should serve to broaden their spiritual outlook and give deeper and clearer meaning to the religious exercises of each day. Morning meditation, the Mass, the particular and general examen, spiritual reading are given their place in the daily program. Particular insistence is placed upon the practice of the monthly retreat. The day is passed in silence and recollection until the Holy Hour before supper. A conference stresses some important aspect of the religious life.

The seminary is a place where the seed (*semen*) of a priestly vocation is nurtured by all possible means. The intellectual training is especially important in our day. It is no less important that the young man be trained in holiness, piety, chastity, and a spirit of detachment and obedience.

SOCIETY OF MARY
(Marianist)

The Reverend Lawrence E. Jordan, S.M.
Chaminade College
Clayton 24, Missouri

Succinctly the Constitutions of the Society of Mary set down the aims of the Marianist training program as follows:

1) to form the religious as a personality to holiness.
2) to form the religious as a professional man to skill in teaching.
3) to form the religious as a religious to zeal for the apostolate.

The novitiate courses are integrated into the fulfillment of the requirements for the regular academic degree, either the B.S. in Education or the B.A., depending upon the college courses pursued later. This integration is possible because newly professed religious take their undergraduate degree from universities under our own auspices, either the University of Dayton at Dayton, Ohio, or St. Mary's University in San Antonio, Texas. Here is the novitiate course of study and its specific evaluation in credit hours. I have taken this data in the order in which I found it on a degree selected at random from the files.

Credited as Religion 103-104 is the course in Mariology. This course in one semester covers general Mariology and in the second semester the specific form of devotion to the Blessed Virgin Mary proper to the Society of Mary, termed Filial Piety to the Blessed Virgin Mary with its unique obligation of the vow of stability professed at the time of final vows in the Society of Mary.

Credited as Philosophy 105-106 is the course in Special Ethics or Problems in Ethics and valued at six credit hours. The subject matter of the course is the ascetic life peculiar to the Society of Mary. The texts are all written by members of the Society of Mary and embrace the study of the religious state; of the interior life; and of the meditation.

Since Latin is not held in high esteem in the curriculum of many high schools, it is necessary to acquaint the novices with the fundamentals of Latin as applied to the office and the Liturgy of the Church. This is achieved by teaching Ecclesiastical Latin, credited as Latin 103-104 and worth four credit hours.

The history of the Church seems to be a subject which serves to enrich the curriculum of the novitiate without immersing the novices too deeply in mundane distractions, so it is offered as a college course catalogued as History 103-104 and valued at six credit hours.

Novices must write themes suited to the courses they are pursuing. These themes carefully supervised by an assistant novice-master degreed in English are accredited as English 101—English composition worth three credit hours.

While in the novitiate the novices become acquainted in a general way with the aims, objectives, and methods of teaching of the Society of Mary. They use a basic text called *Manual of Christian Pedagogy* composed by excellent early educators of the Society. For this course they receive two semester hours of credit as Education 101: Introduction to Education.

No novitiate would be complete without the study of Gregorian chant and the holding of regular singing practice. For this necessary complement of novitiate training, college credit valued at two semester hours is accorded as Music 201: Introduction to Music.

Even the organized games are not overlooked as having some value other than recreational and healthful, for they are credited as Physical Education 101-102: Physical Education.

By this arrangement of novitiate courses the candidate actually achieves the equivalent of one year of college work.

When the young religious leaves the novitiate, he is not sent immediately to the university where he would come too abruptly into contact with the world. For one year he is assigned to college studies in the motherhouse at Kirkwood, Missouri, in an atmosphere which the rule prescribes must be "a happy continuation of the novitiate." At this stage in his formation a turn to a definite subject matter field is given his college work. He begins to major in a field usually of his own choice and to take as minors sufficient hours in education to meet the requirements in Missouri and sufficient hours in one other teaching field. The first summer after the novitiate is also spent in college work at the motherhouse. After this the scholastic, as he is now called, spends two years in residence on the campus of either Dayton or St. Mary's University in a house of studies reserved to the scholastics. The religious formation goes on apace during these two years and two summers in residence at the University.

Upon completion of the courses required for the Bachelor's degree, the religious are employed in teaching. Neither the religious training nor the professional training stops here. During the summer the religious follow courses at various universities to acquire the Master's degree. This work may not be begun, however, until after the profession of final vows. In most cases the religious choose the field of their own interest for this further study, and in many instances they even select the college they wish to attend. Only at the doctorate level are they given time off for study. Here too the religious expresses preference for the institution he desires to attend and the field of study he wishes for his advanced work. One religious selected Oxford, and the superiors agreed!

No matter what the status of the religious is, he must pursue studies in religion and pass examinations in them for eight years after the first scholasticate. This is plainly prescribed in the *Book of Customs of the Society of Mary:*

"In order to stimulate the zeal of the members for the study of religion and to give to clergy and parents a guarantee that efficient teaching is being done, a Diploma of Religious Instruction, comprising two degrees, is awarded to the religious who have passed written and oral tests before a committee appointed by the Provincial Superiors."

Subjects of the First Degree

Christian Doctrine
Mariology: General, Special
Liturgy
Liturgical Chant
Ecclesiastical Latin
Holy Scripture:
  Old Testament
  New Testament
Asceticism:
  Interior Life
  Mental Prayer
  Particular Examen

Religious State
History of Religious Orders
History of Society of Mary
Catholic Dogma
Catholic Moral
Reconstruction, Social Order
  Encyclicals on State
  Encyclicals: Education, Biblical
  Encyclicals: Catholic Action
Mariology:
  Marian Studies, Vol. II
  Munificentissimus Deus
  Theology of St. Joseph

Subjects of the Second Degree

The Sacraments
Moral
Scripture: Old Testament
Catholic Action

History of the Society of Mary
  in America
Apologetics
Liturgy

These required studies in religion serve as an integrating factor; they do not suffer the religious to forget that he is first and foremost an apostle and a catechist.

After three, five, or more years in active life the religious are taken out of circulation and brought to a second novitiate or, as it is sometimes more sophisticatedly called, "The Institute of Marianist Studies" at Glencoe, Missouri. Up to now we have sent six to eight religious to the second novitiate each year—all at their own request. The ideal we have in mind is that each novitiate group as a group be brought together again for the second novitiate.

The second novitiate is perhaps the most telling factor in the integration of the religious and professional life of the members of the Society of Mary. The primary objective of the second novitiate is to develop a strong and profound interior life. The secondary objective is to develop a spirit of loyalty, responsibility, and maturity. The means for achieving the first objective are these:

1) insistence on prayer, especially mental prayer
2) the active use of the examination of conscience, especially particular examen
3) the cultivation of a more serious type of spiritual reading
4) the carrying out of serious and frank spiritual direction.

In the realm of the secondary objective the means used are these:

1) to develop a sense of loyalty
   a) by systematic study of the documents of the Society of Mary
   b) by engaging in creative writing on the doctrines of the Society of Mary
2) to develop a spirit of responsibility
   a) in the spiritual life—by striving to live by the spirit of the rule
   b) in the professional life—by striving for a sense of adequacy, a desire to be interested in "work-to-be-done"
3) to develop maturity
   a) by acquiring a clearer understanding of the principles underlying the religious life

     b) by striving actually to live a life of maturity, that is,
       by allowing principles and not feeling to dominate
       actions and decisions

Each Wednesday evening a seminar is held on topics of practical interest to members of the group. Problems in high school education are most often discussed. Here are some seminar topics.

    Examination and evaluation of a proposed form for the Perpetual Vow Application
    Discussion on Father Hoffer's "Directory of the Postulates"
    The problem of discipline in our schools and the problem of the "habitual offender"
    The role of the priest in the Society of Mary
    The relation of home-room guidance to the guidance program
    The character of scholasticate education
    Catholic literature

A separate committee works on Sodality projects and makes periodical reports to the group at large. This year a pamphlet, *The Imitation of Mary,* is in preparation for dissemination through the office of *The Queen's Work.*

In addition to the second novitiate other factors in integration are the circulars of the superiors general and their assistants, one of whom is specifically charged with supervising the spiritual life in the Society of Mary, and another who supervises instruction in the Society. In addition, there is each week a spiritual conference given in community by a priest of the Society. There are visitations by the Father Provincial and the Brother Supervisor; there are the provincial chapters which study the status of the province from the point of view of the religious life and the procedures in education; there are the directors' meetings; principals' institutes; pedagogical conferences; there are publications such as the *Pedagogical Annual* for the whole Society, and the *Marianist Educator* for the American Provinces. In all our endeavors we strive to bear in mind the words of our Venerated Founder, the Very Reverend William Joseph Chaminade, "Let no one look upon himself as just another teacher, but let him always remember that he is an apostle, a missionary of Mary . . .

a good Brother imparts a Christian lesson by every word, every gesture, and every look."

SOCIETY OF MARY
(Marist Fathers)

The Reverend John L. White, S.M.
Director of Education
Marist College
Washington, D.C.

The training and equipment of our priests require the envisioning of various objectives. It is imperative for us to impart to our students not only the standard ecclesiastical knowledge required in any priest, but also a specialized training for teaching. We are under the constant necessity of seeing that our men procure degrees, and indeed graduate degrees, for the proper fulfillment of our obligations in the college departments of our seminaries. We have to meet state requirements for the proper certification of our teachers on the high school level. All this puts a serious strain upon a limited body of men.

In order to give an overall picture of the training given to the Marist aspirant, I will begin with the minor or preparatory seminary. We approach the problem this way. The preparatory seminary has important functions to fill for both the alumni who go on to the clerical life and the many who leave the seminary to enter the other professions and walks of life. In the early years of training for the priesthood, we train for the priesthood; but we also try to be realistic enough to appreciate the fact that many who enter the minor seminary, and sometimes spend the full six years there, will not go on to that exalted goal. Much of the education imparted in the minor seminary has the same objectives and nature as that found in high school and junior college.

The junior college department of our preparatory seminary is a liberal arts college, the primary purpose of which is to give preparation for the study of philosophy in the senior college and, for those who embrace the clerical life, the post-graduate work of the courses in theology. Of equal importance, of course, is the formation, broadening, and instructing of the student's mind in itself. The life of the priest demands sound character based on moral principles, a cultivated intellect, and good health. Hence the necessity of a solid religious training, a comprehensive curriculum of the liberal arts, and an intensive guidance program to cultivate the mind and the will of the students and to further the formation of character. Hence, too, the necessity of a sensible athletic program to fit them for the exertion entailed in higher studies and the later priestly ministry.

To attain these objectives, our preparatory seminary, St. Mary's Manor at Penudel, Pennsylvania, first of all meets the requirements of the Code of Canon Law and the decrees of the Church. The high school meets the requirements of the Department of Instruction of the State. Its program is geared to the standards of the typical college entrance requirements. The Junior College courses are supervised by Villanova University, and the credits are issued through that institution. To glance briefly at the content of the courses, we give three semester hours in introduction to education, six to college English (composition), three of English literature, three of world literature, six semester hours of French, six of Greek, six in American history, three of Latin syntax in prose and poetry, three in the history of classical Latin literature, and six semester hours of Ecclesiastical Latin. In sciences we have three semester hours of college algebra, three also of trigonometry, and eight semester hours of college physics. There is also a three semester hour course in general psychology. In religion, the program embraces an English survey of fundamental and special theology over a period of two years, two semester hours per week. The idea is to provide a sound basis for the more special studies of the major seminary. Since public speaking is such an essential requisite for the fruitful preaching of the Word of God, special attention is given it during the whole six years of the minor seminary training.

The guidance program aims to achieve the integration of the intellectual and spiritual formation of the young seminarian. We

230 The Reverend John L. White, S.M.

try to place special emphasis in counselling, individual counselling. A guidance director is always at the service of the students for systematic direction and for counselling on special problems. This school director offers general guidance to all students, especially through conferences given three times a week for a half-hour period. Over and above this general guidance, each student is required to choose from among the members of the faculty, a personal counsellor to whom he will go at least once a month for an interview or chat. On external matters, the rector regularly interviews each member of the student body as part of a program of administrative guidance. The purpose of this guidance is to make seminarians better adjusted to school environment.

Since each of us knows what a fruitful period the year of the novitiate is in the spiritual formation of the religious, it suffices that we merely mention it. I pass on to the training given in the major seminary, or as we call it, the scholasticate. After attempting to cope with the problem of securing Bachelor's degrees for our scholastics (major seminarians), and specialized training in the field which they will later teach, we have come to the conclusion that the Catholic University provides the best answer to our needs. Our scholasticate is situated on the fringe of the University campus. It is a five minute walk to class. Our candidates follow the University's Bachelor degree program in philosophy. Aside from the straight philosophical disciplines, the auxiliary program is heavily weighted in the natural sciences, and thus our seminarians take courses in college mathematics, experimental psychology, college physics and chemistry, biology, and also pedagogy. In the ordinary seminary curriculum, the physical sciences always seem to be subjects quite neglected, and I am sure that each of us here knows how basic and essential a good scientific background is, even if only from the point of view of being properly accredited for a teacher's certificate.

The theological courses, embracing the last four years of the seminarian's training, are given at our own institution and by our own professors. Moreover, each summer the whole student body undertakes courses at the Catholic University in view of graduate degrees for the subjects which they will later teach. The students who are sufficiently healthy and mentally capable are sent to the International Scholasticate of the Marist Fathers in Rome where they pursue courses leading to graduate degrees in moral and dogmatic theology, canon law, and Sacred Scripture.

VINCENTIAN FATHERS
(Congregation of the Mission)

The Very Reverend Daniel Martin, C.M.
Provincial Dean of Studies
St. Mary's Seminary
Perryville, Missouri

It is readily admitted by all, in practice as well as in theory, that the function of the seminary is to train priests, to prepare men to fulfill the divine commission given to the Church to teach the truths of supernatural revelation to all men. With due reservations, much the same might be said about any program of training of religious men or women. Any short-sighted policy which would neglect the basic fact of religious training would be doomed to failure and would be disastrous alike to the individuals thus trained and to the religious body that would rely on them to carry on its work and its spirit. Hence, in the seminary, any program of teacher training in the ordinary professional sense of the word is quite secondary to the study of the ecclesiastical sciences and to those branches of the liberal arts which they necessarily presuppose.

In the teacher training program of the Vincentian Fathers, there is a second factor that goes far toward determining the nature of that training. Most of our teachers are engaged in the work of seminaries. Seminaries must be staffed by priests; and thus, priest-teachers must be provided for whatever needs there are in the seminary curriculum. It is possible at times to use the services of a layman for one or another course in the seminary, but only by way of exception. Seminary training is such that the faculty must be not merely instructors in the classroom, but also men authorized as spiritual guides for the seminarians, and men responsible for passing judgment on the fitness of the seminarian not only for academic promotion but chiefly for ecclesiastical promotion. This necessity imposes a certain rigidity on the selection of men to work in specialized fields of academic study; we cannot give free range to the preferences of the individual. We attempt not to put men into fields of study in which they would be misfits; and if there is a misplacement of this kind, we do correct it as soon as it is detected. But in many instances, the seminarian as well as the priest is called upon to cultivate a taste in a field of study in which he has not particular interest or for which he has not special liking.

It is impossible for the ordinary seminary to attempt to be a university or a college of liberal arts and sciences in the full scope of that term. To say nothing of other reasons, such a policy as that would be ruinous both in finances and in personnel. The teacher-training program as carried out at the seminary presupposes, therefore, that the bulk of professional training will be received in universities both before and after ordination. We content ourselves at the seminary with a strong basic curriculum of the arts and sciences with a program of concentration leading to the degree of Bachelor of Arts in philosophy. We do insist in this curriculum on French and German as a preparation for graduate work. Further, we give the undergraduate courses in pedagogy that make up the least common denominator of the five states in which our community conducts high schools or preparatory seminaries. This means that in most instances the young priest assigned to teach in a high school will have some work to complete after ordination in order to qualify for his assignment; but he is close enough to qualification that this additional work is not an insurmountable obstacle.

As a general rule, the training of the seminarians is confined to the seminary campus at Perryville, Missouri, until the completion of their college course—which usually coincides with their final profession in the community. At that time, they are given a field of special study to which they devote themselves during summer sessions in one of the universities where housing facilities are available for them. During the seminary scholastic year, they devote what time they can to reading and study in the field of their specialization, but without formal courses. The geographical location of the seminary precludes their attending any college or university during the seminary scholastic year; and the demands of the theological training would make this inadvisable, in my opinion, even if it were physically possible. This does mean that the completion of work toward a Master's degree must wait until after ordination to the priesthood; but many are within easy striking distance by that time. After ordination, the teacher training continues in the same field as before ordination, on either a part-time or a full-time basis, according to the circumstances.

In integrating teacher training, intellectual development, and the spiritual life of the seminarians, each of the spiritual and ascetical practices common in all communities plays its part. But to give special point and motivation to the integration of professional teacher training and spiritual development, I think it is most useful to stress in conferences and in the classroom the dignity of the teaching office in the Church. For the growth and perfection of the Mystical Body, the office of teaching ranks second only to those of the apostolate and of prophecy (which latter has much in common with the general notion of teaching). It is far more important to the Church than the working of miracles or the speaking in unknown tongues or the various offices of social and charitable ministrations. An appreciation of these facts can hardly leave a young man or woman in religion unmoved to the spiritual motivation of his teaching career.

VINCENTIAN FATHERS

The Reverend Joseph Hogan, C.M.
Dean, Graduate School
St. John's University
Brooklyn, New York

This paper concerns itself with the educational training program in effect throughout the Eastern Province of the Congregation of the Mission. For reasons that will appear, the particular slant and emphasis in this presentation will be on teacher training for religious instruction.

Until the recent revision of our constitutions, completed this year, the work of education did not appear among the specific ends of our community. The reason was that we had been founded principally to engage in missionary activity at home and abroad along with training seminarians for the priesthood. However, with the gradual expansion of educational activities, more and more members of the community were appointed to that field of the apostolate. Yet even now the number is not significant.

In our teacher training program we offer the usual courses in education, namely, the problems, the psychology of education, mental hygiene, and a specialized course in catechetics. Our courses are aimed specifically towards high school teaching because, with rare exceptions, it is in high school that we have our first teaching experience. These young priests are taken in hand by the principal, tutored by an experienced teacher in the subject to which he is assigned, and for six months he observes and is observed.

After one, two, or several years in the high school, the young priest earns his Master's or Doctor's degree from the parent university, or some other university to which he was assigned.

We feel that because of his maturity, his teaching experience in high school, his observance of the various defects and excellences in his instructors and professors, that the confrere will have formed a method of presentation that will be effective on the college and seminary level. If he has not done so, the matter will not long remain a secret, and he will be advised to improve himself and in a spirit of humility and charity, he will be practically aided towards this improvement.

The following breakdown of the teaching load of our confreres at St. John's University on the college level will bear witness to the emphasis on religious teaching. Of the 268 periods a week on the college level taught by our confreres, the following distribution was discovered: Religion (117 hours); Philosophy (83); Latin (3); Sociology (12); French (12); Economics (4); English (9); Art (10); Political Science (6); Ethics (4); and Education (8).

As is evident the preponderance of instruction is in religion and philosophy. Consequently, at Mary Immaculate Seminary, Northampton, Pennsylvania, a rather intensive course in catechetics is conducted. Although there is but one hour of lecture a week, there are several hours of actual catechetical instructions given by the scholastics.

The formal class consists in general and special catechetics with much emphasis placed on the various methods of instructing; lesson plans are drawn up, used in the class of children, recorded as taught in the classroom, and then replayed for the professor who evaluates and criticizes the individual lesson for content and method. Although only one class attends the formal course, usually the third year theologians, yet both the third and fourth theologians engage in the actual teaching program.

This program consists in classes held at the seminary for those area children who attend public schools and cannot attend religious instructions in their own parishes when it is given. In addition to the above group, our scholastics go out each Sunday afternoon into two nearby parishes to conduct catechism classes for the children of these parishes who attend the public schools. During the summer months, the numbers of parishes so served during the summer vacation school program is increased. In this way the young scholastic integrates theory and practice during his last two years in the seminary which is quite valuable for its transfer value in the priesthood.

We have found that his catechetical program is one of the more effective means for perfecting methodology on the part of the scholastics, intensifying their study of the various tracts in theology, and a most important factor in stimulating interest in teaching as a priestly career.

As a supplementary means we have invited throughout the scholastic year, outstanding priest-educators to lecture on the importance of the priest in the classroom, stressing the fact that teaching is another form of preaching the message of Christ, and pointing out to them the very realistic fact of statistics, namely, the number ever increasing of confreres who are now engaged full-time in education.

Another means that we have used in forming the mind of the

scholastic toward teaching as a career is the conference hall. This is effected by indicating to them the end of the congregation, namely, education, and that for one preparing to become a priest in the community it is necessary to develop himself completely in conformity with the objective proposed. Furthermore, this objective can never be realized until a spirit of generosity and dedication is formed during the formative years of training. He is impressed in the conference and in private interviews with the necessity of spending himself and unselfing himself for the educational and moral needs of the students later entrusted to his care. Unless he has this, then, all the techniques, degrees, and science will be so much expert equipment without a principle of vital and generous application.

These are the various means of both an intellectual and spiritual nature that we have employed in the training of our men toward the all important and steadily increasing work of the apostolate in the classroom.

BROTHERS OF HOLY CROSS

The Reverend Brother John Baptist, C.S.C.
Director of Studies
Notre Dame, Indiana

Brother Dominic Elder, C.S.C.
Master of Novices, St. Joseph Novitiate
Rolling Prairie, Indiana

Brother Maurus O'Malley, C.S.C.
Brooklyn, New York

Brother Charles Andersen, C.S.C.
Principal, Notre Dame High School
Sherman Oaks, California

It is our conviction that the person who is religiously or spiritually well grounded, morally strong, socially conscious, intellectually prepared, emotionally stable, and physically fit is the perfect Holy Cross product.

All of these objectives have some place in the various training programs for the Brothers of Holy Cross. The particular emphasis on each, and the means used to achieve each objective will, however, necessarily vary in the different phases of training.

During the year of novitiate training the emphasis is on religious or spiritual objectives as provided by canon law and our constitutions. Courses on the vows and such other subjects as life of Grace, the infused theological and moral virtues, the Gifts of the Holy Ghost, the Mystical Body of Christ, the Holy Sacrifice of the Mass, and so on, provide a very intensive spiritual training. Practical conferences on such subjects as self-discipline, religious manliness, religious etiquette, religious modesty, the meaning of work, and other subjects geared to the more external practical aspects of life as a Holy Cross Brother are also given. These courses and conferences, coupled with an exacting discipline and the fervent day-to-day religious life, provide, we feel, a solid religious foundation for future years of fruitful apostolic labor.

In the scholasticate the emphasis falls on the intellectual objectives, although the scholasticate program is aimed at providing the opportunity to grow in the spiritual life while the scholastic is working toward his Bachelor's degree and doing student teaching.

In view of the time allotted for this discussion we would like to limit the remainder of our remarks to the more specific aspects of the pre-service training program in our scholasticates, our in-service training program for beginning teachers, and our in-service training for veteran teachers. We will then briefly consider the means used for evaluating these programs as well as the effectiveness of our whole system of spiritual and intellectual formation. This last point involves integration and, as we will point out, the integrators are the active administrators and inspiring teachers who consciously develop and direct a balanced program by providing guidance at all levels—in the juniorates, the novitiate, the scholasticate, and in our schools.

Pre-Service Training in the Scholasticate

The Brothers of Holy Cross have scholasticates on the campuses of Notre Dame University, Notre Dame, Indiana, and St. Edward's University, Austin, Texas, where the Brothers pursue their Bachelor's degrees in the arts and sciences. St. Joseph High School in South Bend, and St. Edward's High School at Austin serve as training schools where our scholastics do observation and practice teaching under the supervision of the Department of Education at each university.

To earn a degree and complete 18 to 24 hours of professional courses usually takes three and a half years and from three to four summers. Except for special classes in religion and Gregorian chant, the scholastics take their courses with the regular university students. This classroom association with lay students is deemed to have social and pedagogical values. Programs are planned to meet state requirements for high school teachers in as many as possible of the twelve states in which the Brothers of Holy Cross conduct schools.

The programs are essentially the same at both universities. The head of the department approves the candidate; holds weekly seminars; and once every three weeks observes the candidate teaching, writes a report, and holds a private interview with him. A copy of this tri-weekly report is presented to both the critic and practice teacher. These written critiques are especially helpful in conducting the interview and in coordinating the work of the critic teacher with that of the university supervisor.

To earn six semester hours of credit for Observation and Practice Teaching the student teachers must first observe a minimum of thirty fifty-minute high school classes and make out a report on his observations. Although most of these observations are made in the classes of critic teachers, the student teachers also visit other classes in order to become acquainted with a variety of techniques. Next, the student teacher must conduct a minimum of sixty fifty-minute classes, presenting his lesson plans, tests, and so on for criticism and discussion to his critic teacher at a weekly conference.

The practice teaching program is administered by the principal of the high school and the supervisor of student teachers. Well in advance of the beginning of each semester the principal confers with the superior of the scholasticate regarding the class programs for the student Brothers. Freshman classes are preferred and so arranged that no class has more than one student teacher in the year. The critic teacher, in each instance, is the actual teacher of the class and his name is listed as such on the high school schedule. He does not leave the room for the first six weeks, after which the student teacher is left on his own for short periods until he acquires sufficient experience and confidence to conduct the class by himself.

Each week during this period of practice teaching the critic teacher prepares a written report on the work of the past week for his student teacher and holds an interview with him to discuss the report and the lesson plan for the coming week. Every three weeks the critic teacher prepares a progress report on the student teacher which is sent to the university supervisor and to the superior of the scholasticate.

The supervisor of student teachers coordinates the program by meeting with student teachers for orientation and discussion of procedures. He also meets with the critic teachers to review the program and to discuss problems and methods. In addition, he collects the various progress reports and draws up an annual report with recommendations which are presented to the province director of studies for discussion at the annual meeting of the province committee on studies.

In-Service Training of Beginning Teachers

Pitfalls and heartaches can be spared the beginning teacher through proper supervision; because of the problems caused by the change from life in the scholasticate to a full teaching program on the missions, the beginning teacher should be helped in every way possible.

In Holy Cross a special vigilance is exercised over those who are beginning their teaching career. The principal or superior, by studying each member's dossier, gives full consideration to the mental and physical qualities, aptitudes, tendencies, and preferences so as to assign classes and positions best suited to the individual. The principal plans his first days of school to give these men all needed assistance. Each beginning teacher has a veteran teacher assigned to aid and encourage him. The beginner is given one class less than the normal load with fewer preparations; he is encouraged to visit other classes, to consult veteran teachers, to experiment with various techniques. By means of this initiation the beginner becomes aware of many things he has yet to learn about teaching. As a consequence, his enthusiasm and zeal, properly guided by expert hands, can be made more efficacious. Furthermore, careful and considerate assistance given to the beginning teacher is a Christlike charity which frequently enables the recipient to practice more easily the virtues of obedience and humility.

In-Service Training for Veteran Teachers

Our in-service training program for veteran teachers aims at developing a high degree of professional competency and leadership. A program of summer session courses leading to the Master's degree is recommended for all and further graduate work is encouraged. By the assignment of capable men as critic teachers, to administrative offices, as chairmen of faculty meetings or research projects, their talents are utilized and their initiative encouraged.

We have found workshops to be a very effective and stimulating method of developing the professional attitude. They offer a splendid opportunity to study and execute community-wide projects. Last summer our Brothers held twenty-three three-day area workshops; fifteen were Marian workshops and eight were English workshops, each developing its own program and reporting minutes, papers, and recommendations to the Provincial Director of Studies. The purpose of the English workshop was to review a new program of study in English which had been drawn up by one of these workshops in the previous summer. Having used the program for one year, the English teachers made valuable recommendations for an addendum to the program. Smaller groups met in daily sessions for six-weeks workshops in Catholic Action, French, and music.

Next summer we plan to conduct three-day area workshops in vocations, Catholic Action, and guidance; and a six-weeks workshop on the teaching of religion. To prepare material for this latter project, some twenty area groups will meet during the coming Christmas vacation to discuss problems in the teaching of religion and make suggestions for the workshop next summer.

Integration and Evaluation

Integration is achieved primarily by the careful formulation and organization of programs aimed at realizing certain objectives. These programs must be executed by active administrators and inspiring teachers who, therefore, become the integrators. Evaluation is necessary to detect and remedy weaknesses in the program or its execution and, therefore, becomes an important integrating factor.

The first step in this process is the formulation of the program and its presentation in a well organized manner to clearly point out the duties and responsibilities of each person involved in its execution. The use of a handbook as a guide and source of information is a most effective means to this end. We are all familiar with the *Ratio Studiorum* of the Jesuits and the Christian Brothers' *Conduct of the Schools,* handbooks which have brought unity of aims and methods without stifling individuality, and have served generation after generation in their old and new editions. Our own community has handbooks on almost every level of training. Our administrative handbook, for instance, details the duties and responsibilities of the superiors and principals in our schools, the direction of faculty and students, and explains our educational objectives. Such a handbook eliminates much doubt and indecision of the superior, promotes efficiency at all levels in the school, and keeps activity in line with our religious and educational objectives.

It can be said that all communities have some type of evaluation in the annual visitation by the provincial or supervisor. When the visitation or evaluation is well organized and extensive, consisting of detailed written reports on the religious life, administration of the house and school, finances and the budget, augmented by interviews with all the members and a visit to the individual's classroom, it can be a most effective means of knowing whether or not the integration implicit in the program for the house being visited is actually taking place.

Written reports are necessary because of the impossibility of inquiring into all phases of the constitutions, the chapter decrees and recommendations, adherence to traditions and procedures outlined by provincial letters and our handbooks. Experience has shown us that an evaluating checklist is of value in the degree that it is specific. The questions, "Do you hold regular faculty meetings?" means little; but "How many faculty meetings were held last year?" and "How many are planned for this year?" are specific and meaningful. The checklist used by the Brothers of Holy Cross covers some five hundred items which serve as reminders to superiors and administrators that the policies and principles of the community as outlined in the various sources are to be effectively administered. Administrators may not relish preparing these reports, but if they are properly designed they can serve as a valuable self-evaluation for the local administrators and a constant reminder that progress for the community is real only to the extent of the progress in perfection of its individual members. The realization of this primary objective is the best assurance of the effectiveness of our other objectives.

In summary, then, we can say that if a program is carefully formulated to achieve certain objectives in relationship to our life as religious, organized so that every person concerned clearly understands its purpose and his part in the plan, and, finally, there is an effective periodic review at all levels, the end result should bring not only realization, but a strengthening of the corporate spirit, an increase in individual perfection, and the blessings of God upon the work of the community. It is a task which requires constant work and ceaseless vigilance, but a necessary one if we are to strive for that perfection which is our common goal.

BROTHERS OF THE SACRED HEART

Brother Louis Cavell, S.C.
Menard Memorial High School
Alexandria, Louisiana

In one of our Community publications, *Manuel de perfection chrétienne*, a detailed portrait of the "ideal Brother" is given in the closing chapters. The Brother of the Sacred Heart is discussed as a man, as an educator, and as a religious.

Candidates for the postulate may be accepted at the beginning of their high school course. The time preceding the six months' canonical postulate is termed the juniorate. Since the young temporary professed, the scholastics, must complete their Bachelor's degree before entering upon the active apostolate, a candidate will spend from four and one half to eight years in training under special masters.

Yet another phase of training must be mentioned. It embodies our in-service training. In the intellectual sphere that training is in the line of graduate work, to which a new impetus has been given. In the spiritual life it takes the form of the grand, or second novitiate. This is a six-month period of intense religious renovation imparted in our General House in Rome, for Brothers already professed for a period of from ten to fifteen years.

The general objective of our program has been thus expressed by Brother Claver, S.C., Ph.D., Master of Studies at our scholasticate:

> "To impart the necessary moral, spiritual and intellectual training to enable our candidates to fulfill their destiny of excellent Catholic elementary and high school teachers."

In a word, our objective is to prepare ideal Brothers of the Sacred Heart. This general objective is spelled out in specific objectives proper to each phase of our program. The three aspects of an ideal Brother in the sketch I have presented are, to be sure, purely speculative analysis. However, with reservations, each becomes the special aim of one of those phases. The formation of

the candidate to the full Christian life is the work of the postulate; his religious formation, the object of the novitiate; his professional training, the scope of the scholasticate.

The objectives of our postulate I should express as follows:

1) Formation of a correct conscience in our youth.
2) Education of the heart.
3) Character training.
4) Initiation into the life of the institute.
5) Development of family spirit.

The aims of the novitiate might be outlined as follows:

1) Character adjustment to the life of the institute.
2) Intensification of all Christian virtues, especially charity and
humility.
3) Study and practice of the counsels.
4) Training and exercise in the life of prayer.
5) Study and practice of asceticism.

The work of the scholasticate tends toward leading the student-
Brother to these goals:

1) Maturation and integration of character in accordance with
the tenor of our institute.
2) Intensification of the religious virtues, especially of those
which are the object of the vows.
3) Formation to a truly Christian spirit of scholarship.
4) Development of a sense of regularity.
5) Guidance in enlightened apostleship.

Our Formation Program: Content

The scholastic prerequisite for admission to the novitiate is the
completion of high school. The content of this course can be
generally described as academic. We feel that such a course is imperative if we are to afford our young people that cultural education which is essential to the understanding of true values, to
the formation of a critical sense, and to the training of an educator.

The one subject of this course specifically demanded in our
Constitutions is Christian Doctrine. Hence, a thorough course is

imparted in dogma, moral, and worship. This is abetted by an introduction to liturgy and Gregorian chant.

The content of the novitiate studies is outlined in the Constitutions. In accordance with its prescriptions, these are the courses of our novitiate: Christian doctrine; Church history; liturgy and chant; introduction to the study of Scripture; Christian and religious perfection; catechism of the religious profession; study of the life of Christ; study of the constitutions; study of the directory of rules; history of the institute.

The study of perfection and of the religious profession is made from manuals published by our institute. A new history of the congregation is now in preparation.

During the scholasticate the content of spiritual formation does not vary from that of the novitiate. It constitutes essentially an intensification of that formation. The intellectual content will depend upon the individual inclinations and talents of each Brother. However, the academic course of high school is implemented for all through a good course in philosophy (18 units) and education (24 units). Our Provincial Chapter of 1946 took these important steps:

1) The erection of a scholasticate at Spring Hill, Alabama, affiliated with Spring Hill College.

2) The decision to keep student Brothers in the scholasticate until completion of their Bachelor degree.

3) The formulation of an integrated course in Christian doctrine to extend over the six years of temporary vows.

The subject fields in which our student Brothers earn degrees are as follows, with an academic major and minor: Humanities (Latin, Spanish, English, history); natural sciences (chemistry, biology, mathematics, physics); and commerce (commercial education in its various branches).

Integration in the program is the special function of the respective masters charged with the formation of candidates. It is performed in particular through conferences, and the personal interview, which is of rule. But all who are in any way charged with the instruction of our candidates must cooperate in achieving this integration. In general, I should say the proper method of realizing it is a concerted effort to form in the candidates a true sense of proportion, the ability to keep first things first.

In the postulate, integration is guaranteed by the following:

1) Emphasis on such aspects of life as are new and beyond the general Christian life in the world: regularity, daily examen of conscience, periods of silence, daily mortification.

2) Emphasis on the moral union of prayer, study, and work.

3) Emphasis on the importance of community life and spirit.

Integration is achieved in the novitiate especially by these means:

1) Emphasis on the character of our life—the mixed life, which demands a wholesome and harmonious blending of prayer and study.

2) Emphasis on the habit of purity of intention.

3) Emphasis on the fact that each member is valuable only insofar as he is serviceable to the mission of our institute.

Our masters of scholastics have worked toward effecting integration through the following:

1) Emphasis on the fact that an apostle cannot give what he does not possess.

2) Emphasis on the sacred character of the horarium, not permitting study to encroach upon prayer, or vice versa.

3) Emphasis on the necessity for each student to prepare himself to serve the institute to the best of his abilities.

In this last endeavor, the master of scholastics is aided by a master of studies, who gives each student personal guidance in the choice and sequence of courses and in the pursuit of the courses themselves. Both masters work in close harmony and cooperation, thus personifying the integration under discussion. The master of scholastics advises the provincial superior upon the placement of young Brothers who are sent on their first mission.

Throughout our program we strive to impress on our candidates that a teaching religious is a better religious for being a better teacher; that he is a better teacher for being a holier religious.

CHRISTIAN BROTHERS

The Reverend Brother Charles Henry, F.S.C.
Community Supervisor
Brothers of the Christian Schools
New York, New York

That you may be able to obtain a rather comprehensive picture of the program of teacher education and formation of the Christian Brothers, I have prepared the two statements which accompany this paper. The first statement is "Aims and Objectives of De La Salle College," the scholasticate of the New York Province of our institute. Therein two points of view are stressed: (1) the scholasticate should impart a superior formation to the spiritual, intellectual, and cultural life of the future religious educator; (2) the scholastic must be encouraged, instructed, and habituated to take an active role in his own formation, spiritual, intellectual, and cultural. Not mentioned in this statement of aims and objectives is the training of the scholastic in the manual arts. Each scholastic takes from his period of formation a manual art in which he has acquired some skill for use in his school and community. Likewise, he is encouraged to become adept in the sports normally played in the high and grammar schools so that he may be ready to act as moderator or even coach of athletics. Colloquially, we refer to the scholasticate program as the Formation of the 3 H's, Head, Heart, and Hand.

If you will refer to the statement of "Aims and Objectives" you will see that the first four paragraphs state the obligations of the scholasticate to the student religious. The succeeding paragraphs state the obligations of the student religious in his own education and formation.

Each student and teacher at De La Salle College has his personal copy of this document to be his guide in the multiphasic program of the scholasticate.

The statement on "Teacher Training Curriculum" outlines the course of intellectual formation. I have arranged it under three heads to make it the easier for us to study its various parts.

Religion Curriculum: This is spread over five years and four summer sessions. The credit evaluations mentioned for the courses are those accepted by the Veterans Administration in granting G.I. educational allowances to veterans, and by the Selective Service Board in granting 4-D draft status to candidates under the legal category "theological students" or "students for the ministry."

During the four years of the scholasticate 22 credits in religion are acquired under a program approved and accredited by the Catholic University of America. These courses are taught by Brothers holding the degrees S.T.L. and M.A. in theology and religious education. Successful completion of this religion program through a five-part comprehensive examination is marked by the conferring of a Diploma of Religious Education, awarded by the superior general of the institute.

Finally, the young religious continues his religious studies in community by means of an organized program of private study and annual examinations, spread over a period of twelve years, comprising three years each of apologetics, asceticism, Scripture, sacred history.

The Academic Curriculum: This is the main work of the four year scholasticate. It is the Catholic University B.A. course, liberal arts with concentration in a major field during the two upper years. The freshman and sophomore years are followed at De La Salle College, an approved extension of Catholic University; the courses are taught by Brothers approved by the secretary general, dean, and the respective departmental chairmen. For approval, the teacher must present an M.A. degree in the subject he proposes to teach, and be pursuing doctoral studies at the University. The junior and senior years are done on the Catholic University campus itself. Electives during these two years are chosen in view of having each student Brother become accredited by the State Departments of Education to teach several secondary school subjects. Graduate study is usually a part time pursuit of the young teaching religious. Most of our M.A. work is now done in the Program of Graduate Study of Manhattan College. This program is approved by the Board of Regents for the Christian Brothers only, and has been accredited by the Middle States Association.

When college graduates are received into the novitiate, their scholasticate period is reduced to three years, during which they are enrolled as graduate students at the Catholic University.

Professional Curriculum: This is exclusively a summer session program, whose first three years are approved and credited by the Catholic University, the fourth year by Manhattan College. Each student Brother begins his teaching career with a theoretical background of 21 credits in education and a semi-practical background of 3 to 6 credits in observation and practice teaching. Since practically all these Brothers will eventually be assigned to secondary school teaching, and since some will be immediately assigned to high school on completion of their training, we strive to give each of them a minimum of 24 credits in education, over and above the credit requirements of the B.A. degree, thus satisfying the spirit if not the letter of the recommendation (requirement, in some cases) of several State Education Boards that a secondary school teacher have spent a fifth year of study to acquire 24 to 30 credits after the B.A., 18 of which should be in education. Just now, we are studying the situation that will arise when secondary school teachers are so plentiful that the States can afford to enforce this "fifth year" rule.

Spiritual formation: I should add a brief statement about the spiritual formation of the young Brother. In the novitiate the course in asceticism is an integral part and a very important part of the spiritual formation of the novice. The course is given by the master of novices himself. The classical ascetical principles, such as they are set forth by Tanquerey, are particularized in this course to fit the spiritual life proper to the future teaching Brother. Instructions on the Holy Rule and on the religious vows are an important section of this course. A special study is made of the spiritual doctrine of the Holy Founder, St. John Baptist de la Salle, through a critical reading of his spiritual writings. The first eight weeks of the course in asceticism are devoted to prayer, liturgical, vocal, and mental. The method of mental prayer of St. De la Salle is taught to each candidate. Thenceforth, he will devote one and three quarter hours to mental prayer each day, forty-five minutes in the morning before Holy Mass, thirty minutes in mid-morning, thirty minutes in the evening. Twice a week the mid-morning mental prayer will be made orally by a novice, each young Brother in turn making this public mental prayer. The novice spends an hour a day in spiritual reading, half of this period in books written by the Holy Founder or by some other member of the Institute, the other half hour in books written by the standard ascetical authors. To facilitate the study of these three sections of the ascetics course, namely, Rules and Vows, Doctrine of the Holy Founder, and Prayer, three books have been published by the Institute, which form the texts for the novice's study.

In both the novitiate and scholasticate the spiritual exercises are much the same, with fewer exercises being prescribed in the scholasticate in order to provide more time for study and classes. In the novitiate, the morning spiritual exercises comprise vocal prayer, mental prayer, and the Holy Mass, totaling in all somewhat more than an hour and a half. The office of Our Lady is recited in choir on all week days, and the rosary is recited in choir every day. At noon particular examen is held, followed by prayers for the deceased, and the Angelus. Night prayers and points for mental prayer take about twenty minutes. Every day the young Brother makes a public avowal of his infractions of Rule, or his external faults against charity, obedience, or good manners, and receives a penance in reparation. Once each week he is publicly advertised for his faults by his fellow novices or scholastics. Every Friday is observed as a day of fast as well as abstinence. Every week the novice, every two weeks the scholastic, is received in private by the master for counsel, personal instruction and encouragement. Every Sunday the Brother provincial or assistant provincial gives the young religious a conference upon some aspect of their vocation or apostolate, or upon the liturgy of the day or the season. Every Sunday the young religious chant the *Missa Cantata* in the morning, Vespers in the evening, and Compline at night. The same is done on all the major feasts.

In the scholasticate the time for mental prayer is reduced by one half hour, and the public mental prayer is discontinued entirely. Except on Sundays, the time for spiritual reading is reduced to one half hour, and the office of Our Lady is omitted entirely. Every first Sunday of a month is kept as a day of recollection by the scholastics.

Aims and Objectives of De La Salle College

The purpose of the scholasticate is to develop the future religious educator. Therefore, everything in De La Salle College—instructors, schedules, courses, activities, libraries—must be directed toward that end. The religious-educator should be characterized by three qualities: (1) deep religious character; (2) broad scholarship, which he is able to impart to others; (3) courtesy and refinement of manners.

The four year period of training should produce a religious educator who is before all else a man of God: prayerful, spiritual in outlook, zealous for the Christian education of youth, well instructed in religion content, practiced in the Christian and religious virtues, especially those cultivated by the rules and constitutions of the Brothers of the Christian Schools, possessed of a sense of the social solidarity of the human race, and of the inviolable dignity of the human personality.

This period should likewise develop a deep spirit of study and should impart the general knowledge expected of a cultured man, as well as the pedagogical knowledge and ability necessary for the Christian educator. These will be acquired partly through formal instruction, partly through voluntary participation in the non-instructional academic activities of the scholasticate.

Thirdly, the scholasticate period should train the future religious teacher in the courtesy and refinement of manners proper to the gentleman and the educator of youth. Such courtesy and refinement must not be a veneer, but the deeply ingrained quality of a personality conscious of its own dignity as Christian and religious, and equally conscious of the dignity of those with whom he comes into contact. Since his whole life will be lived in community with his confreres, the spirit of community life, a spirit of thoughtfulness of others and of forgetfulness of self, based on supernatural considerations, must be given emphasis in his training.

Although the scholastic will always need guidance and direction, his growth in years and in experience should be marked by increasing initiative and self-reliance in all three phases of his training. He must be taught to live the spiritual and religious life through personal conviction, saying his prayers because deeply conscious of his need of close union with God; practicing recollection and silence through a realization of their importance in maintaining the Presence of God; observing his Holy Rules and practicing his Holy Vows as the God-given means of growing in holiness; living a reverent sacramental life in order to keep in close touch with Christ through these sources of divine life.

Self-reliance in study must be required of him as early as possible, that the process of education may become one of self-education to a great extent. This will imply initiative and research, intellectual curiosity, and proportioned attention both to detail and to the larger issues in the acquisition of knowledge. He should be encouraged to be productive in his scholarship as well as acquisitive. He should be given opportunities to develop his appreciation of the fine arts through lectures, concerts, and by means of visits to the art and museum collections of the city and to points of interest.

In the matter of courtesy and refinement, the scholastic should be encouraged to adopt a practice of self-criticism and self-evaluation leading to self-improvement. His personal appearance and those places assigned for his use should be characterized by a modest neatness and cleanliness, not because of the system of external control that is in vogue in the house, but because of a personal conviction that such carefulness is important to his own life, and is also a matter of courtesy toward others. In his intercourse with his confreres he will voluntarily adopt the conventional modes of polite behavior and practice them with grace and cheerfulness.

In order that these important principles may never be lost sight of by either the instructional staff or the scholastics, there shall be publicly read in the refectory once each year the following Circular Letters of the Most Honored Brothers Superior: "Our Life of Prayer"; "Our Life as Religious Educators"; "Refinement in the Religious Educator."

Teacher-Training Curriculum

This curriculum is arranged under three headings to allow an easier study of its component elements. In actual operation, this is an integrated program of teacher training, with all of the phases considered essential to the full preparation of the future educator.

The Religion Course: this course extends over a five school year, four summer session period.

(a) Novitiate Program—14 months

Asceticism (6 credits)	Old Testament (3 credits)
New Testament (3 credits)	Church History (3 credits)
The Creed (6 credits)	Methods in Religion (4 credits)

(During the four years following this course in Methods, one "model" demonstration lesson is given by the students in succession every week of the school year.)

(b) Scholasticate Program—4 years

   Freshman Year: The Creed (2 credits); General Moral (2 credits); Summer Session: The Church (2 credits).

   Sophomore Year: The Commandments (2 credits); Grace, Sacraments in General (2 credits); Summer Session: Catholic Social Principles (2 credits).

   Junior Year: Particular Sacraments (2 credits); Scripture (2 credits); Summer Session: Apologetics (2 credits).

   Senior Year: Scripture (2 credits); Liturgy (2 credits).

(c) Post-Graduate Program: a series of four courses, each of three years, in which the student develops by private study and research fifty theses a year, and then sits for an all day examination to test the thoroughness of his mastery of the subject. These four courses cover Apologetics, Sacred history, Asceticism, Sacred Scripture. For the completion of each course a diploma in religious education is conferred by the superior of the institute.

The Academic Course: the first two years are taken at De La Salle Extension of the Catholic University, the final two years in the Catholic University proper.

(a) Freshman Year:

   English (6); Foreign Language (6); Latin or Mathematics (6-8); History (6).

(b) Sophomore Year:

English (6); Foreign Language (6); Latin or Mathematics (6-8); Elective (6-10); Philosophy (6).

(c) Junior Year:

Philosophy (6); Major Subject (12); Electives (12).

(d) Senior Year:

Philosophy (6); Major Subject (12); Electives (12).

(The "electives" in the upper two years are chosen in view of secondary school accreditation in 2 or 3 subjects over and above the major subject.)

(e) Graduate Study: this is pursued by the young Brother as a part-time student during his early years of teaching; he is encouraged to take one course each semester and one each summer session, and to complete his comprehensive exams and his thesis within six years of his B.A. graduation. During this period, too, he is encouraged to study for one or two of the diplomas of religious education, mentioned above.

The Professional Course: the courses in education are taken during the four summer sessions of the scholasticate, under the jurisdiction of the Catholic University during three summer sessions, under Manhattan College following graduation from Catholic University.

(a) First S.S.:

Introduction to Education (2); Principles of Philosophy of Education (2); Teaching (2).

(b) Second S.S.:

Psychology of Education (2); Visual-Auditory Aids (2); Elementary School Methods (2).

(c) Third S.S.:

Secondary Methods (2); Guidance (2); Tests and Measurements (2).

(d) Fourth S.S.:

Classroom Management and School Organization (3); Observation and Practice Teaching (3-6).

(By thus utilizing the summer sessions, the student Brother acquires the 24 credits over and above the B.A. requirements which certain states require or suggest for a secondary school teacher, sometimes called "the fifth year.")

CHRISTIAN BROTHERS

Brother Frederick, F.S.C.
Vocational Director, La Salle Institute
Glencoe, Missouri

Young men are admitted to the institute of the Brothers of the Christian Schools at either the high school or graduate level. Limitation of age is dependent on the adaptability of the candidate.

Four divisions comprise the training program: juniorate (high school), three to six months of postulancy, one year novitiate, and a three year scholasticate program during which time the Bachelor of Arts is completed by the teaching Brother.

With few exceptions the young teachers return to our own St. Mary's College, Winona, Minnesota for summer sessions for graduate work toward the M.A. degree. Graduate work is continued by some of those thus completing the M.A. in various universities in the midwest. Five or six Brothers are in continual release to work for the doctorate degree.

*   *   *

At the end of the novitiate a Brother states his intention of whether he wishes to teach or not. Years ago we did not make efforts to recruit non-teaching Brothers, but recently we are admitting about two to each class of novices. Non-teaching Brothers receive a three year program of training in the scholasticate as do those working for degrees.

A temperament test is given to novices to help them determine their temperament. The test used is based on the characterology of Wiersma and is published in Canada.

Temporary vows made at the end of the novitiate continue to the age of twenty-five. Candidates who enter at an older age have a minimum of five years of temporary vows preceding perpetual profession. A thirty day retreat is made precedent to perpetual profession.

*   *   *

The testing program administered to the student Brothers is given mainly to help choose the major field of study; tests are used only experimentally as an aid in character study. The tests include: Kuder Preference Record, American Council of Education Battery, Ohio Psychological, and the Minnesota Multiphasic Personality Inventory. This last test was introduced this year for the first time.

Each student Brother chooses his own major field under the direction of the vice-provincial, the director of student life. Each Brother receives approximately 24 hours in religion, 21 in philosophy and 20 in education.

*   *   *

Non-teaching Brothers carry about eight to ten hours of scholastic work in fields adapted to the individual. These courses are in religion, philosophy, science, literature, and drafting. The remainder of the day is spent in learning various skills under the direction of an elderly Brother assigned to their care. Brother Norman, director of this group of Brothers, conducts a seminar weekly with the group to clarify this special vocation to the non-teaching Brother. Brothers in this vocation receive special training during summers at Stout Institute, Menominee, Wisconsin after completing the scholasticate program.

*   *   *

'Reliance is based considerably on the principles given us by our founder, St. John Baptist de la Salle, for integrating the spiritual and intellectual training. De la Salle has left us in his "Collection of Short Treatises" the means we are to use to attain this integration.

*   *   *

A sixty day retreat is conducted annually as a means of spiritual renovation for Brothers in the thirties and forties. This retreat takes place during the summer months on Beaver Island,

Lake Michigan. Each of the five United States provinces sends five or six Brothers to this retreat.

A second novitiate is conducted in Rome at the motherhouse for a delegate of each of the 57 provinces in the institute. This year is compulsory for those who direct the houses of formation.

CHRISTIAN BROTHERS OF IRELAND

The Reverend Brother J. B. Darcy, F.S.C.H.
Superior, St. Gabriel's Scholasticate
West Park, New York

The objectives of our training program are, I presume, similar to those of other teaching Orders, that is, to prepare our Brothers for their lives as religious educators: (a) by developing their spiritual lives to such an extent that they will be able, after leaving the houses of formation, to assume responsibility for their own spiritual growth, and be capable, not only of withstanding the temptations of later life, but of making steady progress under these more difficult conditions; (b) by giving them sufficient education to meet the requirements of the various school boards under which they will teach and to be able to deal effectively with the subject matter they will be required to present to their pupils.

Before outlining briefly our training program, I should mention that the program as at present constituted is not considered an ultimate solution to the problem. Considerable experimentation has been carried on in recent years to improve it, and, though the present program has so far proved very satisfactory, it is as yet too soon to arrive at a final verdict as to its effectiveness. Secondly, it should be pointed out that since the greater part of our work is in high schools, the program is intended to emphasize preparation on that level.

For some years past, it has been the policy of our higher superiors to insist that each Brother have his B.A. or B.S. degree before beginning his teaching career, all pressures to the contrary notwithstanding. These degrees have been chosen in preference to the B.S. in Education because it is felt that they offer a more solid educational discipline and prepare better for higher studies.

In addition, because of the far-flung nature of our Province, the educational requirements of states as far apart as New York and Washington, two provinces of Canada, and the Union of South Africa must be provided for.

Various aspects of the spiritual life, also, have to be taken into consideration; in particular, how to carry out this program without unduly interfering with the spiritual growth of the Brothers and, on the other hand, without prolonging too much the time spent in the houses of formation, for it is highly desirable that the Brothers gain sufficient practical experience in the schools so that their suitability for a life of teaching be established before they make their final vows, which, in our case, is after the completion of six annual vows.

The training program begins in the summer after the completion of high school either in our own juniorate (where they are accepted after first year) or elsewhere. The postulants assemble at the juniorate where they spend six weeks during which they begin their college work with courses in logic and economics, receive a short course in the history of the Congregation and, in general, acquire an *esprit de corps* and are screened for any obvious undesirable characteristic before proceeding to the novitiate.

During the novitiate year, they are, of course, restricted in their educational advancement by the requirements of canon law. They do, however, in addition to the regular novitiate training, take two courses, both suited to the novitiate, one in religion—The Life of Christ, and the other in education—Special Methods of Teaching Religion. During the summer they take two non-credit courses, typing—which will considerably facilitate their college work—and a review of English and mathematics, which has been found particularly beneficial for those whose high school background has been somewhat deficient.

After the completion of their novitiate in September, they are sent to the scholasticate where they continue their regular college work. Here they take the basic courses of a liberal arts program:

religion, English, history, modern language, mathematics, and philosophy. All receive the same courses except in the case of mathematics, where those who show a marked ability are given a more advanced course.

During the summer of their scholasticate year, those who intend to major in science do a five-point course in general chemistry, while the others take two educational courses. The purpose of beginning the science major at this time is to relieve some of the pressure on the next two years, for, as you know, the science program is an exceptionally heavy one.

After the summer vacation, the students move to the campus of the college, which is Iona. Here they have a separate residence, but attend classes with the regular student body. They begin work on their majors, which may be in either the liberal arts, science, or business divisions. Within a period of two years and two summers they finish their degree requirements and obtain over thirty additional credits in education.

The method of working in the educational courses is as follows: Each summer three educational courses are taken with one additional course which I would like to mention especially. This is a three-hour-a-day three week course entitled Library Science for School Teachers. It is given in June of the senior year by the library staff and is intended to teach the students how to make the best possible use of the library in their teaching.

The necessary practice-teaching is taken care of in the following manner. During the scholasticate year, and again at Iona, released-time work is carried on one day a week under supervision. During their junior and senior year, two three-week periods when the college is not in session, in December and June, are utilized for observation and practice-teaching in the various Brothers' schools in the New York area under the supervision of the education faculty.

In the scholasticate the usual class-load is 16 credits; at Iona it is between 18 and 22. This might appear to be excessive, but, because of the regular study, the assistance available from the faculty and from each other, it has been found to be practical. Besides, allowances are made for individual differences, each one is carefully guided in choosing a major field within his ability and interest, and, if the ordinary load is found too taxing, it is lightened until it can be carried successfully. Since the program provides for over 160 credits, 30 more than the requirements for a degree, this can be done without causing any delay in graduation.

So, four years after he enters the novitiate, the Brother has received his degree with a full college course in religion, philosophy, English, history, and modern language, besides his major field and approximately 32 credits in education. He is qualified to teach in any of the elementary or high schools under our charge.

After graduation the Brothers begin teaching and at the same time continue their work on higher degrees by the familiar laborious process of attending classes after school or during the summer. The only eventual limits placed on them are those of opportunity and ambition.

So much for the educational program. I would like to add a few words on the religious formation as affected by this educational program.

As was mentioned in the beginning, one of the purposes of the religious formation is to enable the Brothers to be spiritually independent, to be able to accept responsibility for their own spiritual growth. We are all aware that one of the most repeated complaints against those just out of the houses of formation is their lack of maturity, of a sense of individual responsibility. This program aims at developing this maturity.

In the oft-debated argument whether it is better to establish a training college with its usually limited facilities and narrowness of program, or to send the students to a regular university with the subsequent danger of relaxation of the religious spirit, we have adopted a middle course, hoping thereby to obtain the advantages of both and the liabilities of neither, by a gradual change from the rigorous discipline of novitiate life to the comparative freedom of campus residence.

However, the Brothers are not even then completely on their own. They live together under a superior and socius who check carefully on their spiritual and intellectual lives, see that they get sufficient exercise, and help them over their difficulties. Help is also given by the members of the faculty who take a deep interest in the younger members of their religious family and are always available for counsel and advice. Further, two confessors, both skilled in guiding young religious, are in attendance.

After two years in this environment, the student-Brother emerges poised and self-confident, but also—and this is more important—solidly religious.

While, as has been said, this program in its entirety has only recently been adopted, the results so far have been highly satisfactory.

CHRISTIAN BROTHERS OF IRELAND

The Reverend Brother J. C. Bates, F.S.C.H.
Superior, Vancouver College
Vancouver, B.C.

The Christian Brothers of Ireland is a Pontifical Congregation founded by Brother Edmund Ignatius Rice at Waterford, Ireland, in the year 1802. In the comparatively short time of about a century and a half, the Congregation has spread from its tiny beginnings in a rented house to every continent on the face of the earth.

The Christian Brothers of Ireland first landed on the shores of the United States in 1906, a community of four invited by Monsignor James Power to open a school in All Saints Parish in New York City. In less than fifty years, the work of those four Brothers expanded until at the present time there are close to five hundred Brothers teaching in some twenty-eight schools across the length and breadth of North America. With such numbers it is necessary to have a well-rounded program of formation for each and every Brother.

*   *   *

When the foundation of the spiritual formation of the Brother has been completed in the novitiate, he is transferred to St. Gabriel's Scholasticate. Here, while the spiritual formation of the Brother continues, the formal preparation for his life in the classroom begins as he starts his first year of college. Those who have already obtained their degrees attend either Iona College in New Rochelle, New York, for courses in education or psychology, or begin graduate work in one or other of the universities in and around New York City. Another phase of life in the scholasticate is the opportunity to put into practice the theory learned in regard to the teaching of religion. Under the released-time program operating in the State of New York, the scholastics teach religion once a week to the public-school boys of nearby Highland or Poughkeepsie. A summer session of education, psychology, and typewriting completes the scholasticate year.

During the novitiate, the emphasis is on obedience and regularity. In the scholasticate, while these continue to be emphasized, equal weight is given to individual responsibility. For this reason, study is largely unsupervised, care of house and grounds is placed in the hands of the scholastics, and they must arrange their own games, outings, and so forth. In meditations and conferences, the same theme—individual responsibility—is developed, until by the end of the year the scholastics are considered sufficiently well-formed to adjust themselves without harm to life on a college campus.

The next two years are spent in residence at Edmund Hall, a house of studies on the campus of Iona College conducted by the Christian Brothers of Ireland. The student Brothers attend classes with the regular students of Iona College and enjoy the same choice of major field and electives. Summer sessions are used to complete a sequence of thirty-five semester hours in education and psychology. Practice teaching is done in five periods, each of one week's duration, in the elementary schools conducted by the Brothers in the New York archdiocese. A rotation plan permits each student Brother to observe in five different schools. The Brothers begin their teaching career upon the completion of the Bachelor's degree.

The campus life provides a gradual change from the discipline of the novitiate and scholasticate to the less rigorous demands of mission life. Furthermore, while still under supervision the student Brothers have limited intercourse with seculars and in this way they can acquire a desirable social maturity while preserving a proper religious reserve.

In general, all Brothers begin their teaching on the elementary level and advance to high school after four or five years of experience. During the first year of teaching, the Brother's time will be occupied completely with getting acclimated to the classroom, and therefore, he is not permitted to begin work on his Master's degree. However, to ensure advancement in religious knowledge and to provide background for the teaching of religion, special courses, such as moral guidance, Scripture, the liturgy, and so on are given to the Brothers of annual profession, on the basis of one course a semester.

During the summer months, all teaching Brothers not engaged in supervisory work attend summer school courses at conveniently located universities in order to secure graduate degrees, or to refresh themselves in subjects taken years before, or to prepare for some special assignment. Hence, the formation of the Christian Brother of Ireland is designed as a life-long process of continuous development and self-improvement.

CONGREGATION OF THE HOLY GHOST
AND OF THE IMMACULATE HEART OF MARY

The Very Reverend Edmund R. Supple, C.S.Sp.
St. Mary's Seminary
Ferndale, Connecticut

The Congregation of the Holy Ghost and of the Immaculate Heart of Mary is a religious institute devoted to the apostolate. It is classified among the religious congregations with simple vows, approved by the Holy See and under the jurisdiction of the Ordinary.

Its first and general end is to procure the glory of God and the sanctification of its members, by the observance of the vows of religion and the practice of the rules and constitutions.

Its special and distinctive end is to undertake humble and toilful ministries, for which Holy Church has difficulty in finding apostolic laborers, the evangelization of infidels especially, and more especially still, those of the black race.

As regards other works, the congregation shall accept them only when expressly requested to do so by the Holy See, and, in exceptional cases, such as are deemed useful to the Church, whilst being, at the same time, conformable to the interests of the institute.

The word "apostolate" has come to mean many things. In our case it refers to missionary activity. This latter, at one time, connoted teaching catechism and administering sacraments to the natives in any land. Today it has come increasingly to include teaching in a much broader sense. As a result, although our objective remains the same, the changed needs of the missions require a change of emphasis in training.

In mission territories where the government subsidizes schools, its support is contingent upon meeting its requirements. If the Fathers have the required degrees, the school receives the money; if not, it does not. Since the school is the principal means of establishing the faith, and money is perennially hard to come by, especially for the missionary, it is easy to see how important a recognized degree becomes for propagating the faith. Here in the United States many of our priests have to act as principals of schools, and certain states require certain qualifications.

St. Mary's Seminary, Ferndale, Norwalk, Connecticut, is the senior seminary of the Holy Ghost Fathers in the United States. It comprises two years of philosophy and four years of theology. The standard courses are taught. The regular spiritual conferences are given. Over and above these, several attempts have been made to prepare the students along lines specifically educational.

The first was attendance at summer school in Duquesne University in Pittsburgh. This included residence for six weeks during four summers. This, together with the work done during the last two years at our junior seminary in Cornwells Heights and the first two years in Ferndale, entitled the student to a Bachelor of Arts degree. This experiment was discontinued because, since all did not attend summer school, it tended to disrupt community spirit, and it was costly.

Next, accreditation by the State of Connecticut of our present courses pursued during the school year was obtained: a Bachelor of Arts at the end of philosophy, a Bachelor of Divinity at the end of theology. We are not accredited by the New England Association of Colleges and Secondary Schools (the regional accrediting association) for the reason given by it that we are too specialized an institution. This Bachelor of Arts degree equips our men to pursue studies in education. They have found no difficulty in being admitted to graduate schools, even in secular universities, though usually on the provisional basis that they finish the first semester's work with a B average, following which they are fully accepted.

Lastly, in an attempt to improve on this, we began, a few years ago, a three year summer school cycle in Ferndale aimed at providing eighteen credits in education. After completing one cycle this was discontinued because the strain on the students made itself felt about the middle of the regular school year.

At present, a few are chosen after their complete formation to study expressly with a view to obtaining a degree in a given field.

·VIII·

ADDRESS GIVEN AT THE FIRST NATIONAL SISTER FORMATION MEETING COLLEGE AND UNIVERSITY DEPARTMENT, N.C.E.A. ATLANTIC CITY, NEW JERSEY

THE SELECTION OF RELIGIOUS FOR GRADUATE STUDY

The Reverend Edwin A. Quain, S.J.
Vice President, Fordham University
New York, New York

A few months ago I received a most cordial invitation to address the First National Meeting of the Sister Formation conference— that is to say, the letter started off in very cordial fashion, but before I got to the end of it I began to think I should rather characterize it as cogent. The invitation was flattering and at the same time somewhat frightening, and when I got through reading the letter there did not seem to be any way in which I could get myself out of it. Just to add to my freedom of choice in the matter, a few days later I received a letter from a fellow Jesuit and very dear friend of mine practically insisting that I must accept; that reminded me of the biblical saying about a brother being "helped" by a brother. At the moment I did not think he was

266

being very much help. The crowning blow which closed the trap in which I found myself was his statement to the effect that "really, nuns are the easiest people in the world to talk to." On that statement I would not be so presumptuous as to pretend to have knowledge and so in the illusion that I was still exercising freedom of choice, I said yes.

I have said above that I found the invitation very flattering and I can sincerely tell you that I am very glad to have the opportunity to talk to so representative a group of superiors and Catholic school administrators from all over the United States, on a topic which I consider the most important single movement for Catholic education that is being carried on within the structure of a National Catholic Educational Association.

Not to burden you with statistics, I may be pardoned for reminding you that there are just short of four million students in Catholic schools at all levels in the United States. Those four million students are being taught by 123,000 teachers. Out of that total almost 90,000 are Sisters. While those figures may stagger you, they are certainly testimony to your supernatural faith and courage as well as your dedication to the apostolate that the Church has almost been able to take it for granted, that the supply of teaching Sisters would be permanently inexhaustible. Consequently, I feel somewhat guilty, as I stand before you today, not, I hope, to add to your problems, but I feel sure, to deepen in you the realization of the burden and responsibility that is yours.

I need not remind you that the demand for increasing numbers of competently trained school personnel, from the elementary through the college departments, will continue to demand from you, for the foreseeable future, ever increasing numbers of subjects who are capable of working in the large area of the educational apostolate of the Church in the United States that has been confided to you. You are, I am sure, also as aware as I am, of the steadily rising requirements in the professional and cultural preparation of teachers for our schools. Since 1946 more than twenty-three states have increased the minimum requirements for the lowest regular elementary teaching certificates. Eleven states have increased minimum requirements for regular certificates for secondary school teachers, in the same period; and twenty-four states have raised the minimum requirements for elementary school principals' certificates; and twenty-one states have done the same in the area of principal certificates for secondary schools. As of the present time, more than twenty-five states and the District of Columbia require the Bachelor's degree for the lowest elementary school teaching certificate. Five other states have set deadlines for the degree requirement to become effective.

Since 1953, four states and the District of Columbia are requiring a minimum of five years of professional preparation for initial teaching certificates and the trend of the movement makes it clear that the Master's degree will eventually be required for all teachers.

A few years ago a study initiated by the federal government set minimum standards for state approval of teacher preparing institutions, and they therein prescribe a minimum, and I may be pardoned for stressing this word "minimum," of 85 percent of teachers in college, who must have the Master's degree in the field of teaching, while 20 percent must have the Ph.D., or annually show evidence of progress toward that degree.

Since there are 115 colleges for women conducted by nuns in the United States, it is perhaps relevant for us to look at the figures of the degree requirements for colleges with enrollments of under five hundred full-time students for the various academic ranks in non-public colleges with enrollments under five hundred full-time students. I believe this would be the category in which most of your institutions would fall. I should like to stress here that these standards are the ones that are going to be demanded by the regional accrediting associations throughout the United States. It is therefore significant that for the rank of professor, 62.7 percent of these colleges require the Doctor's degree. For the associate professorship, 28.4 percent. For assistant professors, 13.6 percent, and for instructors, 3.9 percent. If on the occasion of an evaluation by your regional accrediting association, you do not come up to these minimum standards, your faculty are bound to be judged sub-standard.

I trust that these standards do not appear to you to be unobtainably high in the foreseeable future because we cannot be satisfied with merely meeting minimum standards, given the importance on the American educational scene of the institutions conducted by Sisters. On the contrary, we must look for outstanding leadership from Sisters in the field of education. While I am not for a moment closing my eyes to the financial burdens that you have to bear, nor to the demands that your educational apostolate makes upon the strength and energy of your devoted subjects, when we consider the vast extent of your educational commitment here in the United States, we may very properly ask, "Have Sisters produced in proportion to their numbers? Are there a proportionate number of outstanding elementary school administrators among nuns? How many on the secondary level, and how many nationally known Sisters' colleges are there in the United States?" And I mean not merely nationally known for the calibre of the lay faculty they have been able to acquire, but rather colleges in which competently trained Sisters can stand up to the competition of privately owned or non-Catholic sectarian schools and colleges. I would not have you think that such comparisons are unfair to our Catholic institutions for we cannot fool ourselves that we need not meet the competition of the field in which we are working on the level of professional training for education. All of us in Catholic education must be convinced that we cannot use education as a means to the salvation of souls unless we have sufficient respect for the means we are using. It is not enough that the end we have in view is supernatural, lest we fall into the difficulty of using education as a mere pretext.

I need not remind you of the resources that are at your disposal in the whole-souled and single-minded devotedness of your subjects to the apostolate of education. To a limited degree in my own teaching I have come to know the apostolic zeal with which Sisters, when given even a slight opportunity, will devote themselves to the achievement of excellence in their field of professional training.

I am reminded here of a Sister who was a student of mine about ten years ago and who during the summer was doing with me a kind of weekly tutorial in addition to a regular course in Medieval Latin Literature. For the second week I gave her an assignment to read Bede on whom I had been lecturing in the regular meetings of the course. When we met on Wednesday afternoon at three I asked her: "How much of Bede's *History of England* have you read?" She very briefly told me, "All of it." I quickly realized that this meant four hundred pages of Latin that she had read since our last meeting the preceding week. With what might appear to be inhuman cruelty but really of set principle, of taking it for granted that a really good student could always do more, I simply said, "Well, what did you get out of it?" Along with being an extraordinarily good student, she was also a well trained religious. She swallowed, and blandly told me that she felt that in some recent lectures she had heard on Bede, justice had hardly been done to the women characters that appeared therein, and she then proceeded for about three quarters of an hour to talk without any notes and in great detail about the outstanding women (all, incidentally, nuns) in Bede's *Ecclesiastical History of the English People.* I am glad to report two things about this incident: two years later she told me she finally understood what I was getting at and she was glad that I had taken that attitude; and the second thing is, that on the Feast of St. Joseph this year, she received word that she had a Fulbright grant to spend the summer at the American Academy in Rome.

From my own personal experience of fourteen years teaching on the graduate level, I can assure you that some Sisters I have taught have been among the very best students that I have ever known.

In order to stress the need for the highest type of professional training for Sisters in education, however, we need not merely look to the requirements of accrediting associations and to national surveys; we have a far better source of stimulus and encouragement in the words of our present Holy Father, who something over a year ago said:

"Good teachers, then, should have perfect human formation, intellectual and moral. For the teaching office is a lofty position which calls for educational discernment and for a goodness of heart, for a capacity of intuition and delicacy of spirit, for adaptability and adjustment as well as human depth, capable of bearing all for the love of our neighbor. Good teachers need a professional competency which should be at least above average, and better yet, outstanding on all levels of instruction and in each of the specialized fields if it is not to be unworthy of a mission which serves not merely the people and the state but also God, the Church, and souls." [1]

Two years ago the Holy Father also said:

"I wish to stress again the formation of your Sisters for the work and duty which is theirs. And here, show no narrowness, but be broad of vision. Whether it be a matter of education, pedagogy, care of the sick, of artistic activity or something else, the Sister must have this feeling: *My Superior gives me a training which places me on a level of equality with my colleagues in the world.* Give them also the possibility of keeping their professional capacities up-to-date." [2]

And further still, we have a summary of the First Congress of Superiors General of Religious Communities in which it was said, "It must be remembered that the Apostolate is also a science and an art and that the Holy See insists on the elevation of the literary, technical and professional culture of the Religious, on the absolute necessity of the degrees required for the exercise of the various professions; on the necessity of aspiring to a greater degree of proficiency, never thinking that one's culture is adequate enough for the present need."

As a result of these quotations, I do not think there can be any longer any doubt that the directives of the Holy Father apply *to all levels* of education and we must meet those standards if the training of our Sisters is not to be unworthy of the apostolate to which they are dedicated.

Given, therefore, the need for substantial numbers of Sisters trained to the highest competence in the various fields of education which flows from the extent of your present and undoubtedly greater future commitments to education in the United States, from the requirements of accrediting organizations, the need for outstanding leadership from Sisters, and the directives that come to you from the Holy See, there is also to be prayerfully considered a further obligation in justice. There is an obligation in justice devolving upon religious superiors to make the best possible selection of the candidates in their community for the highest type of educational training that your resources will make possible. I need only mention in passing how important it is for the personal spiritual development of the religious whom God has confided to you that they be given the human means and opportunities that will fit them for the job which obedience has imposed upon them. The selection of Sisters for graduate work cannot any longer be carried out in haphazard fashion or determined by merely chance considerations. There is need for serious study and hard-headed consideration of the needs in your community for a competently trained dean or principal, professor of philosophy, literature, history, science, or mathematics.

In this connection, I should like to draw upon the principles of moral theology and the notion of distributive justice. Briefly, there is an obligation on the superiors of the community to make an equal distribution of the goods of the community among its members. Conversely, the members of a community have a right, since they are parts of a community, that they be helped by the community in the attainment of its end. By this, of course, I do not mean that each individual Sister has a right to make a declaration of total independence and to make demands upon her superiors. It is, however, true that superiors do have duties with regard to their subjects. In any community, both superiors and subjects have an obligation before God to devote themselves wholeheartedly to the attainment of the end of the community. Each individual religious has an obligation to contribute toward the attainment of that end. The Sister who takes care of the kindergarten has an obligation to bring the resources of the community, insofar as lies within her power, to the accomplishment of her work in her restricted field.

Now, I need not remind you that of all the resources and blessings that Almighty God has given you in your communities, none can compare with the devoted lives, talents, energies, and competence of the Sisters in your community. The utilization of these talents must, in accordance with the principle of distributive justice, be apportioned among all members of your community for the accomplishment of your end and purpose. I have said above that there must be an "equal" distribution of the goods of the community. It is very important to mention here, however, that distributive justice does not mean that training for educational work must be apportioned *in exactly the same measure* to every Sister in your community. There must be a proper basis for the distribution that you make of the goods of your community, in this case, the talents and competence of your members. The mere fact that a Sister is one member out of one hundred members, let us say, in a community, does not give her the right to graduate training, in the schools of your community.

Given as a first foundation the size and extent of the school or college that you are running, you will have individual needs for different people in positions of varying competence. It is in the selection of the individual to fill this specific job, that the principle of distributive justice enters in. The choice of person for that job must be made on the basis of the personal internal qualifications of each individual in your community. In the context of educational training, one Sister will have the right on the basis of her talents and brains to complete the Bachelor's degree. For her, that may well be the end of her educational training. Another, because of her personality and temperament should receive training that will fit her, according to modern educational standards, to be a first class teacher of freshman English. Another perhaps, by her experience before she entered your community, may have the qualities that some of us like to think are required in educational administrators: objectivity of mind, efficiency in administration, patience with a multitude of picayune details, and that sublime gift of God, the ability to leave your job at the desk in your office and not take it to the chapel with you during prayers, or to your room at night when you should be getting some sleep.

I have said that each individual Sister has a right to such training. By that I mean, she has a right to have her talents and qualifications used by the superior for the good of the community. The obligation of the superior is partially to the individual, but most importantly to the community. The obligation of the superior consists in the judgment to be made of the proportion that exists between the qualities of the subject and the end to be attained.

The moral theologians tell us that the fault against distributive justice is *acceptio personarum*. *Acceptio personarum* would happen when the choice made of Sisters to go on to graduate work is made on the basis of other factors than the intelligence, emotional stability, and talent that would be required for the particular field of graduate study to which she should be sent. It will be well known to all of you that the best teacher is going to be an extrovert. Some would go so far as to say that there should be a little of "ham" in every great teacher. The great teacher will also have energy, independence of mind, and devotion to principle. Now it is conceivable, I am sure, that a person of such qualifications might, considering the way God has made us, be considered to be somewhat lacking in that quality which tends to make the life of a superior somewhat comfortable, namely the blessed virtue of tractability. Let us not make the mistake of confusing an apparent external conformity with a true obedience of the mind and will. I have no illusions that the making of the judgment involved is going to be an easy task. It is there, I believe, that the real genius for spiritual government lies: in making the best possible use of each member of the community, always safeguarding the essentials of the religious life and at the same time giving due consideration to the qualities of the individual person.

It has sometimes been said, not altogether without some basis in fact, that communities have not always sent on their really best members for graduate training. Obviously, factors other than intellectual need serious consideration, particularly where graduate work, as so often, will withdraw a Sister from the normal framework of the religious life of her community. But without being unfair, I think there can be a justifiable suspicion that tractability and docility and perhaps, even in some cases, merely the personal acceptability to a superior, have been more highly valued than real ability, maturity of judgment, and individual prudence.

Now, lest I even give the slightest suspicion that I consider the intellectual formation of Sisters as more important than their solid grounding and development in spiritual things, let me say with all possible emphasis, that I know—having been a religious for thirty-one years—that our primary object is the personal, interior life of the individual religious who has vowed herself to the service of God. *That must come first.* A person lacking in the fundamental virtues of a member of your community, with its traditional ideals and objectives, no matter what brains or talents she may have, is not to be chosen above a good religious of equal intellectual competence. Presupposing, therefore, the basic qualities of a good religious, the choice of a Sister for graduate studies should be made on the basis of intellectual competence and maturity. This, however, I should hope, does not demand that you delay sending a Sister to graduate studies until she has celebrated her Silver jubilee; the religious communities of men can send their subjects to graduate studies while they still have the youth, energy, and adaptability that the work requires. I cannot believe that supernatural prudence could not allow the same judgment to be made in the case of Sisters.

The failure to observe distributive justice in this matter by *acceptio personarum* can do real harm to a community and its work for God; it can also do real harm to the personal spiritual development of the individual, who may by this means be rendered incapable of proper peace of mind for the service of God. I need only advert to the personal hurt and consequent bitterness and disillusionment that can arise in a subject who has been unfairly treated.

After all this, at long last, I shall presume to offer you several positive suggestions toward a procedure for the objective selection of candidates for graduate study among your subjects.

First and foremost, prayerful consideration and petition to the Holy Spirit for guidance in a matter that is fraught with such importance for the ultimate good of your community and the good of its individual members. Second, a positive effort must be made, hard-headedly, to come to a detailed knowledge of the qualifications of your subjects. Out of the wealth of your experience in handling your subjects, and from the resources for their evaluation that are the heritage of your communities from your sainted founders, you have the primary means for selection. In this context, we may take for granted as already established the normal judgment as to stability in vocation that would be made at the time of profession by the community, in accordance with its own practices. Above and beyond that, however, the choice of candidates for graduate study demands a relatively high level of intellectual ability and the right kind of personality stability in the person, so that she can be expected, effectively, to carry out the task that is assigned to her. Steady dedication to graduate work is difficult at best for any student; in the case of a religious, it perhaps may be even more difficult given the added obligations that flow from religious life. Graduate studies are of their very nature a competitive undertaking, so that in exposing a Sister to it, you are putting her under a strain. It is mere elementary prudence, therefore, to have much knowledge beforehand on this factor. I have personally seen cases where students were thrown in over their heads with disastrous results to both health and the general good of the community. Besides being a waste of the community's money, this is grossly unfair to the individual.

Beyond, however, the normally adequate means of evaluation that lie within the resources of your community, because of the investment of money and persons involved, it would be desirable that these normal means be supplemented by a judicious use of intelligence and psychological tests which can in many cases give a more rounded view of the person concerned. Of course, in the case of an obviously suitable person, all the tests in the world won't make it any more true that this person has the qualities of mind and personality to make a success of graduate studies. I am not, of course, saying that the answer to all our problems lies in psychology. Too often it may be merely a substitute for, and an avoidance of thinking. The prudent use, however, of psychological and intelligence tests can be a valuable objective criterion in the decisions that you must make.

Thirdly, it is very important that there be an enunciation of a clear and consistent policy that will be known to all in the community. Fourth, I should like to suggest what I consider as a very important basis for the procedure of selection that I have outlined: it is obvious that no one will do well in graduate study unless she has something of a natural attraction for the life of learning and scholarship. In this connection I feel very strongly that from the earliest years of our training in the religious life, it is desirable that there be instilled into our candidates a respect for intellectual eminence as one of the very important means for promoting the greater glory of God. I am fully aware, since I have it from St. Ignatius himself, that our primary concern should be "the interior things from which force must flow to the exterior for the end proposed to us," but I should like to insist that perfection for the religious teacher also encompasses the highest possible competence in the field of intellectual endeavor.

In conclusion I want to assure you that it shall be my prayer, and suggest that it be yours, that you will be remembered in your community as the superior who made the most substantial contribution to the community by bringing the intellectual and cultural formation of your subjects up to the level of their spiritual formation to which you have been dedicated.

FOOTNOTES

1. Pius XII, "The Secret of Good Schools," Radiomessage to the Fifth Inter-American Congress on Catholic Education at Havana. From *The Pope Speaks*, I (First Quarter, 1954), 20. *AAS*, 46 (1954).
2. Address to Religious Superiors, Sept. 15, 1952. "On Religious Vocations," *The Catholic Mind*, 51 (June, 1953), 381. *AAS*, 44 (1952).

INDEX OF CONTRIBUTORS

INDEX OF SUBJECTS